lonely planet

COSTA RICA

TOP SIGHTS, AUTHENTIC EXPERIENCES

THIS EDITION WRITTEN AND RESEARCHED BY

Mara Vorhe

Contents

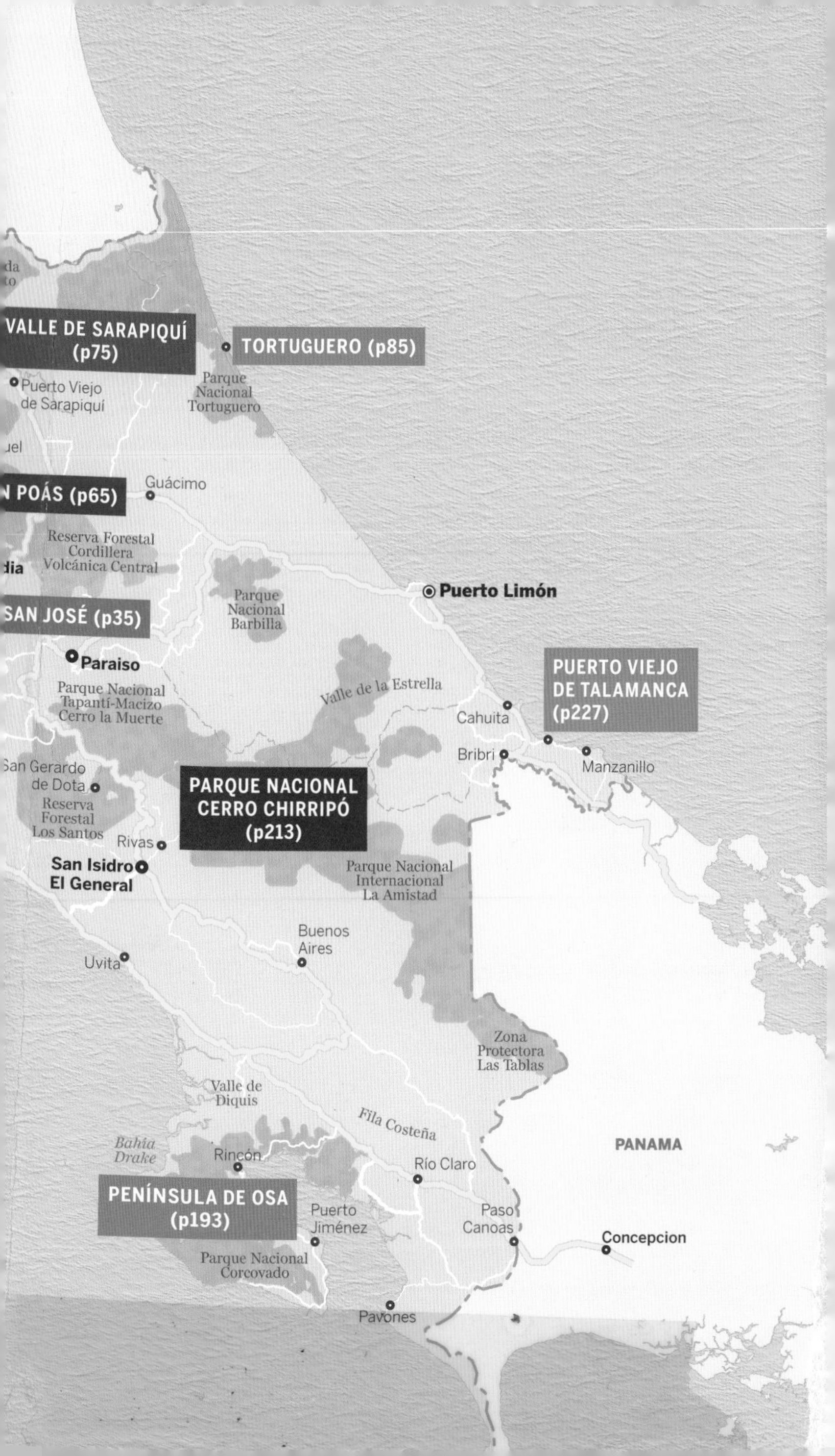

VALLE DE SARAPIQUÍ (p75)

TORTUGUERO (p85)

Puerto Viejo de Sarapiquí

Parque Nacional Tortuguero

N POÁS (p65)

Guácimo

Reserva Forestal Cordillera Volcánica Central

dia

Parque Nacional Barbilla

Puerto Limón

SAN JOSÉ (p35)

Paraiso

PUERTO VIEJO DE TALAMANCA (p227)

Parque Nacional Tapantí-Macizo Cerro la Muerte

Valle de la Estrella

Cahuita

San Gerardo de Dota

Bribri

Manzanillo

Reserva Forestal Los Santos

PARQUE NACIONAL CERRO CHIRRIPÓ (p213)

Rivas

San Isidro El General

Parque Nacional Internacional La Amistad

Buenos Aires

Uvita

Zona Protectora Las Tablas

Valle de Diquis

Bahía Drake

Fila Costeña

PANAMA

Rincón

Río Claro

PENÍNSULA DE OSA (p193)

Puerto Jiménez

Paso Canoas

Concepcion

Parque Nacional Corcovado

Pavones

Welcome to Costa Rica

All trails lead to waterfalls, misty crater lakes or jungle-fringed, deserted beaches. Explored by horseback, foot or kayak, Costa Rica is a tropical choose-your-own-adventure land.

As the eco- and adventure-tourism capital of Central America, Costa Rica has a worthy place in the cubicle daydreams of travelers around the world. With world-class infrastructure, visionary sustainability initiatives and no standing army since 1948 (when the country redirected its defense funds toward education, healthcare and the environment), Costa Rica is a peaceful green jewel of the region. Taking into account that more than a fourth of the land enjoys some form of environmental protection and there's greater biodiversity here than in the USA and Europe combined, it's a place that earns the superlatives.

And then there are the people. Costa Ricans, or Ticos as they prefer to call themselves, are proud of their little slice of paradise, welcoming guests to sink into the easygoing rhythms of the *pura vida* (pure life). This greeting, farewell, catchy motto and enduring mantra gets to the heart of Costa Rica's appeal – its simple yet profound ability to let people relax and enjoy their time. Combined with the highest quality of life in Central America, all the perfect waves, perfect sunsets and perfect beaches seem like the *pura vida* indeed.

> *sink into the easygoing rhythms of the* pura vida *(pure life)*

Waterfall near Parque Nacional Volcán Poás (p65)

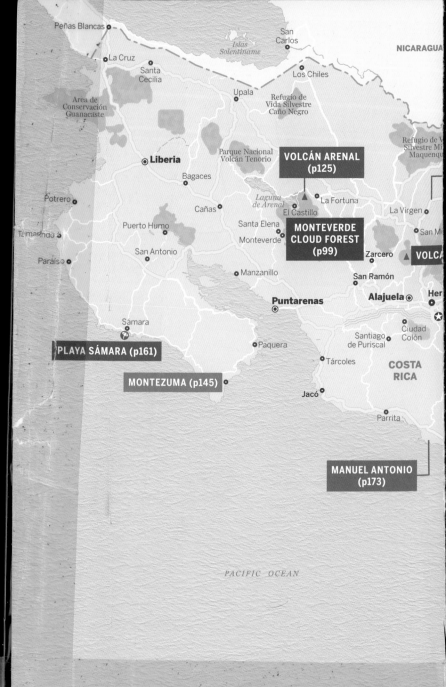

Peñas Blancas

La Cruz

Santa
Cecilia

*Islas
Solentiname*

San
Carlos

NICARAGUA

Área de
Conservación
Guanacaste

Upala

Los Chiles

Refugio de
Vida Silvestre
Caño Negro

Refugio de V
Silvestre Mi
Maquenqu

Liberia

Parque Nacional
Volcán Tenorio

**VOLCÁN ARENAL
(p125)**

Bagaces

*Laguna
de Arenal*

El Castillo

La Fortuna

La Virgen

Potrero

Cañas

Santa Elena

Monteverde

**MONTEVERDE
CLOUD FOREST
(p99)**

San Mi

Tamarindo

Puerto Humo

Zarcero

VOLCÁ

Paraíso

San Antonio

Manzanillo

San Ramón

Alajuela

Her

Puntarenas

Sámara

Ciudad
Colón

PLAYA SÁMARA (p161)

Santiago
de Puriscal

Paquera

**COSTA
RICA**

MONTEZUMA (p145)

Tárcoles

Jacó

Parrita

**MANUEL ANTONIO
(p173)**

PACIFIC OCEAN

N

0
0

100 km

50 miles

Poison-dart frog (p276)
MLORENZPHOTOGRAPHY/GETTY IMAGES ©

Plan Your Trip
Costa Rica's Top 12

Monteverde

A pristine expanse of virginal forest

Monteverde Cloud Forest (p99) owes much of its impressive natural beauty to Quaker settlers, who helped foster conservationist principles with Ticos of the region. But fascinating as the history is, the real romance of Monteverde is in nature: a mysterious Neverland shrouded in mist, dangling with mossy vines, sprouting with ferns and bromeliads, gushing with creeks, blooming with life and nurturing rivulets of evolution. Left: Cloud forest, Monteverde; Right: A resplendent quetzal (p275)

1

Manuel Antonio

Alive with the call of birds and monkeys

Although droves of visitors pack Parque Nacional Manuel Antonio (p173), the country's most popular (and smallest) national park remains an absolute gem. Capuchin monkeys scurry across its idyllic beaches, brown pelicans dive-bomb its clear waters and sloths watch over its trails. It's a perfect place to introduce youngsters to the wonders of the rainforest; indeed, you're likely to feel like a kid yourself.

Top: White-faced capuchin (p277); Bottom: Parque Nacional Manuel Antonio (p176)

2

Volcán Arenal

Iconic volcano, bubbling springs and a stunning lake

While the molten night views are gone, this mighty, perfectly conical giant (p125) is still considered active and worthy of a pilgrimage. There are beautiful trails to explore, especially the magnificent climb to Cerro Chato. At its base, you are just a short drive away from its many hot springs. Some of these springs are free, and any local can point the way. Others are, shall we say, embellished, dressed up, luxuriated – dip your toes into the romantic Eco Termales, for starters.

3

4

Montezuma
Wild ocean meets lush jungle

If you dig artsy-rootsy beach culture, enjoy rubbing shoulders with neo-Rastas and yogis, or long to lounge on sugar-white coves, find your way to Montezuma (p145). Strolling this intoxicating town and rugged coastline, you're never far from the rhythm of the sea. From here you'll also have easy access to the famed Cabo Blanco reserve, or you can hike to a triple-tiered waterfall. And when your stomach growls, the town has some of the best restaurants in the country.

5

Península de Osa
Off-the-beaten-track wilderness

Muddy, muggy and intense, the vast, largely untouched rainforest of Parque Nacional Corcovado (p196) is anything but a walk in the park. Here travelers with a sturdy pair of rubber boots thrust themselves into the unknown and come out the other side with the story of a lifetime. The further into the jungle you go, the better it gets: the best wildlife-watching, most desolate beaches and most vivid adventures lie down these seldom-trodden trails. Bahía Drake (p207)

'YADID LEVY'/GETTY IMAGES ©

SAM CAMP/GETTY IMAGES ©

COLIN33362/GETTY IMAGES ©

Tortuguero

Sea-turtle spotting and jungle tours

Canoeing the canals of Parque Nacional Tortuguero (p85) is
a boat-borne safari. Get up close with caimans, river turtles,
crowned night herons, monkeys and sloths. Under the cover of
darkness, watch the awesome, millenia-old ritual of turtles building nests and laying their eggs. Sandwiched between wetlands
and the wild Caribbean Sea, this is among the country's premier
places to spot wildlife. Sloth (p277)

6

Puerto Viejo de Talamanca

Laid-back charm and surf scene

By day, lounge in a hammock, cycle to uncrowded beaches, hike to waterfall-fed pools and visit remote indigenous territories. By night, dip into zesty Caribbean cooking and sway to reggaetón at open-air bars cooled by ocean breezes. The village of Puerto Viejo de Talamanca (p227), an outpost of this unique mix of Afro-Caribbean, Tico and indigenous culture, is the perfect laid-back base for such adventures.

7

Parque Nacional Cerro Chirripó

Spectacular views above the clouds

The view from Costa Rica's highest peak (p213) – of wind-swept rocks and icy lakes – may not resemble the Costa Rica of the postcards, but the two-day hike above the clouds is one of the country's most satisfying excursions. A pre-dawn expedition rewards hardy hikers with the real prize: a chance to catch the fiery sunrise and see both the Caribbean Sea and the Pacific Ocean in a full and glorious panoramic view from 3820m high.

View from the summit of Cerro Chirripó

MARIO GYSS/SHUTTERSTOCK ©

CHRISTIAN KOBER/GETTY IMAGES ©

PANORAMIC IMAGES/
GETTY IMAGES ©

9

Playa Sámara

A picturesque crescent of sand

Playa Sámara (p161) is a pretty stretch of coast, spanning two rocky headlands, offering the opportunity to surf, stand-up paddle board, kayak or snorkel. Or, just sit on the sand, sipping fruity cocktails and watching other people exert energy. It's all good. Nearby, nature-backed beaches and coves are easy to access, making this prime for families, or anyone who enjoys a palpable sense of ease and tranquility. Far left: Horseback riding along Playa Sámara; Left: Surfing Sámara's breaks

KRYSIA CAMPOS/GETTY IMAGES ©

Volcán Poás

A bubbling, steaming cauldron

Poás (p65) is a fairy-tale land of verdant mountains, hydrangea-lined roads and the largest and most accessible volcanic crater on the isthmus. Although a 6.2 earthquake rocked the region in 2009, the area's most intriguing attractions endured. The windy drive past strawberry farms, waterfalls and coffee plantations still culminates in the smoking volcano and emerald-green crater lake.

Top: Crater of Volcán Poás; Above left: La Paz Waterfall (p73); Above right: Coffee beans

10

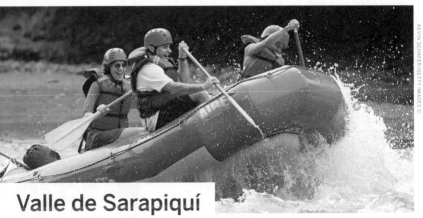

KEVIN SCHAFER/GETTY IMAGES ©

Valle de Sarapiquí
White-water adventures

Sarapiquí Valley (p75) rose to fame as a principal port in the nefarious old days of United Fruit dominance, only to be reborn as a paddler's paradise, thanks to the frothing serpentine magic of its namesake river. These days it's still a mecca for adventure-seekers, and it's also dotted with fantastic ecolodges and private forest preserves in that steaming, looming, muddy jungle. White-water rafting (p78), Río Sarapiquí

WOLFGANG KAEHLER/LIGHTROCKET/GETTY IMAGES ©

San José
Historic neighborhoods, vibrant culture, local cuisine

The heart of Tico culture lives in San José (p35), as do university students, intellectuals, artists and politicians. While not the most attractive capital in Central America, it does have graceful neo-classical and Spanish-colonial architecture, leafy neighborhoods, museums housing pre-Columbian jade and gold and sophisticated restaurants. Street art adds unexpected pops of color and public discourse to the cityscape. Interior of the Teatro Nacional (p40)

Plan Your Trip
Need to Know

When to Go

Tamarindo
GO Nov–Apr

Puerto Limón
GO Jan–Apr

San José
GO Dec–Apr

Parque Nacional
Manuel Antonio
GO Dec–Feb

Puerto Jiménez
GO Feb, Mar, Sep & Oct

■ Tropical climate, rain year-round
■ Tropical climate, wet and dry seasons

High Season (Dec–Apr)

○ 'Dry' season still sees some rain; beach towns fill with domestic tourists.

○ Accommodations should be booked well in advance; some places enforce two- or three-day minimum stays.

Shoulder (May–Jul & Nov)

○ Rain picks up and the stream of tourists starts to taper off.

○ Roads are muddy and rivers begin to rise, making off-the-beaten-track travel more challenging.

Low Season (Aug–Oct)

○ Rainfall is highest, but storms bring swells to the Pacific, and the best surfing conditions.

○ Rural roads can be impassable due to river crossings.

○ Accommodations prices lower significantly.

Currency
Costa Rican colón (₡)

Language
Spanish, English

Visas
Generally not required for stays of up to 90 days.

Money
Both US dollars and Costa Rican colones are accepted every-where and dispensed from ATMs across the country. With the ex-ception of the smallest towns and shops in rural areas, credit cards are accepted.

Cell Phones
Both 3G and 4G systems available, but those compatible with US plans require expensive international roaming.
Prepaid SIM cards are cheap and widely available.
Of the four cellular providers, Kolbi has the best coverage in remote areas and Movistar has the worst.

Time
Central Standard Time (GMT/UTC minus six hours)

Daily Costs

Budget: Less than US$40

- Dorm bed: US$8–15
- Meal at a *soda* (inexpensive eatery): US$3–7
- DIY hikes without a guide
- Travel via local bus: US$1 or less

Midrange: US$40–100

- Basic room with private bathroom: US$20–50 per day
- Meal at a restaurant geared toward travelers: US$5–12
- Travel on an efficient 1st-class bus company such as Interbus: US$50–60

Top End: More than US$100

- Luxurious beachside lodge or boutique hotel: from US$80
- Meal at an international fusion restaurant: from US$15
- Guided wildlife-watching excursion: from US$30
- Short domestic flight: US$50–100
- 4WD rental for local travel: from US$60 per day

Useful Websites

Anywhere Costa Rica (www.anywherecostarica. com) Excellent overviews of local destinations; run by a tour agency that gets good reviews.

Essential Costa Rica (www.visitcostarica.com) The Costa Rica Tourism Board (ICT) website has general travel information, as well as planning tips and destination details.

The Tico Times (www.ticotimes.net) Costa Rica's English-language newspaper's website; its searchable archives can be helpful for trip planning around specific destinations.

Lonely Planet (www.lonelyplanet.com/costa-rica) Destination information, hotel bookings, traveller forum and more.

Opening Hours

Opening hours vary throughout the year. The following are high-season opening hours; hours will generally decrease in the shoulder and low seasons.

Banks 9am to 4pm Monday to Friday, sometimes 9am to noon Saturday.

Bars & clubs 8pm to 2am

Government offices 8am to 5pm Monday to Friday. Often closed between 11.30am and 1.30pm.

Restaurants 7am to 9pm. Upscale places may open only for dinner. In remote areas, even the small *sodas* (inexpensive eateries) might open only at specific meal times.

Shops 8am to 6pm Monday to Saturday.

Arriving in Costa Rica

Aeropuerto Internacional Juan Santamaria (San José) Alajuela–San José buses (US$1.10) from the airport to central San José run between 5am and 10pm. Taxis charge from US$25 to US$30 (depending on your destination in San José) and depart from the official stand; the trip takes 20 minutes to an hour. Interbus (www.interbusonline. com) runs between the airport and San José accommodations (US$15 per adult, US$7 per child under 12). Many rental-car agencies have desks at the airport.

Getting Around

Air Inexpensive domestic flights between San José and popular destinations such as Quepos and Tortuguero will save you the driving time.

Bus Very reasonably priced, with extensive coverage of the country, though travel can be slow and some destinations have infrequent service.

Car Driving allows you to access more remote destinations not served by bus, and frees you to cover as much ground as you like. Cars can be rented in most towns. Renting a 4WD vehicle is advantageous (and essential in some parts of the country); avoid driving at night.

Private shuttle For door-to-door service between popular destinations, shuttles like Interbus or Gray Line allow you to schedule to your needs.

For more on **getting around**, see p292

Plan Your Trip
Hotspots for...

Beaches

Costa Rica has 1466km of glorious coastline on two different oceans; it's time to find your place in the sand (and sun).

Birding

Even for those who don't know their snowy-bellied emerald from their grey-breasted wood wren, Costa Rica's birds are a thrill. Nearly 900 bird species fill Costa Rica's skies – more than in the entire US and Canada combined.

Volcanoes

Four connecting mountain chains run down the center of the country, offering loads of opportunities for challenging hikes and soothing soaks.

White-Water Rafting

With Costa Rica's ample waterways and excellent operators, the opportunities for rushing down frothing white-water rapids will satisfy even the greatest thirst for adventure.

Playa Manuel Antonio
This beach is worth the park fee, thanks to mischievous monkeys, perfect sand and turquoise water (p179).

Top Tip
Arrive early – the number of entrants is limited each day.

Punta Uva
Southeast of Puerto Viejo de Talamanca (p227), this point is lined with beaches, each lovelier than the next.

Top Tip
Bike to the beach (it's only a 7km pedal).

Playa Sámara
A gorgeous in-town beach with sunset views and locals playing soccer on the sand (p161).

Top Tip
The waves are just big enough for surfing beginners.

Península de Osa
Although rare in the country, scarlet macaws frequent the skies around Parque Nacional Corcovado (p200).

What to Spot
Macaws along the Agujitas–Corcovado trail (p207).

Bosque Nuboso Monteverde
Keep your eyes peeled for cloud forest species in this fragile environment (p105).

What to Spot
The resplendent quetzal and three-wattled bellbird.

Parque Nacional Tortuguero
The bird list is a mile long at this wildlife-rich park (p85), home to over 400 bird species.

What to Spot
Herons, kites, ospreys, kingfishers and macaws.

Volcán Poás
Drive right up and take a peak into the steaming, belching bubbling crater of this active volcano (p65).

Best Way to See It
Get there early to beat the crowds. And the clouds.

Cerro Chato
It's a tough hike up this dormant volcano, but your reward is a dip in a true blue crater lake (p131).

Best Way to See It
Start at the Arenal Observatory Lodge (*in* the grounds).

Volcán Arenal
Hike along the lava flows, then recover with a soak in volcano-heated pools. Bliss (p132).

Best Way to See It
Enjoy the serenity at Eco Termales Hot Springs.

La Virgen
Take on runs of Class II to IV rapids on the country's best white water (p80).

Tour Operator
As much as you can handle, by Aguas Bravas (p263).

Río Sarapiquí
Less populated by people but crowded with wildlife, this is a great place to raft or learn how to kayak (p78).

Tour Operator
Sarapiquí Outdoor Center (p79), based in La Virgen.

Río Savegre
Gentle rapids that pick up in the rainy season serve as a great intro to rafting; trips depart from Quepos (p187).

Tour Operator
For kayaking or tubing, try H2O Adventures (p182).

Plan Your Trip
Local Life

MICHAEL BOYNY/GETTY IMAGES ©

✪ Activities

Miles of shoreline, endless warm water and a diverse array of national parks and reserves provide an inviting playground for active travelers. Whether it's the solitude of absolute wilderness, hiking and rafting adventures that kids can enjoy, or surfing and jungle trekking you seek, Costa Rica offers fun to suit everyone.

Be sure to pack for your adventure. Although the coastal areas are hot and humid, calling for shorts and short sleeves, you'll want to pack a sweater and light-weight jacket for popular high-elevation destinations such as Monteverde. If you plan to hike up Chirripó, bring lots of layers and a hat and gloves. Additionally, while hiking through the rainforest is often a hot and sweaty exercise, long sleeves and lightweight, quick-drying pants help keep the bugs away.

✪ Shopping

Avoid purchasing animal products, including turtle shells, animal skulls and anything made with feathers, coral or shells. Wood products are also highly suspicious: make sure you know where the wood came from.

Coffee is the most popular souvenir, available pretty much everywhere, even at the local grocery store. The most popular alcohol purchases are Ron Centenario, Café Rica (the coffee liqueur) and guaro (the local firewater).

Tropical-hardwood items include salad bowls, plates, carving boards, jewelry boxes and a variety of carvings and ornaments.

✪ Entertainment

Live music, dance performances, parades, soccer matches and bullfights are the primary forms of entertainment around Costa Rica. All of these can be found in San José on a regular basis. Nearly every

ESDELVAL/GETTY IMAGES ©

town has its own fiesta once in a while, complete with carnival games, rides and bullfighting spectacles.

✖ Eating

The most popular eating establishment in Costa Rica is the *soda*. These are small, informal lunch counters dishing up a few daily *casados* (set meals). Other popular cheapies include the omnipresent fried- and rotisserie-chicken stands.

A regular *restaurante* is usually higher on the price scale and has slightly more atmosphere. Many *restaurantes* serve *casados*, while the fancier places refer to the set lunch as the *almuerzo ejecutivo* (literally 'executive lunch').

For something smaller, *pastelerías* and *panaderías* are shops that sell pastries and bread, while many bars serve *bocas* (snack-sized portions of main meals).

☻ Drinking & Nightlife

In the more touristy areas of Costa Rica, you'll find no shortage of bars and nightclubs.

San José has the most going on, with all the dive bars, lounges and dance clubs you could ask for. From thumping electron-ica and hip-hop to salsa, merengue and reggaetón, Chepe's clubs offer a galaxy of musical styles to help you get your groove on. Most spots open at around 10pm, and don't truly get going until after midnight. When leaving a bar late at night, keep your wits about you and take a taxi.

At the beach, Montezuma and Puerto Viejo are top spots to tie one on, but almost every beach town in the country has at least one lively local night spot.

From left: Bosque Nuboso Monteverde (p102); *Casado* (set meal) of pork, rice, beans and salad

Plan Your Trip
Month by Month

January

Every year opens with a rush, as North American and domestic tourists flood beach towns to celebrate. January sees dry days and occasional afternoon showers.

February

February is the perfect month, with ideal weather and no holiday surcharges. The skies above Nicoya are particularly clear, and it's peak season for turtle-nesting.

March

Excellent weather continues through the early part of March, though prices shoot up during Semana Santa, the week leading up to Easter (and North American spring break).

✪ Día del Boyero

A colorful parade, held in Escazú (near San José) on the second Sunday in March, honors oxcart drivers and includes a blessing of the animals.

April

Easter and Semana Santa can fall early in April, which means beaches crowd and prices spike. Nicoya and Guanacaste are dry and hot, with little rain.

✪ Día de Juan Santamaría

Commemorating Costa Rica's national hero, who died in battle against American colonist William Walker's troops in 1856, this weeklong celebration includes parades, concerts and dances.

✪ FIA (Festival de las Artes)

This multidisciplinary arts festival descends upon venues all across San José in alternating years during April (or March).

May

Attention budget travelers: wetter weather patterns begin to sweep across the country in May, which begins the county's

MARCODIAZPHOTO/500PX ©

low season. So although the weather is decent, prices drop.

✪ Día de San Isidro Labrador

Visitors can taste the bounty of San Isidro and other villages of Costa Rica during the nation's largest agricultural fairs, on May 15.

June

The Pacific coast gets fairly wet during June, though this makes for good surfing. The beginning of the so-called green season, this time of year has lots of discounted rates.

July

July is mostly wet, particularly on the Caribbean coast, but the month also occasionally enjoys a brief dry period that Ticos call *veranillo* (summer). Expect rain, particularly late in the day.

Top Festivals

Día de los Muertos, November

Independence Day, September

Día de Juan Santamaría, April

Las Fiestas de Zapote, December

✪ Día de Guanacaste

Celebrates the annexation of Guanacaste from Nicaragua. There's also a rodeo in Santa Cruz. It takes place on July 25.

August

The middle of the rainy season doesn't mean that mornings aren't bright and sunny. Travelers who don't mind some rain will find great hotel and tour deals.

From left: Good Friday procession;
Costa Rican masquerade costumes

✪ La Virgen de los Ángeles

The patron saint of Costa Rica is celebrated with an important religious procession from San José to Cartago on August 2.

September

The Península de Osa gets utterly soaked during September, which is in the heart of the rainy season and what Ticos refer to as the *temporales del Pacífico.* It's the cheapest time of year to visit the Pacific.

✪ Costa Rican Independence Day

The center of the Independence Day action is the relay race that passes a 'Freedom Torch' from Guatemala to Costa Rica. The torch arrives at Cartago on the evening of September 14, when the nation breaks into the national anthem.

October

Many roads become impassable as rivers swell and rain continues to fall in one of the wettest months in Costa Rica. Lodges and tour operators are sometimes closed until November.

November

The weather can go either way in November. Access to Parque Nacional Corcovado is difficult after several months of rain, though by the month's end the skies clear up.

✪ Día de los Muertos

Families visit graveyards and have religious parades in honor of the dead – a lovely and picturesque festival on November 2.

December

Although the beginning of the month is a great time to visit – with clearer skies and relatively uncrowded attractions – things ramp up toward Christmas and advance reservations become crucial.

✪ Las Fiestas de Zapote

In San José between Christmas and New Year's Eve, this weeklong celebration of all things Costa Rican (rodeos, cowboys, carnival rides, fried food and booze) draws tens of thousands of Ticos to the bullring in the suburb of Zapote every day.

Plan Your Trip
Get Inspired

Above: Red-eyed tree frog (p276)

Read

Costa Rica: A Traveler's Literary Companion (ed Barbara Ras) A collection of short stories by modern Costa Rican writers.

Tropical Nature: Life & Death in the Rain Forests of Central and South America (Adrian Forsyth and Ken Miyata) Easy-to-digest natural-history essays.

Travelers' Tales Central America (eds Larry Habegger and Natanya Pearlman) Essays from writers including Paul Theroux.

Naturalist in Costa Rica (Alexander Skutch) Beautiful descriptions of flora and fauna in an enchanting memoir and natural history guide.

Watch

El Regreso (The Return; 2012) Featuring a realistic, contemporary plot, the first Tico film to earn international acclaim.

Agua Fría de Mar (Cold Ocean Water; 2010) This social commentary unfolds at a paradisical Pacific beach; the film won several international awards.

El Cielo Rojo (The Red Sky; 2008) A comedic coming-of-age story of young Ticos on the cusp of adulthood in contemporary Costa Rica.

Endless Summer II (1994) Surfers Pat O'Connell and Robert 'Wingnut' Weaver ride Costa Rica's magical waves.

Listen

Various Artists, SíSan José (2011) A collaboration between a WFMU engineer and nine of Costa Rica's indie rock acts.

Chavela Vargas, Coleccion Original RCA (1946) Long out of print, this 2011 reissue of Costa Rican–born singer features hauntingly beautiful folk ballads.

Malpaís, Un Día Lejano (2009) Costa Rica's innovative and now defunct rock band mixes calypso, jazz and Latin American balladry.

Various Artists, Calypsos: Afro-Limonese Music From Costa Rica (1991) A raucous collection which captured the heart of Costa Rico's Afro-Caribbean folk scene.

Plan Your Trip
Five-Day Itineraries

Pacific Dreams

Spend your days exploring dreamy beaches, swimming in turquoise waters and spying on playful monkeys. Spend your nights indulging in amazing seafood, sunset views and rolicking nightlife.

3 Montezuma (p145) Hike to waterfalls, ride the surf and do sun salutations in open-air studios. This is the good life.

1 San José (p35) Devote a day to exploring the neighborhoods, perusing the museums and sampling the dining and drinking scene.
✈ 1 hr to Quepos

2 Manuel Antonio (p173) The park is prime for hiking, swimming and kayaking, followed by sundowners at nearby bars. 🚌 to Jacó, then ⚓ 1 hr to Montezuma

Northeastern Escapade

Steaming volcanoes, raging rivers, jungle-clad canals... Visit the northeast and enter a world where the power of the earth is palpable.

2 Valle de Sarapiquí (p75) Prime territory for riding rapids, sampling local specialties and wildlife watching. 🚌 2 hrs to La Pavona then ⛴ 1 hr to Tortuguero

3 Tortuguero (p85) Paddle through luscious, greenery-draped canals, where birds and animals hide around every corner.

1 Volcán Poás (p65) Alajuela is your base for visiting this bubbling, belching cauldron of geothermic activity. 🚌 2 hrs to the Valle de Sarapiquí

FROM LEFT: KEVIN SCHAFER/GETTY IMAGES ©; FERRAN VEGA VALLRIBERA/GETTY IMAGES ©

Plan Your Trip
10-Day Itinerary

Essential Costa Rica

This is the trip you've been dreaming about: a romp through paradise with volcanoes, tropical parks, cloud forests and sun-kissed beaches.

3 Playa Sámara (p161) Next up: beach time. In this charming coastal town, surfing, snorkeling and swimming are at your doorstep. **3**

NICK LEDGER /GETTY IMAGES ©

1

1 Volcán Arenal (p125) Head for La Fortuna, where adventure awaits. Hike to crater lakes, swim beneath waterfalls and spot a sloth.
🚌 4 hrs to Monteverde

2 Monteverde (p99) Zip through the treetops on a canopy tour or learn about your favorite morning drink on a coffee tour. 🚌 3 hrs to Playa Sámara

Plan Your Trip
Two-Week Itinerary

Southern Adventure

Satisfy your adventurous spirit with a journey into the southern sector. Climb the country's highest peak, then recover on its glorious beaches.

1 San José (p35) Before leaving civilization, spend a day soaking up some culture in San José. 🚗 3 hrs to San Gerardo de Rivas

2 San Gerardo de Rivas (p220) If you're planning to climb Chirripó, this is the place for supplies and a good night's rest. 🚌 to Parque Nacional Chirripó

3 Cerro Chirripó (p216) It's a challenging 20km hike on well-marked trails to the summit of Cerro Chirripó. 🚌 to San Gerardo, then 🚗 4 hrs to Puerto Jiménez

4 Puerto Jiménez (p202) Take a day or two to recover with local farm tours, mangrove kayaking or beach lounging. 🚗 ½ hr to Los Brazos

5 Parque Nacional Corcovado (p196) Undertake the ambitious two-day hike across Corcovado, or the more manageable El Tigre loop.

Plan Your Trip
Family Travel

MIKE TAUBER/GETTY IMAGES ©

In a land of such dizzying adventure and close encounters with wildlife, waves, jungle zip-lines and enticing mud puddles, it can be challenging to choose where to go. Fortunately, your options aren't limited by region, and kids will find epic fun in this accessible paradise (that parents will enjoy too).

Costa Rica for Kids

Mischievous monkeys and steaming volcanoes, mysterious rainforests and palm-lined beaches – Costa Rica sometimes seems like a comic-book reality. The perfect place for family travel, it is a safe, exhilarating tropical playground that will make a huge impression on younger travelers. The country's myriad adventure possibilities cover the spectrum of age-appropriate intensity levels – and for no intensity at all, some kids might like the idea of getting their hair braided and beaded by a beachside stylist in Puerto Viejo de Talamanca. Whatever you do, the warm, family-friendly culture is extremely welcoming of little ones.

In addition to amazing the kids, this small, peaceful country has all of the practicalities that rank high with parents, such as great country-wide transportation infrastructure, a low crime rate and an excellent health-care system. But the reason to bring the whole family is the opportunity to share unforgettable experiences like spotting a dolphin or a sloth, slowly paddling a kayak through mangrove channels, or taking a night hike in search of tropical frogs.

Eating with Kids

○ Hydration is particularly crucial in this tropical climate, especially for children who aren't used to the heat and humidity; fortunately, Costa Rica's tap water is safe everywhere (except for the rare exception, usually in remote areas).

○ If you're traveling with an infant or small child, stock up on formula, baby food and

👍 Best National Parks for Kids

Parque Nacional Manuel Antonio (p173) Beach visits are usually enlivened by monkeys, coatis and iguanas.

Parque Nacional Tortuguero (p94) Boat tours through Tortuguero canals uncover wildlife all around.

Parque Nacional Volcán Poás (p291) One of the most accessible national parks, Poás has a stroller-friendly walkway along the observation area.

snacks before heading to remote areas, where shops are few and far between.

○ Kids love refreshing *batidos* (fresh fruit shakes), either *al agua* (made with water) or *con leche* (with milk); the variety of novel tropical fruits may appeal to older kids.

○ Coconut water might be old news back home, but watching a smiling Tico hack open a *pipa fría* (cold young coconut) for you with a machete is another thing entirely.

○ Many restaurants offers kids' menus but these tend to be international rather than Costa Rican.

Getting Around

○ Children under the age of 12 receive a 25% discount on domestic-airline flights, while children under two fly free (provided they sit on a parent's lap).

○ Children (except for those under the age of three) pay full fare on buses.

○ Car seats for infants are not always available at car-rental agencies, so bring your own or make sure you double (or triple) check with the agency in advance.

Family Activities

Ecocentro Danaus (p134) Walk the trails to look for monkeys and sloths, visit a pond with caimans and turtles, delight in the butterfly garden and ogle frogs in the ranarium (frog pond).

Jaguar Centro de Rescate (p234) No jaguars here, but you may get to hold a howler monkey or a baby sloth. You'll also see colorful snakes (in terrariums), raptors and frogs.

Playa Sámara (p161) Warm water and moderate surf make this a great place to learn to surf.

Río Sarapiquí (p75) Family-friendly rafting and 'safari trips' happen year-round on the calmer stretch of this river.

From left: Zip-lining on a canopy tour; Jaguar (p277)

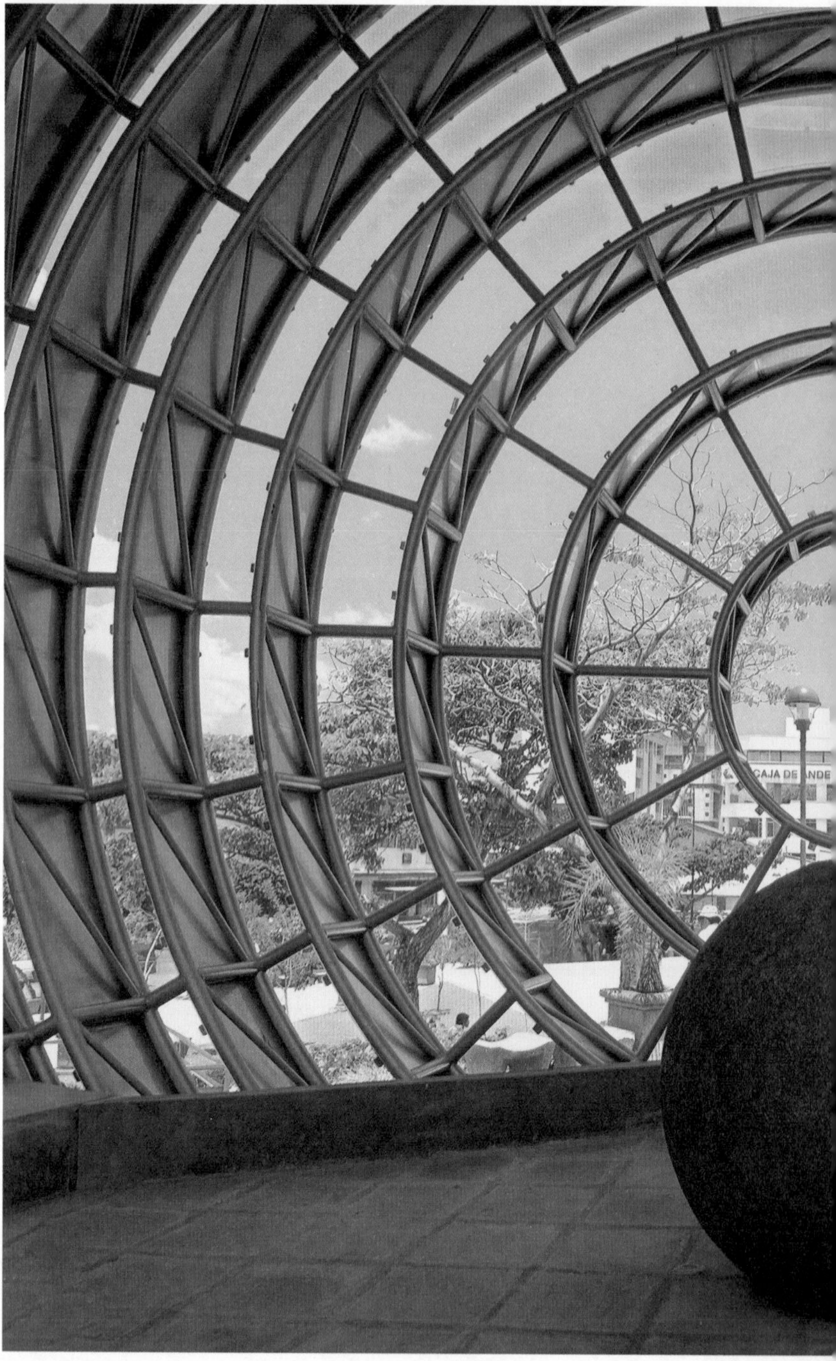

JOHN COLETTI/GETTY IMAGES ©

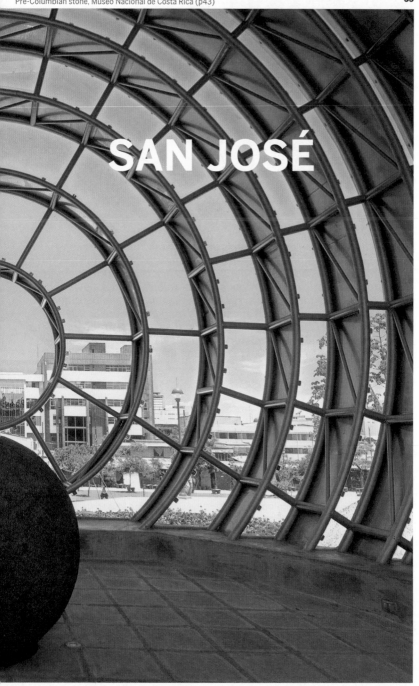

SAN JOSÉ

San José at a glance...

It's true that Chepe – as San José is affectionately known – doesn't make a great first impression, with its unremarkable concrete structures and honking traffic, but dig deeper and you'll discover the city's charms. Poke around historic neighborhoods, where colonial mansions have been converted into contemporary art galleries, restaurants and boutique hotels. Stroll with shoppers at the farmers market, join the Sunday crowds in Parque La Sabana, dance the night away, or visit the museums of gold, jade, art and natural history. Then you'll begin to understand the multidimensional appeal of Costa Rica's largest city and cultural capital.

One Day in San José

Peek inside the city's most beautiful building, the 19th-century **Teatro Nacional** (p40), then head into the nearby **Museo de Oro Precolombino y Numismática** (p41) to peruse its trove of pre-Columbian gold treasures. Lunch on the terrace of **Kalú Café & Food Shop** (p57) or among the vertical gardens of **Al Mercat** (p55). Afterwards, browse the shops of historic Barrio Amón. End your afternoon sampling local microbrews at **Stiefel** (p57) or sipping cocktails at **Café de los Deseos** (p51).

Two Days in San José

Start your second day at the **Museo Nacional de Costa Rica** (p43), then cross Plaza de la Democracia to the newly expanded **Museo de Jade** (p42). After a stroll through the neighboring **Mercado Artesanal** (p43) for handicrafts, head to the **Mercado Central** (p47) to shop for Costa Rican coffee and cigars. In the evening, grab dinner at **Park Café** (p54), then venture to Los Yoses and San Pedro for a rollicking nightlife scene.

Arriving in San José

International flights arrive at **Aeropuerto Internacional Juan Santamaría** (fly2sanjose.com) in nearby Alajuela.

An official taxi to downtown San José should cost around US$30, as measured on the meter. Reserve a pickup with **Taxi Aeropuerto** (☎2221-6865).

Interbus (www.interbusonline.com; ☎4100-0888; US$15/7 per adult/child under 12) runs shuttles in both directions between the airport and San José hotels.

Where to Stay

Accommodations in San José run the gamut from simple but homey hostels to luxurious boutique retreats. If you're flying into or out of Costa Rica from here, it may be more convenient to stay in Alajuela, as the town is minutes from the international airport.

For information on what each neighborhood has to offer, see the table on p63.

San Jose

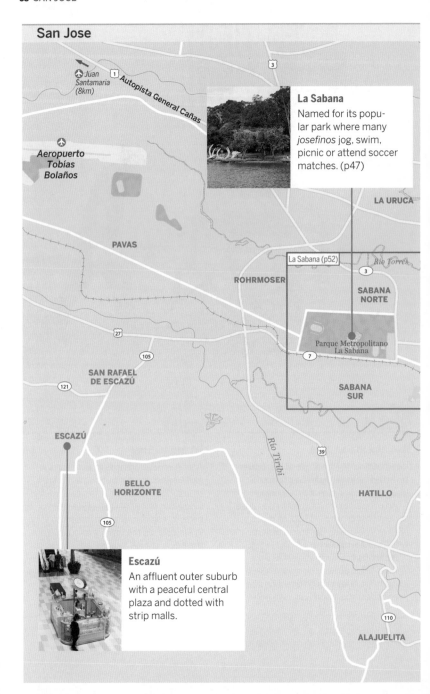

✈ Juan Santamaria (8km)

Autopista General Cañas ①

③

✈ Aeropuerto Tobías Bolaños

La Sabana
Named for its popular park where many *josefinos* jog, swim, picnic or attend soccer matches. (p47)

LA URUCA

PAVAS

La Sabana (p52)

Río Torres

③

ROHRMOSER

SABANA NORTE

㉗

⑩⑤

SAN RAFAEL DE ESCAZÚ

⑫①

Parque Metropolitano La Sabana

⑦

SABANA SUR

ESCAZÚ

BELLO HORIZONTE

Río Tiribí

㊴

HATILLO

⑩⑤

Escazú
An affluent outer suburb with a peaceful central plaza and dotted with strip malls.

⑪⓪

ALAJUELITA

N 0 ⸺ 2 km
0 ⸺ 1 miles

Río Virilla

⑤

Central San José
The city's congested center is where you'll find its cultural and commercial hubs. (p46)

Barrio Escalante
Home to some of San José's trendiest bars and restaurants. (p55)

㊲

TOURNON

⑤ ㉜

Central San José (p48)

⑥

MÉXICO

⑥ **OTOYA**

Río Torres

⑥

㉒

Museo de Insectos

SAN FRANCISCO

AMÓN Estación del Atlántico

DENT

㊲

PLAZA DE LA CULTURA

SAN JOSÉ

CALIFORNIA

SAN PEDRO

Cementerio General

PLAZA DE LA DEMOCRACIA

LOS YOSES

LA GRANJA

Estación del Pacífico

④

ZAPOTE

㉑㉓

Río María Aguilar

Parque Recreativo La Paz

㊲

SAN SEBASTIÁN

④

Los Yoses & San Pedro
These contiguous neighborhoods are home to a rollicking nightlife scene. (p55)

㉑㉔

㉑㉔ **DESAMPARADOS**

Teatro Nacional

Plaza de la Cultura

This architecturally unremarkable concrete plaza in the heart of downtown is usually packed with locals slurping ice-cream cones and observing street life: juggling clowns, itinerant vendors and cruising teenagers.

Great For...

☑ **Don't Miss**

The Teatro Nacional's most famous painting, *Alegoría al café y el banano*.

Teatro Nacional

On the southern side of the Plaza de la Cultura resides the **Teatro Nacional** (National Theater; Map p48; 🕿2010-1110; www.teatronacional.go.cr; Av 2 btwn Calles 3 & 5; US$10; ⊙9am-7pm), San José's most revered building. Constructed in 1897, it features a columned neoclassical facade that is flanked by statues of Beethoven and famous 17th-century Spanish dramatist Calderón de la Barca. The lavish marble lobby and auditorium are lined with paintings depicting various facets of 19th-century life. The hourly tours here are fantastic, and if you're looking to rest your feet, there's also an excellent on-site cafe.

The theater's most famous painting is *Alegoría al café y el banano*, an idyllic canvas showing coffee and banana harvests. The painting was produced in Italy and

Teatro Nacional lobby

⊙ Need to Know

Map p48; Avs Central & 2 btwn Calles 3 & 5

✕ Take a Break

Enjoy an espresso at the Teatro Nacional's atmospheric Alma de Café (p53).

★ Top Tip

Tours are offered every hour on the hour in Spanish and English.

Performances

Costa Rica's most important theater stages plays, dance, opera, symphony, Latin American music and other major events. The main season runs from March to November, but there are performances throughout the year.

shipped to Costa Rica for installation in the theater, and the image was reproduced on the old ₡5 note (now out of circulation). It seems clear that the painter never witnessed a banana harvest because of the way the man in the center is awkwardly grasping a bunch (actual banana workers hoist the stems onto their shoulders).

Museo de Oro Precolombino y Numismática

The three-in-one **Museo de Oro Precolombino y Numismática** (Map p48; ☎2243-4202; www.museosdelbancocentral. org; Plaza de la Cultura, Avs Central & 2 btwn Calles 3 & 5; adult/student/child US$11/8/free; ☺9:15am-5pm) houses an extensive collection of Costa Rica's most priceless pieces of pre-Columbian gold and other artifacts, including historical currency and some contemporary regional art. The museum, located underneath the Plaza de la Cultura, is owned by the Banco Central and its architecture brings to mind all the warmth and comfort of a bank vault. Security is tight; visitors must leave bags at the door.

Tours

On this fascinating **tour** (Map p48; ☎2010-1143; www.teatronacional.go.cr/Visitenos/turismo; Av 2 btwn Calles 3 & 5; tours US$10; ☺9am-5pm), guests are regaled with stories of the art, architecture and people behind Costa Rica's crown jewel, the national theater. The best part is a peek into otherwise off-limits areas, such as the Smoking Room, which feature famous paintings, lavish antique furnishings and ornate gold trim.

Museo Nacional de Costa Rica

STEFANO PATERNA/ALAMY STOCK PHOTO ©

Plaza de la Democracia

Between the national museum and the Museo de Jade is the stark Plaza de la Democracia, which was constructed by President Oscar Arias in 1989 to commemorate 100 years of Costa Rican democracy.

Great For...

☑ **Don't Miss**

Mural by César Valverde Vega in the Museo de Jade.

Museo de Jade

Reopened in its brand-new home in mid-2014, the **Museo de Jade** (Map p48; ☎2521-6610; www.museodeljadeins.com; Plaza de la Democracia; adult/child US$15/5; ☽10am-5pm) houses the world's largest collection of American jade (*ha-day* in Spanish). The ample new exhibition space (five floors offer six exhibits) allows the public greater access to the museum's varied collection. There are nearly 7000 finely crafted, well-conserved pieces, from translucent jade carvings depicting fertility goddesses, shamans, frogs and snakes to incredible ceramics (some reflecting Maya influences), including a highly unusual ceramic head displaying a row of serrated teeth.

Pre-Columbian jade jewelry, Museo Nacional de Costa Rica

WOLFGANG KAEHLER/LIGHTROCKET/GETTY IMAGES ©

ⓘ Need to Know

Map p48; Avs Central & 2 btwn Calles 13 & 15

✕ Take a Break

Touristy Nuestra Tierra (p54) is a fine spot for lunch and sangria after a visit to the nearby museums.

★ Top Tip

The elevated terraces provide lovely views of the mountains surrounding San José (especially at sunset).

Museo Nacional de Costa Rica

Entered via a beautiful glassed-in atrium housing an exotic butterfly garden, the **Museo Nacional de Costa Rica** (Map p48; ☑2257-1433; www.museocostarica.go.cr; Calle 17 btwn Avs Central & 2; adult/child US$8/4; ⊘8:30am-4:30pm Tue-Sat, 9am-4:30pm Sun) provides a quick survey of Costa Rican history. Exhibits of pre-Columbian pieces from ongoing digs, as well as artifacts from the colony and the early republic, are all housed inside the old Bellavista Fortress, which served historically as the army head-quarters and saw fierce fighting (hence the pockmarks) in the 1948 civil war.

It was here that President José Figueres Ferrer announced, in 1949, that he was abolishing the country's military. Among the museum's many notable pieces is the fountain pen that Figueres used to sign the 1949 constitution.

Don't miss the period galleries in the northeast corner, which feature turn-of-the-20th-century furnishings and decor from when these rooms served as the private residences of the fort's various commanders.

Mercado Artesanal

The **Mercado Artesanal** (Crafts Market; Map p48; Plaza de la Democracia, Avs Central & 2 btwn Calles 13 & 15; ⊘8:30am-5pm) is a touristy open-air market that sells everything from handcrafted jewelry and Bob Marley T-shirts to elaborate woodwork and Guate-malan sarongs.

Asamblea Legislativa

Costa Rica's congress meets in the grand **Asamblea Legislativa** (Legislative Assembly; Map p48) in the center of San José.

San José Walking Tour

Historic Barrio Amón is home to a cluster of *cafetalero* (coffee grower) mansions from the late 19th and early 20th centuries. You'll find everything from art-deco concrete manses to brightly painted tropical Victorian structures, many of which house hotels, cafes and boutiques.

Start Parque España
Distance 1.4km
Duration 2 hours

4 Stroll north on Calle 7 to find cutting-edge contemporary art gallery **TEOR/éTica** (p46), housed in a pair of gorgeous historic mansions.

④

Av 9

Calle 7

Calle 9

⑤

Av 7

5 Back on Av 7, **Galería Namu** (p51) has the country's best selection of indigenous handicrafts.

6 End your tour at **Parque Morazán** (p46), which is particularly lovely in the evenings.

⑥

Parque Morazán

Calle 9

Av 3

Calle 7

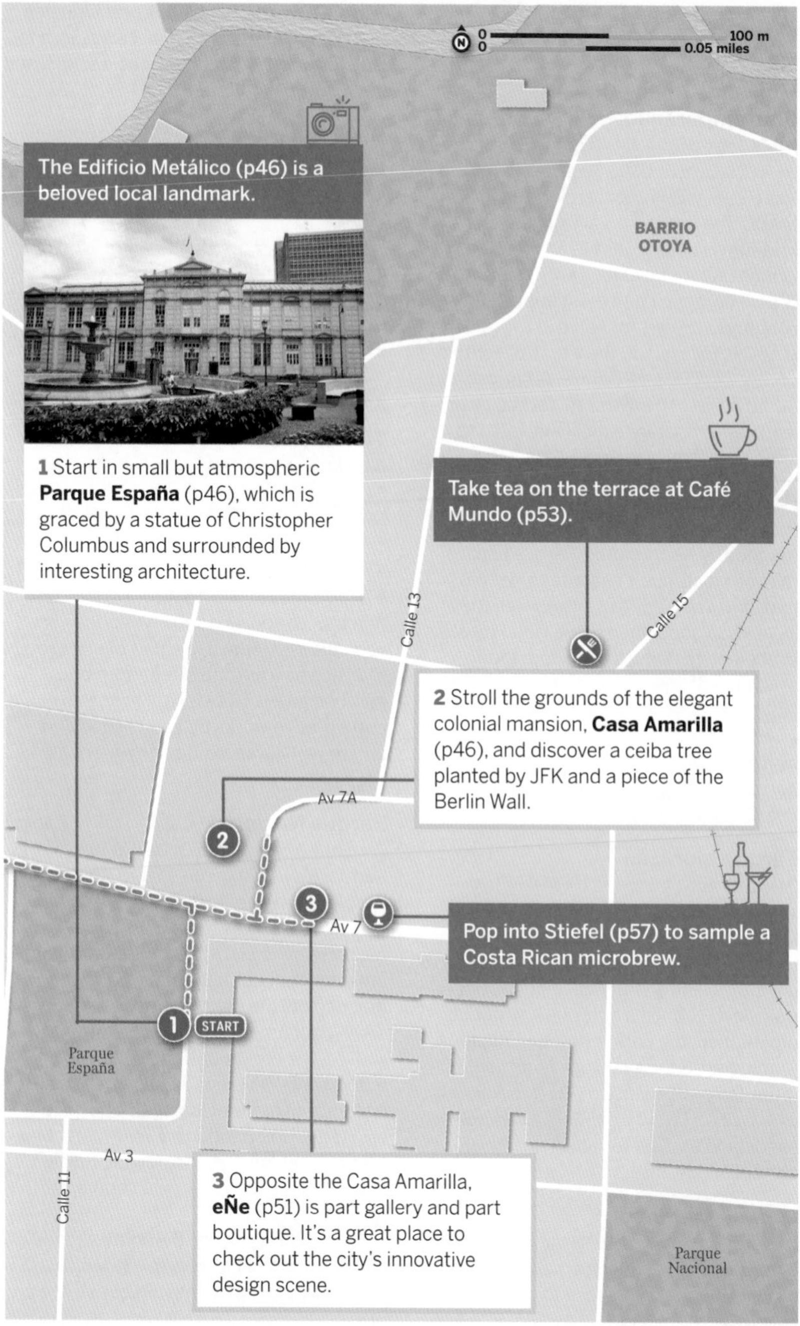

0
0
100 m
0.05 miles

The Edificio Metálico (p46) is a beloved local landmark.

BARRIO OTOYA

1 Start in small but atmospheric **Parque España** (p46), which is graced by a statue of Christopher Columbus and surrounded by interesting architecture.

Take tea on the terrace at Café Mundo (p53).

Calle 13

Calle 15

2 Stroll the grounds of the elegant colonial mansion, **Casa Amarilla** (p46), and discover a ceiba tree planted by JFK and a piece of the Berlin Wall.

Av 7A

Pop into Stiefel (p57) to sample a Costa Rican microbrew.

Av 7

START

Parque España

Av 3

Calle 11

3 Opposite the Casa Amarilla, **eÑe** (p51) is part gallery and part boutique. It's a great place to check out the city's innovative design scene.

Parque Nacional

◎ SIGHTS

◎ Central San José

Museo de Arte y Diseño Contemporáneo   Museum

(MADC; Map p48; ☑2257-7202; www.madc.cr; cnr Av 3 & Calle 15; US$3, Mon free; ☺9:30am-5pm Mon-Sat) Commonly referred to as MADC, the Contemporary Art & Design Museum is housed in the historic National Liquor Factory building, which dates from 1856. The largest and most important contemporary-art museum in the region, MADC is focused on the works of contemporary Costa Rican, Central American and South American artists, and occasionally features temporary exhibits devoted to interior design, fashion and graphic art.

Parque España   Park

(Map p48; Avs 3 & 7 btwn Calles 9 & 11) Surrounded by heavy traffic, Parque España may be small, but it becomes a riot of birdsong every day at sunset when the local avian population comes in to roost. In addition to being a good spot for a shady break, the park is home to an ornate statue of Christopher Columbus that was given to the people of Costa Rica in 2002 by his descendants, commemorating the quincentenary of the explorer's landing in Puerto Limón.

Parque Morazán   Park

(Map p48; Avs 3 & 5 btwn Calles 5 & 9) To the southwest of the Parque España is Parque Morazán, named for Francisco Morazán, the 19th-century general who attempted to unite the Central American nations under a single flag. Once a notorious center of prostitution, the park is now beautifully illuminated in the evenings. At its center is the Templo de Música (Music Temple; Map p48; Avs 3 & 5 btwn Calles 5 & 9), a concrete bandstand that serves as an unofficial symbol of San José.

Edificio Metálico   Landmark

(Map p48; cnr Av 5 & Calle 9) One of downtown San José's most striking buildings, this century-old, two-story metal edifice on Parque España's western edge was prefabricated in Belgium, then shipped piece by piece to San José. Today it functions as a school and local landmark.

Casa Amarilla   Historic Building

(Map p48; Av 7 btwn Calles 11 & 13) On Parque España's northeast corner, this elegant colonial-style yellow mansion (closed to the public) houses the ministry of foreign affairs. The ceiba tree in front was planted by John F Kennedy during his 1963 visit to Costa Rica. If you walk around to the property's northeast corner, you can see a graffiti-covered slab of the Berlin Wall standing in the rear garden.

TEOR/éTica   Gallery

(Map p48; ☑2221-1051; www.teoretica.org; cnr Calle 7 & Av 11; ☺9am-5pm Mon, Tue & Thu, to 6pm Wed, to noon Fri, 10am-4pm Sat) **FREE** This contemporary-art museum is the bricks-and-mortar gathering space for the TEOR/éTica Foundation, a nonprofit organization that supports Central American art and culture. Housed in a pair of vintage mansions across the street from one another, each of its elegant rooms exhibits cutting-edge works by established and emerging figures from Latin America and the world.

Parque Nacional   Park

(Map p48; Avs 1 & 3 btwn Calles 15 & 19) One of San José's nicest green spaces, this shady spot lures in retirees to read newspapers and young couples to smooch coyly on concrete benches. At its center is the Monumento Nacional, a dramatic 1953 statue that depicts the Central American nations driving out American filibuster William Walker. The park is dotted with myriad monuments devoted to Latin American historical figures, including Cuban poet, essayist and revolutionary José Martí, Mexican independence figure Miguel Hidalgo and 18th-century Venezuelan humanist Andrés Bello.

Across the street, to the south, stands the Asamblea Legislativa (p43), which also bears an important statue: this one a depiction of Juan Santamaría – the young man who helped kick the pesky Walker out of Costa Rica – in full flame-throwing action.

Mercado Central   Market

(Map p48; Avs Central & 1 btwn Calles 6 & 8; ☺6am-6pm Mon-Sat) Though *josefinos* mainly do their shopping at chain supermarkets, San José's crowded indoor markets retain an old-world feel. This is the main market, lined with vendors hawking everything from spices and coffee beans to *pura vida* souvenir T-shirts made in China. It's all super cheap, and likely made in China or Nicaragua.

In December Mercado Central is also open on Sundays.

◉ La Sabana & Around

Parque Metropolitano
La Sabana   Park

(Map p52) Once the site of San José's main airport, this 72-hectare green space at the west end of Paseo Colón is home to a museum (Map p52; ☑2256-1281; www.musarco.go.cr; east entrance of Parque La Sabana; ☺9am-4pm Tue-Sun; ♠), a lagoon and various sporting facilities – most notably Costa Rica's national soccer stadium (p60). During the day, the park's paths make a relaxing place for a stroll, a jog or a picnic.

⊕ TOURS

Really Experience
Community   Tour

(Triángulo de la Solidaridad Slum Tour; ☑2297-7058; www.elninoylabolacr.org; per person US$12-25) Nonprofit Boy with a Ball wants to be clear: this is a slum tour. It may seem exploitative, but visiting El Triángulo, a squatter development of 2000 people north of San José, is anything but. Promising young residents lead the tours, introducing guests to neighbors and community entrepreneurs. No cameras are allowed, but the conversations make a lasting impression.

 Kid Stuff in San José

If you're going to be hanging out with kids in San José, it won't be too hard to keep them busy.

Museo de Insectos (Insect Museum; ☑2511-5318; www.miucr.ucr.ac.cr; San Pedro; US$2; ☺8am-noon & 1-5pm Mon-Fri) Reputedly Central America's largest insect museum, this place has an extensive collection assembled by the Facultad de Agronomía at the Universidad de Costa Rica. After viewing the specimens, visitors are invited to sample meal worms, scarabs and crickets. Curiously, the museum is housed in the basement of the music building (Facultad de Artes Musicales), a brutalist structure painted an incongruous shade of Barbie pink.

Museo de los Niños & Galería Nacional (Map p48; ☑2258-4929; www.museocr.org; Calle 4, north of Av 9; adult/child US$4.20/3.80; ☺8am-4:30pm Tue-Fri, 9:30am-5pm Sat & Sun; ♠) If you were wondering how to get your young kids interested in art and science, this unusual museum is an excellent place to start. Housed in an old penitentiary built in 1909, it is part children's museum and part art gallery. Small children will love the hands-on exhibits related to science, geography and natural history, while grown-ups will enjoy the unusual juxtaposition of contemporary art in abandoned prison cells.

Museo de Ciencias Naturales La Salle (Map p52; ☑2232-1306; www.museolasalle.ed.cr; Sabana Sur; adult/child US$2/1.60; ☺8am-4pm Mon-Sat, 9am-5pm Sun; ♠) Ever wanted to see a spider-monkey skeleton or a herd of stuffed tapirs? This natural-history museum near Parque La Sabana's southwest corner has an extensive collection of taxidermic animals and birds from Costa Rica and far beyond, alongside animal skeletons, minerals, preserved specimens and a vast new collection of butterflies.

Central San José

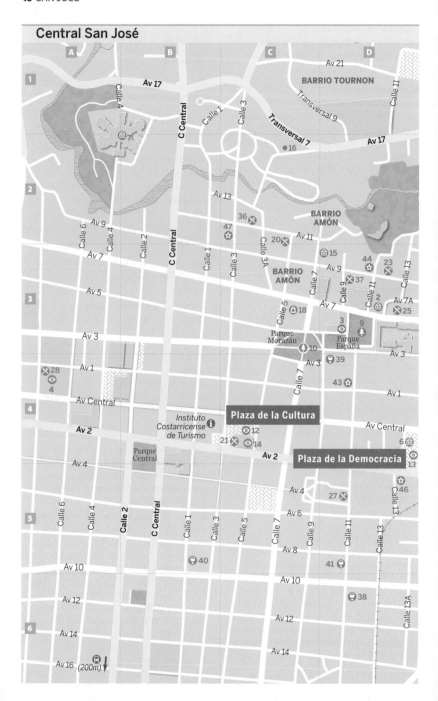

BARRIO TOURNON

BARRIO AMÓN

BARRIO AMÓN

Parque Morazán

Parque España

Parque Central

Instituto Costarricense de Turismo

Plaza de la Cultura

Plaza de la Democracia

Av 21
Av 17
Av 17
Av 13
Av 11
Av 11
Av 9
Av 9
Av 7
Av 7A
Av 7
Av 5
Av 3
Av 3
Av 3
Av 1
Av 1
Av Central
Av Central
Av 2
Av 2
Av 2
Av 4
Av 4
Av 6
Av 8
Av 10
Av 10
Av 12
Av 12
Av 14
Av 14
Av 16 (200m)

Calle 4
C Central
Calle 1
Calle 3
Calle 11
C Central
Calle 6
Calle 4
Calle 2
Calle 1
Calle 3
Calle 3A
Calle 5
Calle 7
Calle 9
Calle 11
Calle 13
Calle 2
Calle 7
Calle 13
Calle 6
Calle 4
Calle 2
C Central
Calle 1
Calle 3
Calle 5
Calle 7
Calle 9
Calle 11
Calle 13
Calle 13A

Transversal 9
Transversal 7

16
36
47
20
15
44
23
37
2
25
18
3
9
10
39
43
28
4
12
21
14
6
13
46
27
40
41
38

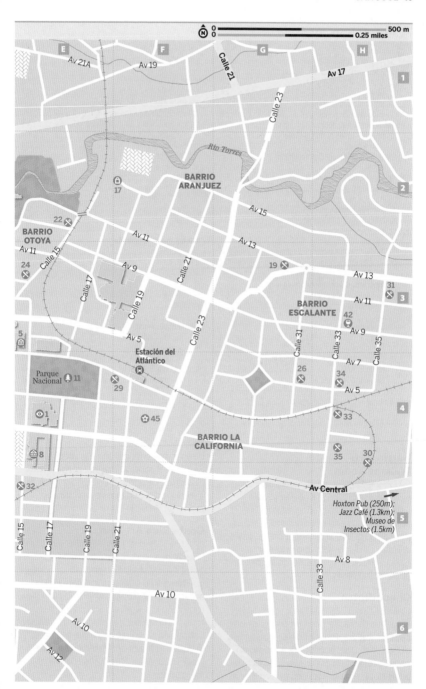

0 _____ 500 m
0 _____ 0.25 miles

Av 21A
Av 19
Calle 21
Av 17

Calle 23

Río Torres

**BARRIO
ARANJUEZ**

17

Av 15

22

**BARRIO
OTOYA**

Av 11

Av 11

Av 13

24

Calle 15

Av 9

19

Av 13

Calle 17

Calle 21

Calle 19

31

Av 11

**BARRIO
ESCALANTE**

42

Av 9

Calle 31

Calle 33

Calle 35

Av 5

Calle 23

Av 7

**Estación del
Atlántico**

26

34

Av 5

Parque
Nacional 11

29

1

45

33

**BARRIO LA
CALIFORNIA**

8

35

30

32

Av Central

*Hoxton Pub (250m);
Jazz Café (1.3km);
Museo de
Insectos (1.5km)*

Calle 15

Calle 17

Calle 19

Calle 21

Av 8

Calle 33

Av 10

Av 10

Av 12

Central San José

Barrio Bird Walking Tours
Walking Tour

(☏6280-6169; www.toursanjosecostarica. com; tours from US$29) Knowledgeable and engaging guides show visitors San José's famous and not-so-famous sights, providing history and insight on the city's architecture, markets and urban art. Specialized tours also cater to foodies and LGBT enthusiasts.

ChepeCletas
Tour

(☏8849-8316, 2222-7548; www.chepecletas. com) This dynamic Tico-run company offers cultural walking tours and free cycling tours of San José (tips accepted), a foodie-oriented exploration of the Mercado Central, a bar-hopping tour focused on traditional downtown cantinas, and a guided visit to San José's parks and green spaces. They also offer a nighttime biking tour once a week and group rides every Sunday morning.

Costa Rica Art Tour
Tour

(☏8359-5571, in USA 877-394-6113; www.costa ricaarttour.com; per person US$150) This small outfit run by Molly Keeler conducts private day tours that offers an intimate look at artists in their studios, where you can view (and buy) the work of local painters, sculptors, printmakers, ceramicists and jewelers. Lunch and San José city hotel pickup is included in the price. Reserve at least a week in advance. Discounts are available for groups.

Carpe Chepe Tour

(☏8326-6142; www.carpechepe.com; guided pub crawls US$20; ⏱7pm Thu & Sat) For an insider's look at Chepe's nightlife, join one of these lively guided pub crawls on Thursday and Saturday evenings, led by an enthusiastic group of young locals. A free welcome shot is included at each of the four bars visited. Online bookings receive a 20% discount.

Swiss Travel Service Walking Tour

(Map p48; ☏2282-4898; www.swisstravelcr.com) This long-standing agency offers a four-hour afternoon city tour of San José that hits all the key sites.

🔒 SHOPPING

Whether you're looking for indigenous carvings, high-end furnishings or a stuffed sloth, San José has no shortage of shops, running the gamut from artsy boutiques to tourist traps stocked full of tropical everything. Haggling is not tolerated in stores (markets are the exception).

In touristy shops, keep watch for 'authentic' woodwork pieces that have 'Made in Indonesia' stamped on the bottom. For the country's finest woodcrafts, it is absolutely worth the trip to Biesanz Woodworks (p54).

Feria Verde de Aranjuez Market

(Map p48; www.feriaverde.org; ⏱7am-noon Sat) For a foodie-friendly cultural experience, don't miss this fabulous Saturday farmers market, a weekly meeting place for San José's artists and organic growers since 2010. You'll find organic coffee, artisanal chocolate, tropical-fruit Popsicles, fresh produce, baked goods, leather, jewelry and more at the long rows of booths set up in the park at the north end of Barrio Aranjuez.

Galería Namu Handicrafts

(Map p48; ☏2256-3412, in USA 800-616-4322; www.galerianamu.com; Av 7 btwn Calles 5 & 7; ⏱9am-6:30pm Mon-Sat year-round, plus 1-4pm Sun Dec-Apr) This fair-trade gallery brings together artwork and cultural objects from a diverse population of regional ethnicities, including Boruca masks, finely woven Wounaan baskets, Guaymí dolls, Bribrí canoes, Chorotega ceramics, traditional Huetar reed mats, and contemporary urban and Afro-Caribbean crafts. It can also help arrange visits to remote indigenous territories in different parts of Costa Rica.

Kiosco SJO Handicrafts

(Map p48; ☏2253-8426; www.kioscosjo.com; cnr Calle 31 & Av 5; ⏱noon-10pm Tue-Fri, 9am-10pm Sat, 9am-4pm Sun) With a focus on sustainable design by Latin American artisans, this sleek shop in Barrio Escalante stocks handmade jewelry, hand-tooled leather boots and bags, original photography, artisanal chocolates, fashion and contemporary home decor by established regional designers. It's pricey, but rest assured that everything you find here will be of exceptional quality.

eÑe Handicrafts

(Map p48; ☏2222-7681; laesquina13y7@gmail. com; cnr Av 7 & Calle 13; ⏱10am-6:30pm Mon-Sat) This hip little design shop across from Casa Amarilla sells all manner of pieces crafted by Costa Rican designers and artists, including clothing, jewelry, handbags, picture frames, zines and works of graphic art.

✕ EATING

From humble corner stands dishing out gut-filling *casados* (set meals) to contemporary bistros serving fusion everything, in cosmopolitan San José you will find the country's best restaurant scene. Dedicated eaters should also check out the dining options in Los Yoses and San Pedro, as well as Escazú.

Top-end restaurants tend to get busy on weekend evenings; make a reservation.

Central San José

Café de los Deseos Cafe $

(Map p48; ☏2222-0496; www.facebook.com/ Cafedelosdeseos; Calle 15 btwn Avs 9 & 11; mains

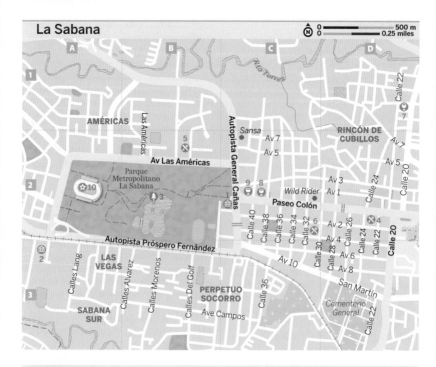

La Sabana

US$5-12; ⊘2-10pm Tue-Sat; 🛜) Abuzz with artsy young bohemians, this cozy, colorful Barrio Otoya cafe makes a romantic spot for drinks (from wine to cocktails to smoothies), *bocas* (handmade tortillas with Turrialba cheese, salads, teriyaki chicken, individual pizzas), and tempting desserts. Walls are hung with the work of local artists and rooms are adorned with hand-painted tables, beaded curtains and branches entwined with fairy lights.

La Ventanita Meraki   Fast Food $
(Map p48; ☑4034-2655; www.facebook.com /laventanitameraki; Av 3 & Calle 21, in front of the train station; mains US$5-8; ⊘noon-9pm Tue-Thu, to 2am Fri, 6pm-2am Sat) Ventanita means 'little window' in Spanish and Meraki means 'artistry' in Greek. Put them together and it's an accurate moniker for this new fusion hole-in-the-wall, a to-go window in front of downtown's train station that serves innovative street food. Expect elaborate spins on typical fare,

along with sandwiches like pumpkin butter cheese madness, and Twinkie *frito* (fried Twinkie) for dessert.

Café Té Ría
Cafe $

(Map p48; ☏2222-8272; www.facebook.com/CafeTeRiaenAmon; cnr Av 7 & Calle 13; mains US$6, cakes US$1.50-3; ⏱10:30am-7:30pm Mon-Fri, noon-7:30 Sat; 🛜🖊🐾) This petite, pet-friendly cafe in Barrio Amón is adorned with local art and replete with homey goodness. It's a perfect place to work over a few cups of morning coffee, then stay for lunch. Specials often include a mouthwatering baked trout with capers and a fresh salad. Sandwiches and pastries are also a big hit, and vegetarians are well served.

Alma de Café
Cafe $

(Map p48; ☏2010-1119; www.almadecafe.net; Teatro Nacional; mains US$6-11; ⏱9am-7pm Mon-Sat, to 6pm Sun) One of the most beautiful cafes in the city, this atmospheric spot evokes early-20th-century Vienna. In other words, it's a perfect place to sip cappuccino, enjoy a crepe or quiche and take in the lovely ceiling frescoes and rotating art exhibitions. The elaborate coffee cocktails are an excellent midday indulgence.

Talentum
Cafe $

(Map p48; ☏2256-6346; www.galeriatalentum.com; Av 11 btwn Calles 3 & 3A; lunch specials US$8-10; ⏱11am-7pm Mon & Tue, to 8pm Wed-Fri) This vibrant, quirky cultural space in a renovated mansion runs the gamut from cafe to art gallery. Sporting local artwork inside and out, with cozy seating on vintage couches and an outdoor deck,
it's a fun place for a midday break. The ever-changing cultural agenda includes book signings, films, anatomical drawing classes and occasional live music.

Café Miel
Cafe $

(Map p48; www.facebook.com/cafemielcostarica; Av 9 btwn Calle 11 & 13; coffee US$1-5, pastries US$2; ⏱9am-6pm Mon-Fri, 2-6pm Sat) This tiny cafe opened to such wild success in 2014 that the owners opened another one right down the street. What's their secret? In

addition to adorable and homey interiors, there are artisanal products from the cafes' chefs and bakers. The mushroom *empanadas* are divine, as is the locally sourced coffee.

Zero Army
Cafe $

(Map p48; ☏2248-2401; www.facebook.com/zeroarmycr; Calle 9 & Av 9; smoothies US$3-4; ⏱6:30am-5:15pm Mon-Fri, 9am-2pm Sat) Named for Costa Rica's nonexistent army, this new smoothie and juice bar in the center of Barrio Amón serves fresh fruit drinks in reusable glass bottles. The smoothies are all-natural, highly refreshing and named for Costa Rican destinations. Breakfast wraps are highly recommended.

La Sorbetera de Lolo Mora
Desserts $

(Map p48; ☏2256-5000; Mercado Central; desserts US$2-5; ⏱9:30am-5:45pm Mon-Sat) Head to the main market for dessert at this century-old local favorite that serves up fresh sorbet and cinnamon-laced frozen custard. Do as the locals do and order *barquillos* (cylindrical sugar cookies that are perfect for dipping).

Alma de Amón
Latin American $

(Map p48; ☏2222-3232; www.facebook.com/AlmadeAmon/; Calle 5 btwn Avs 9 & 11; small plates US$6-9; ⏱11am-10pm Mon-Wed, to midnight Thu-Sat) With entrées from nearly a dozen Latin countries and considerable Caribbean influence, this new restaurant is raising the bar in Barrio Amón. Popular menu items include *mofongo* (a Puerto Rican dish with fried plantains) and *coxinhas* (Brazilian croquettes with chicken). The mixologist whips up spicy and delicious cocktails; El Chapulin has tequila, ginger beer, lime and sugar-cane syrup.

Café Mundo
Italian $$

(Map p48; ☏2222-6190; cnr Av 9 & Calle 15; mains US$8-36; ⏱11am-10pm Mon-Wed, to 10:30pm Thu, 5pm-11:30 Sat; 🖊) This longtime Italian cafe and expat favorite is set on a sprawling terrace in a vintage Barrio Otoya mansion. It's a perfect spot to enjoy a glass

Biesanz Woodworks

Located in the hills of Bello Horizonte in Escazú, the workshop of **Biesanz Woodworks** (☑2289-4337; www.biesanz.com; ☺8am-5pm Mon-Fri, 9am-2pm Sat) can be difficult to find, but the effort will be well worth it. This shop is one of the finest woodcrafting studios in the nation, run by celebrated artisan Barry Biesanz.

His bowls and other decorative containers are exquisite and take their inspiration from pre-Columbian techniques, in which the natural lines and forms of the wood determine the shape and size of the bowl. The pieces are expensive (from US$45 for a palm-size bowl), but they are unique – and so delicately crafted that they wouldn't be out of place in a museum. Indeed, Biesanz pieces are part of the collections of the Queen and Prince of Spain, as well as five US Presidents. While Biesanz crafts boxes of all sorts, his specialty is nesting boxes (a set of three or four, which fit inside each other).

Behind Biesanz Woodworks, there is a small botanical garden, replete with medicinal plants, rare wood trees, and plenty of edibles. Labels along the paths encourage independent wandering.

Wooden items made at Biesanz Woodworks
IMAGE SUPPLIED BY BIESANZ WOODWORKS

of wine and good (if not earth-shattering) pizzas and pastas within sight of a splashing outdoor fountain. At lunchtime on weekdays, don't miss the good-value *plato del día* (plate of the day; US$8).

Lubnan   Lebanese $$
(Map p52; ☑2257-6071; www.facebook.com/lubnancostarica; Paseo Colón btwn Calles 22 & 24; mains US$8-25; ☺11am-3pm & 6pm-midnight Tue-Fri, noon-4pm & 6pm-midnight Sat, 11am-5pm Sun; ℗) This atmospheric Lebanese place is a great date spot, with creamy hummus, flavorful tabbouleh and an array of succulent meats – some cooked, some deliciously raw. Waiters wear fezzes and a live belly-dancing performance goes down every Thursday at 8:30pm.

Nuestra Tierra   Costa Rican $$
(Map p48; ☑2222-2223, 2258-6500; cnr Av 2 & Calle 15; mains US$6-22; ☺6am-midnight; ☷) Touristy but fun, this bustling eatery maintains a calculatedly rustic atmosphere, with picnic-style tables, mounted bull heads and strings of metal cups dangling from the rafters. Cheery waiters deliver well-prepared if overpriced Tico food, from tasty pork tamales to wooden platters piled with heaping *casados* (set meals). A fine spot for lunch and sangria after a visit to the nearby museums.

La Esquina de Buenos Aires   Argentine $$$
(Map p48; ☑2223-1909; cnr Calle 11 & Av 4; mains US$15-29; ☺11:30am-3pm & 6-10:30pm Mon-Thu, 11:30-11pm Fri, 12:30pm-11pm Sat, noon-10pm Sun; ☑) White linens and the sound of old tango evoke the atmospheric bistros of San Telmo, as does the menu, featuring grilled Argentine cuts of steak, house-made *empanadas* and an extensive selection of fresh pastas in exquisite sauces. The excellent South American–centric wine list, attentive service and flickering candlelight make this an ideal place for a date. Reservations recommended.

🝔 La Sabana & Around

Park Café   European $$$
(Map p52; ☑2290-6324; parkcafecostarica.blogspot.com; tapas US$6-15; ☺5-9:15pm Tue-Sat) At this felicitous fusion of antique shop and French restaurant, Michelin-starred chef

Traditional Costa Rican *casado* (set meal)

Richard Neat offers an exquisite dégustation menu featuring smaller sampling plates (Spanish tapas style) and a carefully curated wine list. The romantic, candlelit courtyard is eclectically decorated with Asian antiques imported by Neat's partner, Louise French. It's near Parque La Sabana's northeast corner (100m north of Rostipollos restaurant).

Restaurante Grano de Oro
Fusion $$$

(Map p52; ☑2255-3322; www.hotelgranode oro.com; Calle 30 btwn Avs 2 & 4; lunch mains US$15-29, dinner mains US$19-42; ☺7am-10pm) Known for its Costa Rican–fusion cuisine, this stately, flower-filled restaurant is one of San José's top dining destinations. The menu is laced with unique specialties such as sea bass breaded with toasted macadamia nuts, and seared duck crowned with caramelized figs, and there's an encyclopedic international wine list. For dessert, don't miss the coffee cream mousse. Dinner reservations recommended.

🍴 Los Yoses, Barrio Escalante & San Pedro

Café Kracovia
Cafe $

(☑2253-9093; www.cafekracovia.com; snacks US$4-10, mains US$8-14; ☺10:30am-9pm Mon, to 11pm Tue-Sat; 🛜) With several distinct spaces, from a low-lit, intimate downstairs to an outdoor garden courtyard, this hip cafe has something for everyone. Contemporary artwork and a distinct university vibe create an appealing ambiance for lunching on crepes, wraps, salads, daily specials and craft beer. It's 500m north of the Fuente de la Hispanidad traffic circle, where San Pedro and Los Yoses converge.

Al Mercat
Gastronomy $$

(Map p48; ☑2221-0783; www.almercat.com; Barrio Escalante; US$13-25; ☺noon-3pm Mon-Fri, 7:30pm-midnight Thu-Sat; 🍴) This exquisite new Barrio Escalante restaurant serves whatever is fresh from the market. Family-style courses such as grilled avocado, and hummus with chickpeas and peach palm fruit, are fresh and flavorful.

And although vegetarians are well served, meat eaters will appreciate the fine cuts of meat. The service here is impeccable, and the atmosphere is enlivened by vertical gardens.

Olio
Mediterranean $$

(Map p48; ☎2281-0541; www.facebook.com/ Restaurante.olio; cnr Calle 33 & Av 3; tapas from US$7; dishes US$12-22; ◷noon-midnight Mon-Fri, from 6pm Sat; ☑) This cozy, Mediterranean-flavored gastropub in a century-old brick building in Barrio Escalante serves a long list of tempting tapas, including divine stuffed mushrooms, goat-cheese croquettes, and house-made pastas. The enticing drinks list includes homemade sangria and a decent selection of beers and wine. It's a romantic spot for a date, with imaginative, conversation-worthy quirks of decor and beautiful patrons.

Sofia Mediterráneo
Mediterranean $$

(Map p48; ☎2224-5050; www.facebook.com/ SofiaMediterraneo; cnr Calle 33 & Av 1; mains US$8-22; ◷6pm-11pm Tue-Fri, noon-11pm Sat, noon-5pm & 6:30-9pm Sun; ☑) This Barrio

Escalante gem serves a superb mix of authentic Mediterranean specialties, including house-made hummus, tortellini, grilled lamb and a rotating selection of daily specials, accompanied by sweet, delicate baklava for dessert. The restaurant doubles as a community cultural center where owner Mehmet Onuralp hosts occasional theme dinners featuring musicians, chefs and speakers from around the world.

Rávi Gastropub
Pub Food $$

(Map p48; ☎2253-3771; www.facebook.com/ ravicostarica; cnr Calle 33 & Av 5; mains US$9-18; ◷3pm-midnight Tue-Sat) This cool corner pub in Barrio Escalante is awash in bright murals, with seating in funky red booths, intimate back rooms or at the convivial bar stools up front. A menu of *bocas*, sandwiches, pizzas and more is served with craft brew on tap and homemade tropical-fruit sodas served in cute little bell jars.

Mantras
Vegetarian $$

(Map p48; ☎2253-6715; www.facebook. com/mantrasveggiecafe; Calle 35 btwn Avs 11 & 13; mains US$8-10; ◷8:30am-5pm; ☑)

Widely recognized as the best vegetarian restaurant in San José (if not all of Costa Rica), Mantras draws rave reviews from across the foodie spectrum for meatless main dishes, salads and desserts so delicious that it's easy to forget you're eating healthily. It's in Barrio Escalante, and for Sunday brunch, the line often stretches out the door.

Lolo's — Pizza $$

(Map p48; ☏2283-9627; pizzas US$14-24; ☺6pm-midnight Mon-Sat) Fans of bohemian chic will appreciate this quirky pizzeria, hidden in a mustard-yellow house (No 3396) along the railroad tracks north of Av Central in Barrio Escalante. The vibrantly colorful, low-lit interior, hung with an eclectic collection of plates and other knickknacks, creates an artsy, romantic setting for sangria and pizzas fired up in the bright-red oven out back.

Kalú Café & Food Shop — International $$$

(Map p48; ☏2253-8426, 2253-8367; www.kalu.co.cr; cnr Calle 31 & Av 5; mains US$15-21; ☺noon-10pm Tue-Fri, 9am-10pm Sat, 9am-

4pm Sun; 🐾) Sharing a sleek space with Kiosco SJO (p51) in Barrio Escalante, chef Camille Ratton's exceptional back-patio cafe serves a global fusion menu of soups, salads, sandwiches, pastas and unconventional delights such as the fish taco trio filled with mango-glazed salmon, red curry prawns and macadamia-crusted tuna. Don't miss the mind-meltingly delicious passion-fruit pie.

🍷 DRINKING & NIGHTLIFE

Whatever your poison, San José has plenty of venues to keep you lubricated.

Stiefel — Pub

(Map p48; www.facebook.com/StiefelPub; ☺6pm-2am Mon-Sat) Two-dozen-plus Costa Rican microbrews on tap and an appealing setting in a historic building create a convivial buzz at this pub half a block from Plaza España. Grab a pint of Pelona or Maldita Vida, Malinche or Chichemel; better yet, order a flight of four miniature sampler glasses and try 'em all!

★ Top 5 for Foodies

Al Mercat (p55)

Park Café (p54)

Kalú Café & Food Shop

Rávi Gastropub

La Ventanita Meraki (p52)

From left: Outdoor produce market; Market eatery; *Casado* (set meal) with meat, rice, beans and plantains

ALFONSE PAGANO/GETTY IMAGES ©

EQROY/SHUTTERSTOCK ©

Costa Rica Craft Brewing   Brewery
(☎2249-0919; www.facebook.com/craftbeer-costarica; Ciudad Colón; ⏱9am-5pm Mon, to 11pm Tue & Wed, to midnight Thu, noon-5pm Fri, 1pm-midnight Sat, noon-6pm Sun) Just when everyone thought it would be Imperial and Pilsen forever, this artisanal brew pub paved the way for craft beer in Costa Rica. The brewery's new location in Ciudad Colón offers facility tours and tastings of its fine products, which include staple ales like Libertas and Segua, along with more experimental drinks like barley wines and Russian Imperil stouts.

It's out of town; ask locally for directions.

Hoxton Pub   Pub
(☎7168-1083; www.facebook.com/hoxtonstag; ⏱9pm-4am Tue-Sat) Good cocktails, great music and a lively dance floor in a cool old Los Yoses mansion just east of Subaru. The place often holds theme nights and brings in good DJs on the weekend. Tuesday's ladies night is the biggest party in town, with women paying no cover and drinking free until midnight. Hundreds show up to rage till dawn.

Wilk   Brewery
(Map p48; www.facebook.com/wilkcraftbeer; Calle 33 & Av 9; ⏱4pm-1am Tue-Sat) This new pub in Barrio Escalante attracts a mixed crowd of Ticos and gringos who share an appreciation for craft brews and seriously delicious burgers (veggie included). The wide selection of craft beer includes all of the inventive concoctions of Costa Rica Craft Brewing (p58), which is a partner in the pub.

Castro's   Club
(Map p52; ☎2256-8789; cnr Av 13 & Calle 22; ⏱6pm-3am Sun-Thu, 5pm-4:30am Fri & Sat) Chepe's oldest dance club, this classic Latin American disco in Barrio México draws crowds of locals and tourists to its large dance floor with a dependable mix of salsa, cumbia and merengue.

Chubbs   Sports Bar
(Map p48; ☎2222-4622; 2nd fl, Calle 9 btwn Avs 1 & 3) Decidedly local, in the heart of the San José tourist belt, this humble little sports bar has reasonably priced drinks, tasty burgers, a stack of TVs displaying the game

Flower stall, Mercado Central (p49)

GARDEL BERTRAND/AGEFOTOSTOCK ©

and a supersized mural of dogs playing poker. Awesome.

Pub
Bar

(☏2288-3062; www.facebook.com/thepubcr; Av 26 btwn Calles 128 & 130; ⏱4pm-2am Sun-Fri, 1pm-2am Sat) This small, friendly expat pub has a list of more than two-dozen international beers, more than a dozen local brews and a selection of shots. Well-priced happy-hour drink specials keep things hopping, and a greasy bar menu is available to soak up the damage.

Club Vertigo
Club

(Map p52; ☏2257-8424; www.vertigocr.com; Paseo Colón btwn Calles 38 & 40; cover US$6-15; ⏱10pm-dawn) Located on the ground floor of the nondescript Centro Colón office tower, the city's premier club packs in Chepe's beautiful people with a mix of house, trance and electronica. Downstairs is an 850-person-capacity sweat-box of a dance floor; upstairs is a chill-out lounge lined with red sofas. Dress to the nines and expect admission charges to skyrocket on guest-DJ nights.

Rapsodia
Lounge

(Map p52; ☏2248-1720; www.rapsodiacr.com; cnr Paseo Colón & Calle 40; ⏱9:30pm-3:30am Fri, to 6am Sat) This hyper-chic, see-and-be-seen club, clad in white and gold, has an extensive list of cocktails and a menu of Mediterranean-inspired dishes and snacks. Guest DJs set the mood with a mix of electronica and other sounds every Friday and Saturday.

ENTERTAINMENT

Pick up *La Nación* on Thursday for listings (in Spanish) of the coming week's attractions. The *Tico Times* 'Weekend' section (in English) has a calendar of theater, music and museum events. The free publication GAM Cultural (www.gamcultural.com) and the website San José Volando (www.sanjosevolando.com) are also helpful guides to nightlife and cultural events.

 LGBT
San José

The city is home to Central America's most thriving gay and lesbian scene. As with other spots, admission charges vary depending on the night and location (from US$5 to US$10). Some clubs close on various nights of the week (usually Sunday to Tuesday) and others host women- or men-only nights; inquire ahead or check individual club websites for listings.

Many clubs are on the south side of town, which can get rough after dark. Take a taxi.

La Avispa (Map p48; ☏2223-5343; www.laavispa.com; Calle 1 btwn Avs 8 & 10; ⏱8pm-6am Thu-Sat, 5pm-6am Sun) A lesbian disco bar that has been in operation for more than three decades, La Avispa (The Wasp) has a bar, pool tables and a boisterous dance floor that's highly recommended by travelers.

Bochinche (Map p48; ☏2221-0500; cnr Calle 11 & Av 10; ⏱8pm-5am Wed-Sat) A club that features everything from classic disco to electronica, as well as special themed nights. As this club is on the south side of town, it can get rough after dark.

Pucho's Bar (Map p48; ☏2256-1147; cnr Calle 11 & Av 8; ⏱8pm-2am Mon-Sat) This gay male outpost is more low-rent (and significantly raunchier) than some; it features scantily clad go-go boys and over-the-top drag shows.

From left: Tile painting in Central San José; Market stalls; Costa Rican soccer fans

El Lobo Estepario
Live Music

(Map p48; ☏2256-3934; www.facebook.com/loboestepariocr; Av 2, corner opposite La Caja de ANDE; ⊙4pm-12:45am Sun-Thu, to 2am Fri & Sat, closed Mon) This artsy dive attracts some of the top local talent for live music gigs.

Casino Club Colonial
Casino

(Map p48; ☏2258-2807; www.casinoclubcolonial.com; Av 1 btwn Calles 9 & 11; ⊙24hr) San José's most elegant casino.

8ctavo Rooftop
Live Music

(☏4055-0588; www.facebook.com/8voRooftop; Hotel Sheraton San José) See and be seen at this swanky rooftop lounge, where international DJs regularly perform. If you want to show up early and dine first, this place is also a hit for the city views, the eclectic menu and the spicy cocktails.

It's right off Hwy 27 on the west side of Escazú.

El Sótano
Live Music

(Map p48; ☏2221-2302; www.facebook.com/sotanocr; cnr Calle 3 & Av 11; ⊙7pm-2:30am Mon, noon-2:30am Tue-Sat, 2-6pm Sun) One of Chepe's most atmospheric nightspots, Só-tano is named for its cellar jazz club, where people crowd in for frequent performances including intimate Tuesday jam sessions. Upstairs, a cluster of elegant high-ceilinged rooms in the same mansion have been converted to a gallery space, stage, and dance floor where an eclectic mix of groups play live gigs.

Jazz Café
Live Music

(☏2253-8933; www.jazzcafecostarica.com; Av Central; cover US$5-10; ⊙6pm-2am Mon-Sat) This intimate San Pedro venue presents a different band every night. Countless performers have taken to the stage here, including legendary Cuban bandleader Chucho Valdés and Colombian pop star Juanes. Its sister club in Escazú (p61) features a similar mix of local and international bands.

Estadio Nacional de Costa Rica
Stadium

(Map p52; Parque Metropolitano La Sabana) Costa Rica's graceful, modernist 35,000-seat national soccer stadium, constructed with funding from the Chinese government and

WENN.COM/AGEFOTOSTOCK ©

opened to the public in 2011, is the venue for international and national Division-1 *fútbol* (soccer) games. Its predecessor, dating to 1924 and located in the same spot in Parque Metropolitano La Sabana, hosted everyone from Pope John Paul II to soccer legend Pelé to Bruce Springsteen over its 84-year history.

Centro de Cine   Cinema

(Map p48; ☑2242-5200; www.centrodecine. go.cr; cnr Calle 11 & Av 9) This pink Victorian mansion houses the government-run film center and its vast archive of national and international flicks. Festivals, lectures and events are held here and in outside venues; check the site for current events.

Jazz Café Escazú   Live Music

(☑2288-4740; Autopista Próspero Fernández, north side; cover US$5-10; ☺6pm-2am) Find a little aural satisfaction at the Jazz Café, the sister club of the San Pedro (p60) standard-bearer. The calendar features a mix of local and international bands. If you're coming from San José, take the exit immediately after the tollbooth.

El Cuartel de la Boca del Monte   Live Music

(Map p48; ☑2221-0327; www.facebook.com/ elcuartelcr; Av 1 btwn Calles 21 & 23; ☺11:30am-2pm Mon-Fri, 6pm-midnight daily) This atmospheric old Barrio La California bar has long drawn cheek-by-jowl crowds for live bands. Friday is a good night to visit, as is Monday, when women get free admission and the band cranks out a crazy mix of calypso, salsa, reggae and rock. It's popular with university students, who indulge in flirting, drinking and various combinations thereof.

❶ INFORMATION

EMERGENCY

Fire ☑118

Red Cross ☑128

Traffic Police ☑2222-9245, 2222-9330

GAY & LESBIAN TRAVELERS

In recent years attitudes toward LGBT locals and travelers have shifted towards acceptance.

Gay pride parades take place regularly, and the city's youth are leading the country's tolerance movement. A good site for all things gay travel is www.costaricagaymap.com, which offers listings of bars, clubs and hotels that cater to the LGBT community.

GETTING THERE & AWAY

All international flights leave from Juan Santamaría (SJO) airport outside Alajuela.

Aeropuerto Internacional Juan Santamaría (p292) Handles all international flights and **NatureAir** (☑2299-6000, in USA 1-800-235-9272; www.natureair.com) domestic flights in its main terminal. Domestic flights on **Sansa** (Map p52; ☑2290-4100; www.flysansa.com) depart from the Sansa terminal.

Aeropuerto Tobías Bolaños (☑2232-2820; Pavas) In the San José suburb of Pavas; services private charter and a few national flights.

GETTING AROUND

Central San José frequently resembles a parking lot – narrow streets, heavy traffic and a complicated one-way system mean that it is often quicker to walk than to take the bus. The same applies to driving: if you rent a car, try to avoid downtown. If you're in a real hurry to get somewhere that's more than 1km away, take a taxi.

CAR

It is not advisable to rent a car just to drive around San José. The traffic is heavy, the streets are narrow and the meter-deep curbside gutters make parking nerve-wracking. In addition, break-ins are frequent, and leaving a car – even in a guarded lot – might result in a smashed window and stolen belongings.

If you are renting a car to travel throughout Costa Rica, there are more than 50 car-rental agencies – including many of the global brands – in and around San José. One excellent local option is **Wild Rider** (Map p52; ☑2258-4604; www.wild-rider.com; Paseo Colón btwn Calles 30 & 32; ◷8am-6pm). They have a fleet of over 60 very reasonably priced 4WD vehicles (from US$380 per week in high season, including all mandatory insurance coverage). Reserve well in advance.

TAXI

Red taxis can be hailed on the street, day or night, or you can have your hotel call one for you. Make sure the *maría* (meter) is operating when you get in, or negotiate the fare up front. Short rides downtown cost from US$2 to US$4. There's a 20% surcharge after 10pm that may not appear on the *maría*.

You can hire a taxi and a driver for half a day or longer if you want to do some touring around the area; for such trips, it is best to negotiate a flat fee in advance. Uber has also become a popular form of transport in the city.

Where to Stay

Reservations are recommended in the high season (December through April), in particular the two weeks around Christmas and Semana Santa (Holy Week, the week preceding Easter).

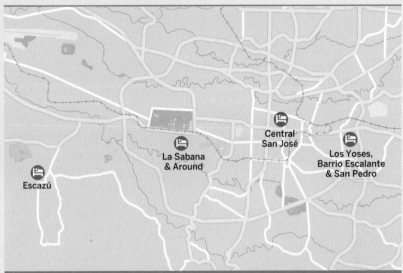

Neighborhood	Atmosphere
Central San José	The best hotels are east of Calle Central, many of which are housed in historic Victorian and art-deco mansions; close to sights, restaurants and nightlife; non-stop traffic jams and street noise.
La Sabana & Around	West of the city center; great variety of accommodations, from hostels to vintage B&Bs; pleasant setting around Parque Metropolitano La Sabana; some good dining venues, though budget options are limited.
Los Yoses, Barrio Escalante & San Pedro	Lively university area, replete with restaurants and nightlife; walking distance to city center; excellent choices for budget travelers.
Escazú	An affluent suburb with accommodations ranging from sleek boutique inns to homey B&Bs, mostly upscale; innovative dining scene; 20-minute drive or bus ride from city center; challenging to navigate.

VOLCÁN
POÁS

In this Chapter

Volcán Poás at a glance...

Just 37km north of Alajuela, by a winding and scenic road, is Parque Nacional Volcán Poás, ideal for those who want to peer into an active volcano without the hardship of hiking one. Volcán Poás (2704m) had its last blowout in 1953, which formed the enormous crater measuring 1.3km across and 300m deep. Poás offers the wonderful opportunity to watch the bubbling cauldron belch sulfurous mud and water hundreds of meters into the air. In recent years, Poás has posed no imminent threat of eruption, though scientists still monitor it closely.

One Day in Poás

Perhaps you have just flown into Juan Santamaría International Airport, or perhaps you're on your way out. Either way, **Parque Nacional Volcán Poás** (p68) is a perfect place to begin or end your Costa Rican adventure. Just be sure to get there early. In Alajuela, treat yourself to dinner at **Xandari** (p73) and go out (or in) in style.

Two Days in Poás

On your second day, make a bee-line to **La Paz Waterfall Gardens** (p73) (perhaps en route to your next destination). Spend the day exploring the trails, admiring the waterfalls and ogling the animals. And if you're spending the night here...lucky you!

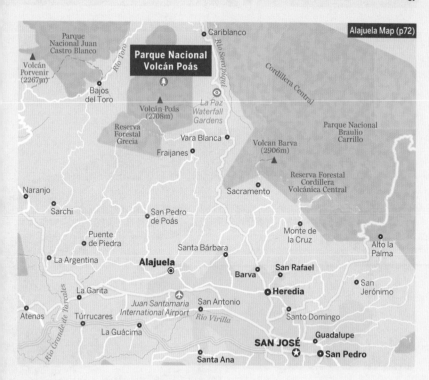

Alajuela Map (p72)

Parque
Nacional Juan
Castro Blanco

Volcán
Porvenir
(2267m)

Bajos
del Toro

Cariblanco

**Parque Nacional
Volcán Poás**

Volcán Poás
(2708m)

La Paz
Waterfall
Gardens

Reserva
Forestal
Grecia

Vara Blanca

Fraijanes

Cordillera Central

Volcán Barva
(2906m)

Parque Nacional
Braulio
Carrillo

Reserva Forestal
Cordillera
Volcánica Central

Naranjo

Sarchí

San Pedro
de Poás

Sacramento

Puente
de Piedra

Santa Bárbara

Monte de
la Cruz

Alto la
Palma

La Argentina

Alajuela

Barva

San Rafael

San
Jerónimo

La Garita

Juan Santamaria
International Airport

San Antonio

Río Virilla

Heredia

Atenas

Túrrucares

La Guácima

Santo Domingo

SAN JOSÉ

Guadalupe

Santa Ana

Santa Ana

San Pedro

Arriving at Volcán Poás

The downside of taking a tour to Poás is that they typically reach the summit at around 10am – right when the clouds start rolling in. To beat the clouds and crowds, hire a car or a taxi and arrive around the park's 8am opening time. If you're driving, the road from Alajuela to the volcano is well signed.

Where to Stay

There are no accommodations inside the park itself, but the area offers a range of options. About 10km before the entrance to the national park, a winding, paved road heads east through bucolic high pastureland en route to the village of Vara Blanca. This scenic, uncluttered countryside is an ideal place to stay.

Alajuela is also close enough to be a convenient base for visiting Poás. It has a good variety of hostels and guesthouses, with the more affordable options concentrated in the downtown area. A few budget hotels also offer dorm rooms.

Crater of Volcán Poás

Parque Nacional Volcán Poás

Here's your chance to get up close and personal with an active volcano without exerting the energy to climb it. You can drive right up, which makes this an ideal outing for families.

Great For...

☑ **Don't Miss**

Gazing out over the picturesque crater lake known as Laguna Botos.

From the visitors center there is a paved, wheelchair-accessible 600m path that leads to a crater lookout. Visitors are prohibited from descending into the crater because of the toxic sulfuric-acid fumes that are emitted from the cauldron.

Sendero Botos

Upon leaving the lookout, you can simply retrace your steps to the parking lot, or continue touring the park on a series of trails that collectively make a 3.6km loop back to the main path. For the longer loop, head east from the the crater lookout onto Sendero Botos, a 1.4km, 30-minute trail that takes you through dwarf cloud forest, which is the product of acidic air and freezing temperatures. Here you can wan-

Montane squirrel

KARIN WASSMER/SHUTTERSTOCK ©

ⓘ Need to Know

📞2482-1226; US$15; ⊘8am-3:30pm

✕ Take a Break

Stop for some steaming French onion soup from Colbert Restaurant (p71).

★ Top Tip

Wheelchair-accessible also means stroller accessible. This is a great stop for kids.

pecially from February to April). Although mammals are infrequently sighted in the park, coyotes and the endemic montane squirrel are present.

Return to the main path via the 400m, 10-minute **Sendero Escalonia**, which will drop you at the restrooms just north of the visitors center.

Crowds & Clouds

Volcán Poás is the most heavily trafficked national park in Costa Rica. Some 250,000 people visit the park annually; weekends get especially jammed. The best time to go is on a weekday in the dry season. In particular, arrive early in the morning before the clouds obscure the view. If the summit is cloudy, hike to the other craters and return to the cauldron later – winds shift and sometimes the cloud cover is blown away.

Be advised that overnight temperatures can drop below freezing, and it may be windy and cold during the day. Also, Poás receives almost 4000mm of rainfall each year; dress accordingly.

der about looking at bromeliads, lichens and mosses clinging to the curiously shaped and twisted trees growing in the volcanic soil. Birds abound, especially the magnificent fiery-throated hummingbird, a high-altitude specialty of Costa Rica. The trail ends at Laguna Botos, a peculiar cold-water lake that has filled in one of the extinct craters.

Sendero Canto de Aves

From here, continue south on Sendero Canto de Aves, a 1.8km, 45-minute trail through taller forest, which gets significantly less traffic than the other parts of the park and is ideal for birdwatching. Species to look for include the sooty robin, black guan, screech owl and even the odd quetzal (es-

Alajuela

Costa Rica's second city is also home to one of the country's most famous figures: Juan Santamaría, the humble drummer boy who died putting an end to William Walker's campaign to turn Central America into slaving territory in the Battle of Rivas in 1856. A busy agricultural hub, it is here that farmers bring their products to market.

Alajuela is by no means a tourist 'destination.' But it's an inherently Costa Rican city, and, in its more relaxed moments, it reveals itself as such, where families have leisurely Sunday lunches and teenagers steal kisses in the park. It's also a good base for exploring the countryside to the north.

◉ SIGHTS

Parque Central   Park

(Avs Central & 1 btwn Calles Central & 2) The shady Parque Central is a pleasant place to relax beneath the mango trees, or people-watch in the evenings.

Museo Juan Santamaría   Museum

(☏ 2441-4775; www.museojuansantamaria.go.cr; Av 1 btwn Calles Central & 2; ⊙10am-5:30pm Tue-Sun) FREE Situated in a century-old structure that has served as both a jail and an armory, this museum chronicles Costa Rican history from early European settlement through the 19th century, with special emphasis on the life and history of Juan Santamaría and the pivotal mid-1850s battles of Santa Rosa, Sardinal and Rivas. Exhibits include videos, vintage maps, paintings and historical artifacts related to the conflict that ultimately safeguarded Costa Rica's independence.

Cathedral   Church

(Calle Central btwn Avs Central & 1) To the east of Parque Central is this 19th-century cathedral, which suffered severe damage in the 1991 earthquake. The hemispherical cupola is unusually constructed of sheets of red corrugated metal. Two presidents are buried here.

Cathedral, Alajuela

ADRIAN HEPWORTH/ALAMY STOCK PHOTO ©

Parque Juan
Santamaría   Plaza

(Calle 2 btwn Avs 2 & 4) Two blocks south
of Parque Central, this plaza features a
statue of the hero in action, flanked by
cannons. Across the way, the Parque de
los Niños has a more parklike scene going,
complete with playground equipment,
chattering toddlers and canoodling
teenagers.

🟢 ACTIVITIES

Ojo de Agua Springs   Swimming

(🖉2441-0655; www.facebook.com/ojodeaguacr;
San Antonio de Belén; US$3, under 3yr free;
🕑7:30am-4:30pm; 👶) About 6km south of
Alajuela, this picturesque working-class
water park gets packed with local families
on weekends. Approximately 20,000L of
water gushes from the spring every minute, powering a small waterfall and filling
various pools (including an Olympic-size
lap pool complete with diving tower) and
an artificial boating lake.

🔒 SHOPPING

Goodlight Books   Books

(🖉2430-4083; www.goodlightbooks.com; Av 3
btwn Calles 1 & 3; 🕑10am-6pm Mon-Sat) Good-
light Books, managed by Alajuelense Rosa
Carballo, offers a selection of over 20,000
well-organized books (both used and new).
She also keeps a worthwhile stock of hard-
to-find books on Costa Rica, a growing
supply of Spanish-language titles and a
sizable array of volumes in other European
languages.

✴ EATING

For the cheapest meals, head to the en-
closed Mercado Central (Calles 4 & 6 btwn Avs
1 & Central; 🕑8am-6pm Mon-Sat).

Jalapeños Central   Mexican $

(🖉2430-4027; Calle 1 btwn Avs 3 & 5; mains
US$4-8; 🕑11:30am-9pm Mon-Sat, to 8pm Sun)
Offering the best Tex-Mex in the country,

🍴 Eating Options
Near Poás

The road up to Parque Nacional Volcán
Poás is lined with stands selling fruit
(especially local strawberries), cheese
and snacks – as well as countless
touristy spots serving typical Tico
fare – so you won't go hungry. Bring
your own bottled water, though, as the
tap water here is undrinkable.

Colbert Restaurant (🖉2482-2776; www.
colbert.co.cr; Vara Blanca; mains US$9-26;
🕑noon-8pm Fri-Tue) At this charming
restaurant 6km east of Poasito, the
toque-clad, mustachioed French chef
Joël Suire looks like he's straight out
of central casting. Naturally, the menu
is loaded with traditional French items
such as onion soup, house-made pâte
and rabbit with beer sauce. A good
wine list (bottles from US$17) is strong
on vintages from South America and
France.

Freddo Fresas (🖉2482-2800; breakfast US$3-7, lunch US$6-10; 🕑7am-4pm)
This homey brunch spot looks like it
was built from oversize Lincoln logs.
It's known for heavenly strawberry
smoothies (milky ones beat watery
ones) and large, piping hot breakfasts
that fuel some serious volcano hikes.
For those returning from Volcan Poás,
a wide soup selection warms the soul.
Find Freddo's a couple of blocks north
of the cemetery.

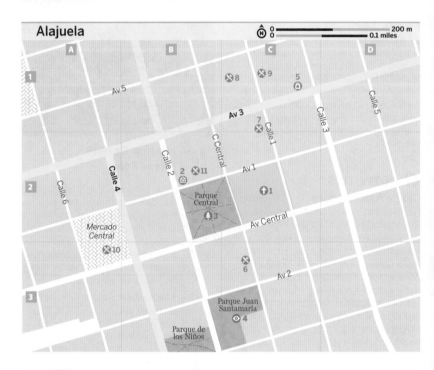

Alajuela

this popular, 11-table spot will introduce some much-needed spice into your diet. The simple and fresh burritos, chimichangas and enchiladas come in a meal deal or on their own, and, regardless, should be devoured alongside a salty margarita.

The devoted staff caters to the whims of customers – lick that guac bowl clean and don't be surprised if a second one lands in front of you!

El Chante Vegano   Vegetarian $

(⌥2440-3528, 8911-4787; www.elchantevegano. com; mains US$7-10; ⊙11am-8pm Tue-Sun; ☑) Two brothers, their mom and a girlfriend run this eatery specializing in healthy, organic food. Vegan treats are served on an open-air, street-facing patio, including garbanzo and portobello-mushroom burgers, falafel, textured-soy-protein nachos, pasta, pizza and sandwiches like the Veggie Lú (grilled veggies, avocado and sprouts on homemade bread).

Puntalitos de Manuela — Cafe $

(📞8855-8650; Museo Juan Santamaría; daily specials US$6; ⏰11am-5:30pm Tue-Sat) Tranquilly tucked into the courtyard of Alajuela's historic museum, this simple cafe with comfy booths and cushioned chairs makes a good spot to relax over sweet and savory snacks or the well-priced *plato del día* (daily special).

Coffee Dreams Café — Cafe $

(📞2430-3970; cnr Calle 1 & Av 3; mains US$5-9; ⏰8am-8pm Mon-Sat, 9am-6pm Sun; 🍴) For breakfast, *bocas* (appetizers) and a variety of *típico* (traditional Costa Rican) dishes, this centrally located cafe is a reliably good place to dine or enjoy a coffee accompanied by one of its rich desserts.

Balcón Mansarda — Costa Rican $$

(📞2441-4390; 2nd fl, Calle Central btwn Avs Central & 2; mains US$5-16; ⏰11am-11pm) Grilled fish and chicken dishes are the specialty at this casual balcony restaurant overlooking the street. The *casados* (set meals) are also large and tasty, but save room for the *flan de coco* (coconut flan) or, better yet, a belt of Flor de Caña rum.

Xandari — International $$$

(📞2443-2020; www.xandari.com; Xandari Resort Hotel & Spa; mains US$9-26; ⏰7am-9pm; 🍴) 🍴 If you want to impress a date, you can't go wrong at this elegant restaurant with incredible views. The menu is a mix of Costa Rican and international, with plenty of vegetarian options. The restaurant utilizes the resort's homegrown organic produce, supplemented by locally grown organic produce whenever possible – making for tasty *and* feel-good gourmet meals.

ℹ GETTING THERE & AWAY

Numerous car rental agencies are located near the airport. **Interbus** (📞4100-0888; www.interbusonline.com) and **Grayline** (📞2220-2126; www.graylinecostarica.com) shuttle buses pick

⛰ La Paz Waterfall Gardens

This storybook **garden complex** (📞2482-2720, reservations 2482-2100; www.waterfallgardens.com; adult/under 13yr US$40/24, package tours from San José adult/child US$88/78; ⏰8am-5pm; 🅿♿) 🍴, just east of Volcán Poás, offers the most enchanting day trip in the Central Valley. Guests walk 3.5km of trails to five scenic waterfalls, and can also wander around a butterfly conservatory, hand-feed hummingbirds and toucans, tour a serpentarium and ranarium (frog garden), and witness wild cat meals (three baby jaguars were born here in 2015).

Ocelot
FRANZ MARC FREI/GETTY IMAGES ©

up at many of the hotels in the vicinity, to take passengers to other parts of the country.

ℹ GETTING AROUND

Taxis charge between US$6 and US$8 (depending on destination) for the five- to 10-minute drive from Juan Santamaría International Airport into Alajuela. Since Alajuela is so close to the international airport, most hotels and B&Bs can arrange airport transfers for a small fee (or for free). If you're driving your own car, note that many places in the city center don't have dedicated parking, but there are many guarded lots available.

VALLE DE SARAPIQUÍ

Valle de Sarapiquí at a glance...

This flat, steaming stretch of finca-dotted lowlands was once part of the United Fruit Company's vast banana holdings. In more recent times, the Río Sarapiquí has again shot to prominence as one of the premier destinations in Costa Rica for kayakers and rafters. With the Parque Nacional Braulio Carrillo as its backyard, this is one of the best regions for wildlife-watching, especially considering how easy it is to get here.

One Day in Sarapiquí

If you only have one day in the Valle de Sarapiquí, you ought to spend it on the river, kayaking or **rafting** (p78) over the thrilling white water. Refuel at the **Rancho Magallanes** (p80) before retiring to your ecolodge to watch the birds.

Two Days in Sarapiquí

Slow things down on day two, with a wildlife-watching **boat tour** (p82) on the Río Sarapiquí or a farm tour (with dégustation!) at **Best Chocolate Tour** (p81) or **Organic Paradise** (p81).

Don't leave town without sampling the *chicharones* and admiring the livestock at **Chicharronera Caballo Loco** (p83).

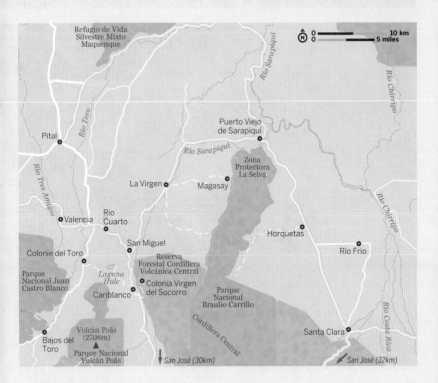

Arriving in Sarapiquí

Rte 4 runs parallel to the river and connects the towns and villages in this region. In the east, the highway hooks up with Rte 32, which continues to the Caribbean coast. In the west, it joins with Rte 32, which turns south toward San José. Soon the new Vuelta Kooper Chilamate highway will head west, connecting the region to the Pacific.

Where to Stay

In addition to raging rapids and prowling animals, there are a slew of stellar lodges in the region, featuring rainforest trails, suspension bridges, pre-Columbian ruins and chocolate tours. Even budget travelers have a few interesting and atmospheric options in and around Chilamate, although the cheapest places to stay are in town (Puerto Viejo or La Virgen).

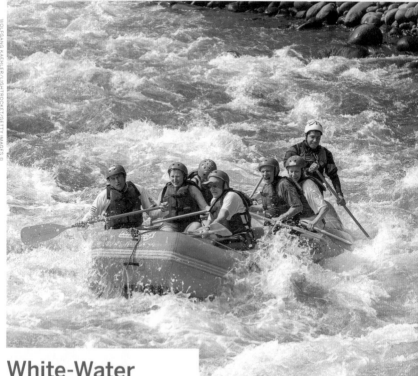

WOLFGANG KAEHLER/LIGHTROCKET/GETTY IMAGES ©

White-Water Rafting

The Río Sarapiquí offers a pretty special package: high-adrenaline kayaking and river-rafting in the midst of wildlife-rich rainforest. Hold on tight as you surf those rapids – but keep your eyes open!

Great For...

☑ Don't Miss

Spotting birds, monkeys and iguanas as you cruise down the river.

The Río Sarapiquí isn't as wild as the white water on the Río Pacuare near Turrialba, but it will get your heart racing. Even better, the dense jungle that hugs the riverbank is lush and primitive, with chances to glimpse wildlife from your raft. All of the outfitters ride the same rapids, offering roughly the same Class II–IV options at similar prices.

Tour Operators

Aventuras del Sarapiquí (☑2766-6768; www.sarapiqui.com; river trips US$60-80) A highly recommended outfitter, offering adventures in land, air and water. Beside white-water rafting (both Class II and III/IV trips), you can also fly through the air on a 14-cable canopy tour. Or, stay down to

Collared aracari

PANORAMIC IMAGES/GETTY IMAGES ©

earth with horseback riding, mountain biking or good old-fashioned hiking.

Sarapiquí Outdoor Center (☎2761-1123; www.costaricaraft.com; 2/4hr rafting trip US$65/90, guided kayak trips from US$90) Here is the local paddling authority. In addition to its own rafting excursions, it offers kayak rental, lessons and clinics. Indie paddlers should check in for up-to-date river information. If you need somewhere to sleep before you hit the water, you can crash in the simple rooms or pitch a tent here.

Green Rivers (☎8341-0493, 2766-6265; www.facebook.com/greenriverscostarica; tours US$60-80) Operating out of the Posada Andrea Cristina B&B, this outfit is run by the ever-amiable Kevín Martínez and his

wife. They offer a wide variety of rafting and kayaking tours, from family-friendly floats to adrenaline-pumping, rapid-surfing rides. They also know their nature, so they do natural-history and bird tours too.

Tropical Duckies (☎8760-3787, 2761-0095; www.tropicalduckies.com; adult/child US$65/50; ☺departs 9am & 1pm) Highly recommended for beginners and families, this outfit does tours and instruction in inflatable kayaks, which allow for a fun paddle even when the river is low. Paddle on flat moving water or Class III rapids (or somewhere in between). Reserve ahead.

Aguas Bravas (☎2766-6525; www.aguas bravascr.com; rafting trips US$75, safari float US$65; ☺9am-5:30pm) This excellent and well-established rafting outfit has set up shop along the Río Sarapiquí (complete with on-site hostel). Aguas Bravas has two tours on offer: take a gentle safari float to spot birds, iguanas, caimans and other wildlife, or sign up to splash through 14km of 'extreme rapids' on the San Miguel section of the river.

La Virgen

Tucked into the densely jungled shores of the wild and scenic Río Sarapiquí, La Virgen was one of the small towns that prospered during the heyday of the banana trade. Although United Fruit has long since shipped out, the town remains dependent on its nearby pineapple fields. And it still lives by that river.

A tremendous earthquake and landslide in 2009 altered the course of the river and flattened La Virgen's tourist economy. Some businesses folded, others relocated to La Fortuna. And a few held on. Now, independent kayakers are starting to come back and there are three river outfitters offering exhilarating trips on the Class II–IV waters of the Río Sarapiquí.

◎ SIGHTS

Nature Pavilion
Reserve, Birdwatching

(☏2761-0801; www.costaricanp.com; admission US$20; ☺7am-5pm) Father-and-son Dave and Dave greet all comers to this 10-acre reserve on the Río Sarapiquí. It's a lovely setting in which to spy on feathered friends. There are several viewing platforms, with feeders attracting toucans, trogans, tanagers and 10 species of hummingbird. From here you can follow along a trail system that winds through secondary forest all the way down to the river. Bonus: free coffee.

Snake Garden
Zoo

(☏2761-1059; www.snakegardencr.com; adult/child US$15/10, night tour US$30/24; ☺9am-5pm) Get face to face with 50 species of reptiles and amphibians, including poison-dart frogs, rattlesnakes, crocs and turtles. The star attraction is a gigantic 80kg Burmese python. Make reservations for the night tour, which shows off many species of frogs you won't be able to see during the day.

☉ TOURS

Hacienda Pozo Azul Adventures
Adventure Tour

(☏2438-2616, in USA & Canada 877-810-6903; www.pozoazul.com; tours US$55-85) Specializes in adventure activities, including horseback-riding tours, a canopy tour over the lush jungle and river, rappelling, mountain biking, and assorted river trips. It's the best-funded tour concession in the area, catering largely to groups and day-trippers from San José.

❌ EATING

La Virgen has a few favorite restaurants serving tried and true Tico favorites. It's nothing extraordinary, but you won't go hungry.

El Chante
Soda $

(☏2761-0032; www.facebook.com/restauranteelchante; mains US$6-10) This La Virgen favorite has recently moved up the street to new digs (next to the old Rancho Leona). The service is welcoming and the food is tasty and filling. The place is popular (and it has televisions) so it can get loud in the evenings.

Restaurante Mar y Tierra
Costa Rican $

(☏8434-2832; mains US$8-10; ☺8am-10pm) You can't miss this roadside restaurant, set in an A-frame in the middle of town. The seafood and steak restaurant is popular with both locals and travelers. Try the *arroz Mar y Tierra*, a Tico take on surf and turf.

Rancho Magallanes
Costa Rican $$

(☏2766-5606; chicken US$5-12; ☺10am-10pm) Rancho Magallanes is a sweet roadside restaurant with a wood-burning brick oven where they roast whole chickens and serve them quite simply with tortillas and banana salsa. You can dine with the truckers by the roadside or in the more upscale riverside dining area, painted with colorful jungle scenes.

🍷 DRINKING & NIGHTLIFE

Bar & Cabinas El Río   Bar

(☏2761-0138; ⊘noon-10pm) At the southern end of town, turn off the main road and make your way down to this atmospheric riverside hangout, set on rough-hewn stilts high above the river. Locals congregate on the upper deck to sip cold beers and nosh on filling Tico fare.

ℹ️ GETTING THERE & AWAY

La Virgen lies on Hwy 126, about 8km north of San Miguel and 17km west of Puerto Viejo de Sarapiquí. It's a paved but curvy route (especially heading south, where the road starts to climb into the mountains). In the very near future, the new Vuelta Kooper Chilamate Hwy, aka Hwy 4, will head west from here, eventually connecting the Sarapiquí Valley to Muelle and beyond.

Puerto Viejo de Sarapiquí

At the scenic confluence of the Ríos Puerto Viejo and Sarapiquí, this was once the most important port in Costa Rica. Boats laden with fruit, coffee and other commercial exports plied the Sarapiquí as far as the Nicaraguan border, then turned east on the Río San Juan to the sea.

Today the town is adjusting to the new economy, as the local polytechnic high school offers students advanced tourism, ecology and agriculture degrees. Visitors, meanwhile, can choose from any number of activities in the surrounding area, such as birdwatching, rafting, kayaking, boating and hiking.

◎ SIGHTS

Heliconia Island   Gardens

(☏2764-5220; www.heliconiaisland.com; self-guided/guided tours US$10/18; ⊘8am-5pm; P ⛽) 🌿 Drive down a rugged road, walk across the bridge and enter a masterpiece of landscape architecture that is home to more than 80 varieties of heliconias, tropical flowers, plants and trees. The

↱ Taking a Farm Tour

While agriculture remains the primary money-maker in the region, many folks recognize that tourism also has a role to play in the local economy. And it doesn't have to be an either/or. Entrepreneurial local farmers have started supplementing their agricultural activities with farm tours, allowing visitors a view into Tico rural lifestyles, sustainable farming practices, and the ins and outs of producing delicious food.

Best Chocolate Tour (☏8815-0031, 8501-7951; per person US$30; ⊘tours 8am, 10am, 1pm & 3pm) Where does chocolate come from? This local Chilamate family can answer that question for you, starting with the cacao plants growing on their farm. The two-hour demonstration covers the whole chocolate-making process, with plenty of tasting along the way.

Organic Paradise (☏2761-0706; www.organicparadisetour.com; adult/child US$$35/14; ⊘tours 8am, 10am, 1pm & 3pm) Take a bumpy ride on a tractor-drawn carriage and learn everything you ever wanted to know about pineapples. The two-hour tour focuses on the production process and what it means to be organic, but it also offers real insight into Costa Rican farm culture, as well as practical tips like how to choose your pineapple at the supermarket. The tour is very educational and surprisingly entertaining. And of course, you get to sample the goods.

Fresh pineapples
WOLFGANG KAEHLER/LIGHTROCKETW/GETTY IMAGES ©

Estación Biológica La Selva

Not to be confused with Selva Verde Lodge in Chilamate, Estación Biológica La Selva is a working biological research station equipped with laboratories, experimental plots, a herbarium and an extensive library. The station is usually teeming with scientists and students researching the nearby private reserve.

The area protected by La Selva is 16 sq km of premontane wet tropical rainforest, much of which is undisturbed. It's bordered to the south by the 476-sq-km Parque Nacional Braulio Carrillo, creating a protected area large enough to support a great diversity of life. More than 886 bird species have been recorded here, as well as 120 mammal species (including 70 species of bat and five species of big cat), 1850 species of vascular plant (especially from the orchid, philodendron, coffee and legume families) and thousands of insect species – with 500 types of ant alone.

Guided Hikes

Reservations are required for three-hour **guided hikes** (☎2766-6565; www.three paths.co.cr; guided hike US$35, birdwatching hike US$50; ⊙guided hike 8am & 1:30pm, birdwatching hike 5:45am) with a bilingual naturalist guide. You'll head across the hanging bridge and into 57km of well-developed jungle trails, some of which are wheelchair accessible. Unguided hiking is forbidden, although you'll be allowed to wander a bit after your guided tour. You should also make reservations for the popular guided birdwatching hikes.

2.3-hectare island overlooking the Río Puerto Viejois is also a refuge for 228 species of bird, including a spectacled owl who returns every year to raise her family. There are resident howler monkeys, river otters, sloths, and a few friendly dogs that will greet you upon arrival.

Dutch owners Henk and Carolien offer guided tours to show off the most memorable plants, including rare hybrids of heliconia found only on the island. They also own swatches of secondary forest on either side of the garden, which offers a wild forest buffer and attracts wildlife. The admission fee is waived for overnight guests, who stay in immaculate raised cabins with stone floors and breezy balconies (double/quad from US$80/100). Heliconia Island is about 5km north of Horquetas.

⊙ TOURS

The boat traffic at the dock in Puerto Viejo is no longer transporting commuters who have somewhere to go. Nowadays, it's used primarily for tourist boats, which cruise the Ríos Sarapiquí and Puerto Viejo, looking for birds and monkeys. On a good day, passengers might spot an incredible variety of water birds, not to mention crocodiles, sloths, two kinds of monkeys and countless iguanas sunning themselves on the muddy riverbanks or gathering in the trees.

Ruta Los Heroes   Boat Tour
(☎2766-5858; 2hr tour per person US$20; ⊙7am-3pm) The pink building near the dock is a boat-captain cooperative, offering river tours with ecological and historical emphasis. Make arrangements to leave as early as possible to beat the heat and see more wildlife. If the office is closed (as it sometimes is in the low season), you can negotiate directly with the captains you find at the dock.

Anhinga Tours   Boat Tour
(☎2766-5858, 8346-1220; http://anhinga. jimdo.com; tours per person US$25) This local guide takes travelers out to explore the Río Sarapiquí and its tributaries.

Oasis Nature Tours   Boat Tour
(☎2766-6260, 2766-6108; www.oasisnature-tours.com; full-day tour incl transportation from

Three-toed sloth (p277)

San José US$65-80) This is just one of several guides that runs boat tours on the local rivers. Also offers zip-lining, rafting and other guided adventures.

🗙 EATING

Most of the lodgings in and around Puerto Viejo have on-site restaurants or provide meals. Otherwise, there are several *sodas* in Puerto Viejo de Sarapiquí and a supermarket at the western end of town.

Chicharronera
Caballo Loco   Steak $

(✐8630-2320; www.facebook.com/chicharroneracaballoloco; mains US$4-8; ⊘6am-8pm Mon-Sat, 11am-10pm Sun) This is an open-air joint, serving up *chicharones* (fried pork or beef rinds) and other meats just outside the livestock auction mart. Take your lunch inside to watch the auction action. The livestock sales can attract quite a crowd of *sabaner-*

os and other local characters, so it's great people-watching (and animal-watching, for that matter).

Restaurante La Casona   Pizza $$

(✐2766-7101; www.hotelaraambigua.com; meals US$8-16; ⊘8am-10pm; 🛜🛉) At Hotel Ara Ambigua, this place is particularly recommended for its oven-baked pizza and typical, homemade cuisine served in an open-air *rancho*. The deck offers a sweet view of the gardens, where birds flutter by as you enjoy your meal.

❶ GETTING THERE & AWAY

Puerto Viejo de Sarapiquí has been a transportation center longer than Costa Rica has been a country, and it's easily accessed via paved major roads from San José, the Caribbean coast and other population centers. There's a taxi stop across from the bus terminal, and drivers will take you to the nearby lodges for US$5 to US$10.

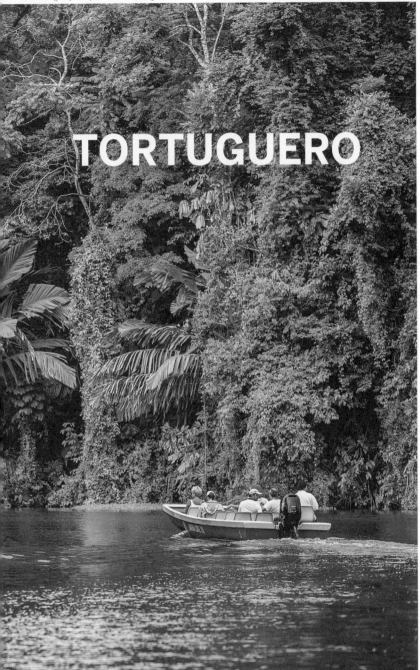

TORTUGUERO

Tortuguero at a glance...

Located within the confines of Parque Nacional Tortuguero, accessible only by air or water, this bustling little village with strong Afro-Caribbean roots is best known for attracting hordes of sea turtles (the name Tortuguero means 'turtle catcher') – and the hordes of tourists who want to see them. While the peak turtle season is in July and August, the park and village have begun to attract travelers year-round. Even in October, when the turtles have pretty much returned to the sea, caravans of families and adventure travelers arrive to go on jungle hikes and canoe the area's lush canals.

One Day in Tortuguero

If you only have one day in Tortuguero, it's going to be a busy one. Start early with breakfast from **Dorling Bakery** (p96), then hit the (aquatic) trails on a **boat tour** (p92), keeping your eyes peeled for wildlife. Rest up in the afternoon so you're ready for a (seasonal) **turtle tour** (p88) at sunset.

Two Days in Tortuguero

With an extra day, you can spread out the action. On the first day, take a **boat tour** (p92), followed by a few hours relaxing at the lodge or sucking down smoothies from **Fresh Foods** (p95). On day two, follow the short **hiking trail** (p94) behind Cuatro Esquinas ranger station in the morning, before taking a **turtle tour** (p88) in the evening.

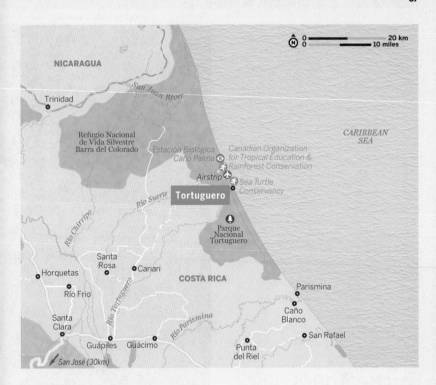

NICARAGUA

Trinidad

San Juan River

Refugio Nacional
de Vida Silvestre
Barra del Colorado

CARIBBEAN
SEA

Estación Biológica
Caño Palma

Canadian Organization
for Tropical Education &
Rainforest Conservation

Airstrip

Sea Turtle
Conservancy

Tortuguero

Río Suerte

Río Chirripó

Parque
Nacional
Tortuguero

Horquetas

Santa
Rosa   Cariari

Río Tortuguero

COSTA RICA

Río Frío

Parismina

Santa
Clara

Río Parismina

Caño
Blanco

Guápiles   Guácimo

Punta
del Riel

San Rafael

San José (30km)

0 — 20 km
0 — 10 miles

Arriving in Tortuguero

If you're coming from San José, the two most convenient ways to get to Tortuguero are by air or all-inclusive bus-boat shuttles – though budget travelers can save money by taking public transit.

If coming from the southern Caribbean, your best bets are the private boat operators from Moín (just outside Puerto Limón) or shuttle deals from Cahuita and Puerto Viejo.

See p96 for information on getting to Tortuguero by shuttle.

Where to Stay

There are essentially two areas of Tortuguero where travelers stay. The village itself has the largest variety and selection of accommodation options, catering especially to budget and mid-range travelers. The higher-end lodges are north of the village (and across a canal, meaning that guests do not have access to the village except by water taxi).

Green turtle, Parque Nacional Tortuguero (p94)

Turtle Tours

One of the most moving experiences is turtle-watching on its wild beaches. Witnessing a massive turtle return to its natal beach and perform its laborious nesting ritual feels both solemn and magical.

Great For...

☑ **Don't Miss**

The scurry of the hatchlings as they set off on their journey to the sea.

★ **Top Tip**

Four species of sea turtle nest in Tortuguero – green, leatherback, hawksbill and loggerhead.

Turtle Nesting

Most female turtles share a nesting instinct that drives them to return to the beach of their birth (their natal beach) in order to lay their eggs. (Only the leatherback returns to a more general region, instead of a specific beach.) During their lifetimes, they will usually nest every two to three years and, depending on the species, may come ashore to lay eggs 10 times in one season. Often, a turtle's ability to successfully reproduce depends on the ecological health of this original habitat.

The female turtle digs a perfect cylindrical cavity in the sand using her flippers, and then lays 80 to 120 eggs. She diligently covers the nest with sand to protect the eggs, and she may even create a false nest in another location in an attempt to confuse predators. She then makes her way back to

sea – after which the eggs are on their own. Incubation ranges from 45 to 70 days, after which hatchlings – no bigger than the size of your palm – break out of their shells using a caruncle, a temporary tooth. They crawl to the ocean in small groups, moving as quickly as possible to avoid dehydration and predators. Once they reach the surf, they must swim for at least 24 hours to get to deeper water, away from land-based predators.

Tours

Because of the sensitive nature of the habitat and the critically endangered status of some species, tours to see this activity are highly regulated. So as to not alarm turtles as they come to shore (a frightened turtle will return to the ocean and dump her eggs), tour groups gather in shelter sites close to the beach and a spotter relays a turtle's lo-

Green turtle covering her nest, Parque Nacional Tortuguero (p94)

cation via radio once she has safely crossed the high-tide mark and built her nest. At this time, visitors can then go to the beach and watch the turtle lay her eggs, cover her nest and return to the ocean. Seeing a turtle is not guaranteed, but licensed guides will still make your tour worthwhile with the wealth of turtle information they'll share. By law, tours can only take place between 8am and midnight. Some guides will offer tours after midnight; these are illegal.

Visitors should wear closed-toe shoes and rain gear. Tours cost US$25, which includes the purchase of a US$5 sticker that pays for the patrols that help protect the

❶ Need to Know

Make arrangements for a turtle tour with Leonardo Tours (p95) or Tinamon Tours (p95).

ADRIAN HEPWORTH/ALAMY STOCK PHOTO ©

nesting sites from scavengers and looters. Nesting season runs from March to October, with July and August being prime time. The next best time is April, when leatherback turtles nest in small numbers. Flashlights and cameras are not allowed on the beach.

Save the Turtles

The area attracts four of the world's eight species of sea turtle, making it a crucial habitat for these reptiles. It will come as little surprise, then, that these hatching grounds gave birth to the sea-turtle-conservation movement. The Caribbean Conservation Corporation, the first program of its kind in the world, has continuously monitored turtle populations here since 1955. Today green sea turtles are increasing in numbers along this coast, but the leatherback, hawksbill and loggerhead are in decline.

Canadian Organization for Tropical Education & Rainforest Conservation This not-for-profit organization operates the Estación Biológica Caño Palma, 8km north of Tortuguero village. This small biological research station runs a volunteer program in which visitors can assist with upkeep of the station and ongoing research projects, including sea-turtle and bird monitoring, mammal, caiman and snake monitoring, and also a community program.

Sea Turtle Conservancy About 200m north of the village, Tortuguero's original turtle-conservation organization operates a research station, visitor center and museum. Exhibits focus on all things turtle-related, including a 20-minute video about the history of local turtle conservation. STC also runs a highly reputable environmental volunteer program. During nesting season, volunteers can observe turtle tagging and assist with egg counts and biometric data collection.

✕ Take a Break

Serving until 10pm, Taylor's Place (p95) will set you up if watching turtles has made you hungry.

Boat tour, Parque Nacional Tortuguero (p94)

ALEX ROBINSON/GETTY IMAGES ©

Boat Tours

Tortuguero teems with wildlife. You'll find howler monkeys in the treetops, green iguanas scurrying among buttress roots, and endangered manatees swimming in the canals – all visible from the seat of a canoe or kayak.

Great For...

☑ Don't Miss

The great green macaw (though you'll need a good guide and some luck).

Aquatic Trails

Four aquatic trails wind their way through Parque Nacional Tortuguero, inviting waterborne exploration. **Río Tortuguero** acts as the entrance way to the network of trails. This wide, beautiful river is often covered with water lilies and is frequented by aquatic birds such as herons, kingfishers and anhingas – the latter of which is known as the snakebird for the way its slim, winding neck pokes out of the water when it swims.

Caño Chiquero and **Canõ Mora** are two narrower waterways with good wildlife-spotting opportunities. According to park regulation, only kayaks, canoes and silent electric boats are allowed in these areas. Caño Chiquero is thick with vegetation, especially red guácimo trees and epiphytes. Black turtles and green iguanas

Great green macaw

GLENN BARTLEY/GETTY IMAGES ©

ⓘ Need to Know

To see the most wildlife, be on the water early or go out following a heavy rain.

✕ Take a Break

Grab a yummy breakfast from Dorling Bakery (p96) before you set out.

★ Top Tip

Small, silent watercraft, like canoes and kayaks, will allow you to get into less trafficked areas.

like to hang out here. Caño Mora is about 3km long but only 10m wide, so it feels as if it's straight out of *The Jungle Book*. **Caño Harold** is actually an artificially constructed canal, but that doesn't stop the creatures (such as Jesus Christ lizards and caimans) from inhabiting its tranquil waters.

Tour Guides

Leonardo Tours (p95) and Tinamon Tours (p95) are recommended for their canoeing and kayaking tours.

Wildlife-Watching

More than 400 bird species, both resident and migratory, have been recorded in Tortuguero – a birdwatchers' paradise. Due to the wet habitat, the park is especially rich in waders, including egrets, jacanas, 14 different types of heron, as well as species such as kingfishers, toucans and the great curassow (a type of jungle peacock known locally as the *pavón*). The great green macaw is a highlight, most common from December to April, when the almond trees are fruiting. In September and October, look for flocks of migratory species such as eastern kingbird, barn swallows and purple martins. The Sea Turtle Conservancy conducts a biannual monitoring program, in which volunteers can help scientists take inventory of local and migratory species.

Certain species of mammal are particularly evident in Tortuguero, especially mantled howler monkeys, the Central American spider monkey and white-faced capuchin. If you've got a decent pair of binoculars and a good guide, you can usually see both two- and three-toed sloths. In addition, normally shy neotropical river otters are reasonably habituated to boats. Harder to spot are timid West Indian manatees. The park is also home to big cats such as jaguars and ocelots, but these are savvy, nocturnal animals – sightings are very rare.

Tortuguero Village

◉ SIGHTS

Parque Nacional Tortuguero Park
(US$15; ◷6-7am, 7:30am-noon & 1-4pm) This
misty, green coastal park sits on a broad
floodplain parted by a jigsaw of canals.
Referred to as the 'mini-Amazon,' Parque
Nacional Tortuguero's intense biodiversity
includes over 400 bird species, 60 known
species of frog, 30 species of freshwater
fish and three monkey species as well as the
threatened West Indian manatee. Caimans
and crocodiles can be seen lounging on river
banks, while freshwater turtles bask on logs.

Over 120,000 visitors a year come
to boat the canals and see the wildlife,
particularly to watch turtles lay eggs. This
is the most important Caribbean breed-
ing site of the green sea turtle, 40,000 of
which arrive every season to nest. Of the
eight species of marine turtle in the world,
six nest in Costa Rica, and four nest in
Tortuguero. Various volunteer organizations address the problem of poaching with
vigilant turtle patrols.

Park headquarters (☏2709-8086;
◷6-7am, 7:30am-noon & 1-4pm) is at Cuatro
Esquinas, just south of Tortuguero village.

Sharks and strong currents make the
beaches unsuitable for swimming.

⊕ ACTIVITIES

Behind Cuatro Esquinas ranger station,
the park currently has just one trail on
solid ground. Visitors can hike the muddy,
2km out-and-back trail that traverses the
tropical humid forest and parallels a stretch
of beach. Green parrots and several species
of monkey are commonly sighted here. The
short trail is well marked. Rubber boots are
required and are available for rent at hotels
and near the park entrance.

At the time of research, the park was pre-
paring to open a second hiking option, Cerro
Tortuguero Trail. To reach the trailhead,
guests will take boats to the town of San
Francisco, north of Tortuguero village, where
they will disembark at a new ranger station
and buy a ticket. The trail then takes visitors
1.8km up a hill for a view of the surrounding
lagoon, forest and ocean.

Rainforest accommodations, Tortuguero Village

🕑 TOURS

Leonardo Tours
Outdoors

(☏8577-1685; www.leonardotours.wordpress.com) With nine years of experience guiding tours in the area, Leonardo Estrada brings extensive knowledge and infectious enthusiasm to his turtle, canoeing, kayaking and hiking tours.

Tinamon Tours
Tour

(☏8842-6561, 2709-8004; www.tinamontours.de) Barbara Hartung, a trained zoologist and Tortuguero resident for 20-plus years, offers hiking, canoeing, cultural and turtle tours in German, English, French or Spanish.

Ballard Excursions
Tour

(www.tortuguerovillage.com/ballardexcursions) Ross Ballard, a Canadian with deep local roots, leads 3½-hour walking tours focusing on the biology and ecology of the species-rich rainforest at the foot of Cerro Tortuguero, the region's tallest hill.

Castor Hunter Thomas
Tour

(☏8870-8634; castorhunter.blogspot.com) Excellent local guide and 42-year Tortuguero resident who has led hikes, turtle tours and canoe tours for over 20 years.

Asociación de Guías de Tortuguero
Tour

(☏2767-0836; www.asoprotur.com) The most convenient place to arrange tours is at the official Asociación de Guías de Tortuguero kiosk by the boat landing. Made up of scores of local guides, the association offers tours in English, French, German and other languages. Although guides are all certified to lead tours in the park, the quality of the tours can vary.

Rates at the time of research were US$20 per person for a two-hour turtle tour and US$40 for a three-hour boat tour. Other options include two-hour walking (US$20), birdwatching (US$35) and fishing (US$15) tours. Tours also involve a US$15 admission fee to the park (not required for the fishing tour).

🍴 Afro-Caribbean Cooking

Thanks to the Afro-Caribbean influence, the food here has more of a kick than what's found on the Pacific coast. Even the country's blandest dish, rice and beans, becomes something special in the southern Caribbean with the simple additions of coconut milk, Panamanian peppers, thyme and ginger, along with red beans instead of black. Mouthwatering lobster and whole fish are ubiquitous, as is the staple *pollo caribeño* (Caribbean chicken). For best results, pair these delights with *agua de sapo* (translation: frog water), a variation of lemonade that uses lemon juice, ginger and sugar cane juice.

🍽 EATING

One of Tortuguero's unsung pleasures is the cuisine: the homey restaurants lure you in from the rain with steaming platters of Caribbean-style food.

Taylor's Place
Caribbean $

(☏8319-5627; mains US$7-14; ⊙6-10pm) Low-key atmosphere and high-quality cooking come together beautifully at this back-street eatery southwest of the soccer field. The inviting garden setting, with chirping insects and picnic benches spread under colorful paper lanterns, is rivaled only by friendly chef Ray Taylor's culinary artistry. House specialties include beef in tamarind sauce, grilled fish in garlic sauce, and fruit drinks both alcoholic and otherwise.

Fresh Foods
Caribbean $

(☏2767-1063; mains US$7-12, smoothies US$3-4) Next to the Morpho grocery store in the commercial center of the village, this family-owned food stand opened in 2013 to offer breakfast, solid Caribbean meals and giant, delicious smoothies in fishbowl glasses. And after a long day on the canals,

Getting to Tortuguero by Shuttle

If you prefer to leave the planning to someone else, convenient shuttle services can whisk you to Tortuguero from San José, Arenal-La Fortuna or the southern Caribbean coast in just a few hours. Shuttle companies typically offer minivan service to La Pavona or Moín, where waiting boats take you the rest of the way to Tortuguero. This is a relatively inexpensive, hassle-free option, as you only have to buy a single ticket, and guides help you negotiate the van-to-boat transfer.

Caribe Shuttle (2750-0626; www.caribeshuttle.com) Shuttles from Puerto Viejo (US$75, five hours) and Arenal-La Fortuna (US$60, six hours).

Exploradores Outdoors (2750-2020; www.exploradoresoutdoors.com; 1-day trips incl 2 meals & transportation from US$99) More expensive package deals that include transport from San José, Puerto Viejo or Arenal-La Fortuna, a mid-journey Río Pacuare rafting trip, and accommodations in Tortuguero.

Jungle Tom Safaris (2221-7878; www.jungletomsafaris.com) Offers one-way shuttles between Tortuguero and San José (US$45). All-inclusive one- and two-night packages (US$99 to US$152) can also include shuttles from Cahuita (US$60), Puerto Viejo (US$60) and Arenal-La Fortuna (US$60), as well as optional tours.

Pleasure Ride (2750-2113) Shuttles from Puerto Viejo and Cahuita (US$70).

Ride CR (2469-2525; www.ridecr.com) Shuttles from Arenal-La Fortuna (US$55).

Riverboat Francesca Nature Tours (2226-0986; www.tortuguerocanals.com) Shuttles from San José to Tortuguero via Moín (US$75, including lunch) plus package deals including accommodation.

Terraventuras (p234) Shuttles from Puerto Viejo (US$65).

a tasty Caribbean-style filet and passion-fruit drink really nail it.

Dorling Bakery Bakery $
(2767-0444; pastries US$2, breakfast US$4-5; 5am-8:30pm Mon-Sat, to noon Sun) Thanks to its predawn opening time, this is a good spot to pick up homemade banana bread, lemon and orange cake or cinnamon rolls before an early-morning flight or canal tour.

Sunrise Restaurant Caribbean $
(mains US$4-10; 9:30am-9pm Wed-Mon) Between the boat dock and the national park, this cozy log-cabin-like place will lure you in with the delicious smoky aroma of its grilled chicken and pork ribs. It also serves breakfast and a full Caribbean menu at lunch and dinnertime, at some of the best prices in town.

Soda Doña María Soda $
(8870-8634; dishes US$5-8; 11am-7:30pm) Recover from a hike in the park at this riverside *soda*, serving *jugos* (juices), burgers and *casados* (set meals). It's about 200m north of the park entrance.

Miss Junie's Caribbean $$
(2709-8029; mains US$13-20; 7-9am, noon-2pm & 6-9pm) Over the years, Tortuguero's best-known and most delicious Caribbean eatery has grown from a personal kitchen to a full-blown restaurant. Prices have climbed accordingly, but the menu remains true to its roots: chicken, fish and whole lobster cooked in flavorful Caribbean sauces, with coconut rice and beans. It's at the northern end of the main street.

Tutti's Restaurant Steak $$
(2767-2218; 9am-9:30pm Tue-Sun) This colorful, open-air surf'n'turf establishment opened up next to Super Las Tortugas in 2014. Hummingbirds zip by and calypso music fills the air as guests feast on juicy steaks, fresh seafood, and mouthwatering coconut flan for dessert. Cash only.

Wild Ginger Fusion $$
(2709-8240; www.wildgingercr.com; mains US$12-22; noon-3pm & 5:30-9pm;) This

Fish with fried plantains and salad

low-lit spot near the beach specializes in fusion cuisine incorporating fresh local ingredients, such as lobster and mango *ceviche* (seafood marinated in lemon or lime juice, garlic and seasonings), Caribbean beef stew and passion-fruit crème brûlée. It's 150m north of the elementary school.

Budda Cafe   European $$

(☏2709-8084; www.buddacafe.com; mains US$10-18, pizzas US$7-9; ☉noon-9pm; ☀) Ambient club music and stenciled 'om' symbols impart a hipster vibe at this cafe between the main road and the river. It's a pleasant setting for pizzas, cocktails and crepes (savory and sweet). Grab a table outside for a prime view of the yellow-bellied flycatchers zipping across the water.

🍷 DRINKING & NIGHTLIFE

Turtle-watching is the most popular night-time activity in these parts. But should you require a *cerveza*, there are occasionally good times to be had in the town's few bars.

La Taberna Punto
de Encuentro   Bar

(☉11am-11pm) Adjacent to the Super Bambú *pulpería,* this popular tavern is mellow in the afternoons, but draws the party people after dark with cold beer and blaring reggaetón.

La Culebra   Club

(☉8pm-close) Next to the public dock in the center of town, this bright-purple night-club – Tortuguero's one and only – plays thumping music and serves beer and *bocas* right on the canal.

ℹ INFORMATION

There are no banks or ATMs in town and only a few businesses accept credit cards, so bring all the cash you'll need.

ℹ GETTING THERE & AWAY

The small airstrip is 4km north of Tortuguero village. **NatureAir** (☏2299-6000; www.natureair.com) has early-morning flights daily to/from San José and twice weekly to La Fortuna. Charter flights land here regularly as well.

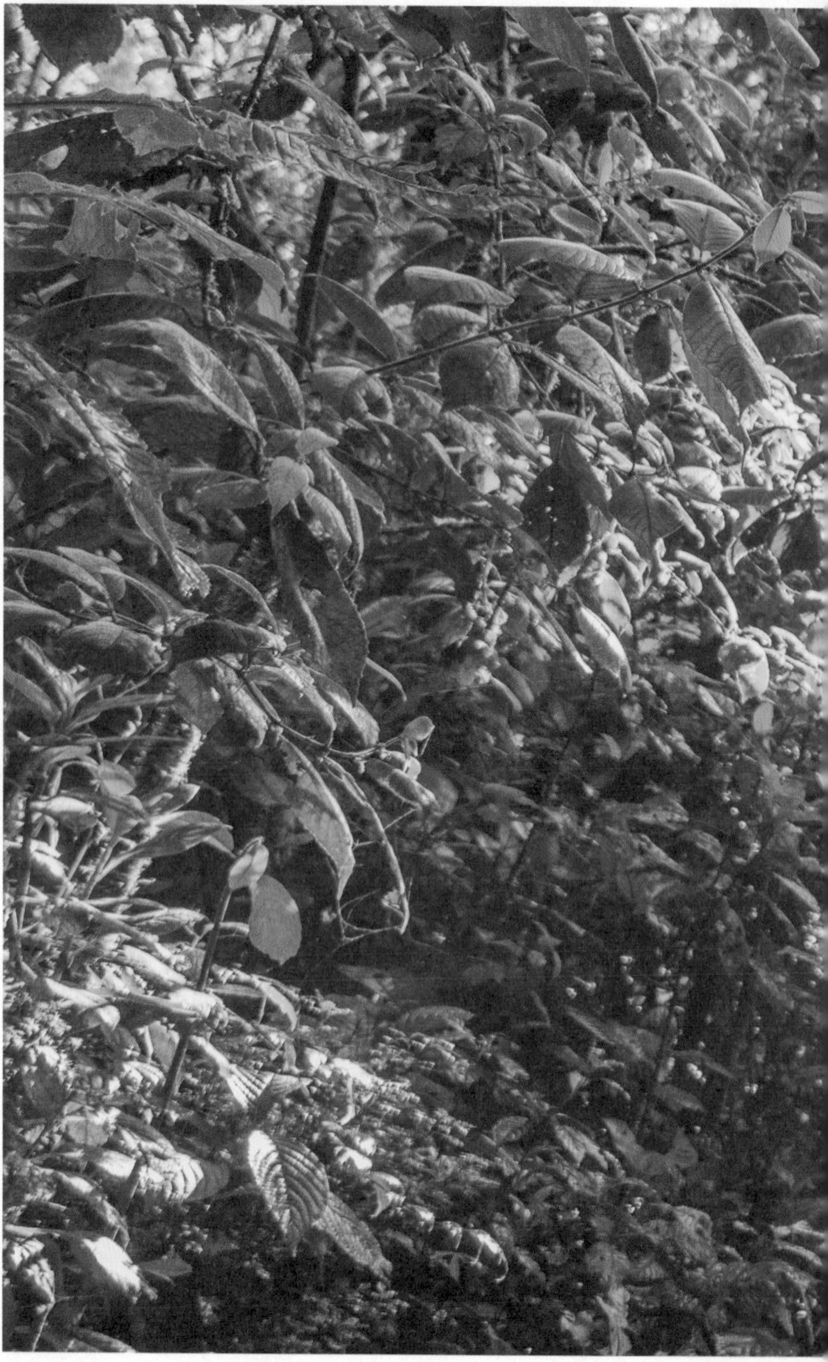

MONTEVERDE
CLOUD FOREST

Monteverde Cloud Forest at a glance...

Spread out on the slopes of the Cordillera de Tílaran, this area is a sprawling chain of villages, farms and nature reserves. The Reserva Bosque Nuboso de Monteverde (Monteverde Cloud Forest Reserve) is the most famous one, but there are properties of all shapes and sizes – from tiny family fincas to the vast Children's Eternal Rainforest – that blanket this whole area in luscious green. As a result, there are trails to hike, birds to spot, waterfalls to swim and adventures to be had everywhere you turn.

Two Days in Monteverde

For your first day, register in advance for a guided tour at the **Bosque Nuboso Monteverde** (p102), taking time afterwards to explore independently. Your second day is devoted to getting your adventure on, either flying through the treetops on a **canopy tour** (p106) or climbing trees and canyoning down waterfalls at **Finca Modelo Ecologica** (p114). Don't miss dinner in a fig tree at **Tree House Restaurant** (p119).

Four Days in Monteverde

On your third day, visit a local farm for an enlightening (and energizing) coffee tour. When the sun sets, check out the area nightlife on a night tour at **Bosque Eterno de los Niños** (p113) or **Santuario Ecológico** (p114). Use your final day to learn about bugs at the **Butterfly Garden** (p110), followed by lunch at **Orchid Coffee** (p117).

Clockwise from top left: Two-toed sloth (p277); Blue morpho butterfly (p277); Coffee beans; Eyelash viper (p276); White-faced capuchin (p277); Orchids

Bosque Nuboso Monteverde

Monteverde & Santa Elena Map (p112)

Arriving in Monteverde

There is no easy way to get to Monteverde. The three access roads to Santa Elena – one to the north via Tilarán, one to the west via Las Juntas, and one to the south via Guacimal – all require an hour of winding and bumping up the mountain. That's all supposed to change when the widening and paving of the southern route is completed in 2016.

Where to Stay

Many lodgings are clustered in the villages of Santa Elena and Monteverde, but many more dot the landscape in the hills above Santa Elena and beyond. Before booking, consider carefully how remote you want to be (keeping in mind whether or not you'll have your own vehicle). This area has a huge variety of accommodations at all price levels. Reservations are practically required during holiday weeks, and recommended throughout the high season. Prices drop 30% to 40% during the low season.

Canopy walkway, Bosque Nuboso Monteverde

Bosque Nuboso Monteverde

Here is a virginal forest dripping with mist, dangling with mossy vines, sprouting with ferns and bromeliads, gushing with creeks, blooming with life and nurturing rivulets of evolution.

Great For...

SANTA ELENA

MONTEVERDE

Bosque Nuboso Monteverde

ℹ Need to Know

Monteverde Cloud Forest Reserve; ☏2645-5122; www.reservamonteverde.com; adult/concession/child under 6yr US$20/10/free; ⊙7am-4pm

★ Top Tip
The reserve's walking trails are almost always muddy, even during the dry season. Bring your boots!

History

This beautiful reserve came into being in 1972, when the Quaker community, spurred on by the threat of encroaching squatters, joined forces with environmental and wildlife organizations to purchase and protect an extra 328 hectares (811 acres) of land. This fragile environment relies almost entirely on public donations to survive. Today, the reserve totals 10,500 hectares (25,946 acres).

Plan Ahead

Because of the fragile environment, the Monteverde reserve allows a maximum of 160 people inside at any time. During the dry season this limit is usually reached by 10am. You can ensure your admission by making a reservation for a spot on a tour. Otherwise, be an early bird and arrive before the gates open.

Hiking

There are 13km of marked and maintained trails – a free map is provided with your entrance fee. The most popular of the nine trails, suitable for day hikes, make a rough triangle (El Triángulo) to the east of the reserve entrance. The triangle's sides are made up of the popular Sendero Bosque Nuboso (1.9km), an interpretive walk through the cloud forest that begins at the ranger station, paralleled by the more open, 2km El Camino, a favorite of bird-watchers. The Sendero Pantanoso (1.6km) forms the far side of El Triángulo, traversing swamps, pine forests and the continental divide. Returning to the entrance, Sendero Río (2km) follows the Quebrada Cuecha past a few photogenic waterfalls.

Bisecting the triangle, the gorgeous Chomogo Trail (1.8km) lifts hikers to 1680m,

Purple-throated mountain-gem hummingbird

the highest point in the triangle. Other little trails crisscross the region.

The trail to the Mirador La Ventana (elevation 1550m) is moderately steep and leads further afield to a wooden deck overlooking the continental divide.

Wildlife-Watching

Monteverde is a bird-watching paradise, with the list of recorded species topping out at more than 400. The resplendent quetzal is most often spotted during the March and April nesting season, though you may get lucky any time of year. Keep your ears open for the three-wattled bellbird, a kind of cotinga that is famous for its distinctive call.

> ☑ **Don't Miss**
> The magical, misty view from the continental divide.

IVAN KUZMIN/GETTY IMAGES ©

If you're keen on birds, a specialized bird tour is highly recommended.

For those interested in spotting mammals, the cloud forest's limited visibility and abundance of higher primates (namely human beings) can make wildlife-watching quite difficult, though commonly sighted species include coatis, howler monkeys, capuchins, sloths, agoutis and squirrels. Most animals avoid the main trails, so get off the beaten track.

Tours

Although you can (and should) hike around the reserve on your own, a guide will provide an informative overview and enhance your experience. Make reservations at least a day in advance for park-run tours. The English-speaking guides are trained naturalists; proceeds benefit environmental-education programs in local schools. The reserve can also recommend excellent guides for private tours.

Bird-Watching (☑2645-5112; per person incl entry fee US$64; ☺tours 6am) These early-morning walks last four to five hours, checking off as many as 40 species of birds (out of a possible 500). There's a three-person minimum, six-person maximum.

Natural History (☑2645-5122, reservations 2645-5112; adult/student excl entry fee US$37/27; ☺tours 7:30am, 11am & 1:30pm) Take a 2½- to three-hour guided walk in the woods. Learn about the characteristics of a cloud forest and identify some of its most unique flora. Your ticket is valid for the entire day, so you can continue to explore on your own.

Night Tours (with/without transportation US$25/20; ☺tours 5:45pm) Observe the 70% of regional wildlife that has nocturnal habits. Tours are by flashlight (bring your own for the best visibility).

> ✕ **Take a Break**
> Stop at Cafe Colibrí (p119) for a post-hike snack and to snap some hummingbird photos.

Brewing coffee

Coffee Tours

If you're curious about the magical brew that for many makes life worth living, tour one of the coffee plantations and learn all about how Costa Rica's golden bean goes from plant to cup.

Great For...

  👓

☑ **Don't Miss**

Taking a ride in a traditional ox cart,

Tour Operators

Café de Monteverde

Stop by **Café de Monteverde** (☎2645-7550; www.lifemonteverde.com; Monteverde; tour per person US$18; ☺coffee tasting 7:30am-6pm, tours 8am & 1:30pm) 🍴 in Monteverde to take a crash course in coffee and sample the delicious blends. Or, sign on for the three-hour tour on sustainable agriculture, which visits organic fincas (farms) implementing techniques like composting and solar energy. Learn how coffee growing has helped to shape this community and how it can improve the local environment.

Kind of makes you want to pour yourself another cup!

Coffee

STIG STOCKHOLM PEDERSEN/GETTY IMAGES ©

back home, as this fair-trade-certified organization sells to Starbucks, among other clients. Tours include a visit to the industrial facility, followed up by some hands-on (mouth-on) quality control. The co-op is located in the village of El Dós, about halfway between Tilarán and Monteverde.

Don Juan Coffee Tour

Don Juan (☑2645-7100; www.donjuancoffeetour.com; Santa Elena; adult/child US$35/15, night tour US$20; ☉7am-4:30pm, tours 8am, 1pm & 6pm) does three in one, where you can learn about all your favorite vices (OK, maybe not all your favorites, but three of the good ones). It's a pretty cursory overview of how sugarcane is harvested and processed; how cacao beans are transformed into dark, decadent chocolate; and how coffee happens, from plant to bean to cup.

El Trapiche

Visit picturesque family finca, **El Trapiche** (☑2645-7650; www.eltrapichetour.com; Santa Elena; adult/child US$32/12; ☉tours 10am & 3pm Mon-Sat, 3pm Sun; 🚻) in Santa Elena, where they grow not only coffee but also sugarcane, bananas and plantains. See the coffee process first-hand, take a ride in a traditional ox cart, and try your hand at making sugar. Bonus: lots of samples along the way, including sugarcane liquor, sugarcane toffee and – of course – delicious coffee. Kids love this one.

Coopeldós RL

Coopeldós (☑2693-8441; www.coopeldos.com) 🍃 is a cooperative of 450 small- and medium-sized organic coffee growers from the area. You might drink Coopeldós blends

Chocolate, too!

And if you're not a coffee drinker, try the **Caburé Chocolate Tour** (☑2645-5020; www.cabure.net; per person US$15; ☉tours 1pm & 4pm Mon-Sat). Bob, the owner of the Caburé chocolate shop in Monteverde, shares his secrets about the magical cacao pod and how to transform it into the food of the gods. There are plenty of opportunities for taste testing along the way, and you'll try your hand at making truffles.

Zip-lining

DREAMPICTURES/SHANNON FAULK/GETTY IMAGES ©

Canopy Tours

The wild-eyed faces and whoop-de-whoop soundtrack are all the proof you need: clipping into a high-speed cable and soaring across the treetops is pure joy.

Santa Elena is the site of Costa Rica's first zip lines, today eclipsed in adrenaline by the many imitators who have followed. If you came to Costa Rica to fly, this is the absolute best place to do it.

Operators

Original Canopy Tour

The storied **zip-line tour** (📞2645-5243; www.theoriginalcanopy.com; adult/student/child US$45/35/25; ⏱7:30am, 10:30am & 2:30pm) that started the trend. With 15 cables, a Tarzan swing and a rappel through the center of an old fig tree, it's a lot more fun than most history museums. Your adrenaline rush may not be as big as at some of the other canopy tours, but you'll enjoy

Great For...

☑ **Don't Miss**

Howling like Tarzan as you sail through the jungle on the aptly named swing.

Hanging bridge

❶ Need to Know

Transportation from your lodging is included in the price.

✖ Take a Break

Zip-liners can refuel at the canopy tour facilities' on-site restaurants.

★ Top Tip

Hanging bridges allow less daring travelers to explore the treetops without the adrenaline rush.

SkyTrek

This seriously fast canopy tour consists of 11 platforms attached to steel towers that are spread out along a road and zoom over swatches of primary forest. We're talking serious speeds of up to 64km/h, which is probably why **SkyTrek** (🗷2645-5238; www.skyadventures.travel; Santa Elena; adult/student/child SkyWalk US$25/21/17, SkyTrek US$77/64/53; ⊙7:30am-5pm; 🚼) was the first canopy tour with a real brake system. The SkyWalk is a 2km guided tour over five suspended bridges; a night tour is also available.

100% Aventura

Aventura (🗷2645-6388; www.aventuracanopytour.com; Santa Elena; canopy adult/child US$50/40, bridges US$30/20; ⊙tours 8am, 11am, 1pm & 3pm; 🚼) boasts the longest zip line in Latin America (which is nearly 1600m in case you were wondering). The 19 platforms are spiced up with a Tarzan swing, a 15m rappel and a Superman zip line that makes you feel as if you really are flying. They also have a network of suspension bridges, laced through secondary forest. Reservations required.

smaller groups and more emphasis on the natural surroundings.

After the tour, you are free to wander the 5km of hiking trails on the grounds of the Cloud Forest Lodge. It's 1km north of town, on the way to Reserva Santa Elena.

Selvatura

One of the bigger games in town, **Selvatura** (🗷2645-5929; www.selvatura.com; canopy US$50, walkways US$30, each exhibit US$5-15; ⊙7:30am-4pm) has 3km of cables, 18 platforms and one Tarzan swing over a stretch of incredibly beautiful primary cloud forest. In addition to the cables, it has 3km of 'Treetops Walkways,' as well as a hummingbird garden, a butterfly garden and an amphibian and reptile exhibition.

Monteverde & Santa Elena

⊙ SIGHTS

The sights in Monteverde and Santa Elena are mostly geared to bringing the wildlife a little closer, whether it's bats, butterflies, frog, snakes or flowers. These stops can be entertaining and educational – especially for children – but it's even more rewarding when you see these creatures in the wild. And you're in the wild, so go out there and see it.

Butterfly Garden   Zoo

(Jardín de Mariposas; ☎2645-5512; www.monteverdebutterflygarden.com; Cerro Plano; adult/student/child US$15/10/5; ⊙8:30am-4pm; 🅟) Everything you ever wanted to know about butterflies, with four gardens representing different habitats and home to more than 40 species. Up-close observation cases allow you to witness the butterflies as they emerge from the chrysalis (if your timing is right). Other exhibits feature the industrious leafcutter ant and the ruthless tarantula hawk (actually a wasp that eats

tarantulas) and lots of scorpions. Kids love this place, and knowledgeable naturalist guides truly enhance the experience.

Monteverde Theme Park   Zoo

(Monteverde Frog Pond; ☎2645-6320; www.monteverdethemepark.com; Santa Elena; per attraction $13-17, canopy tour adult/child $35/20; ⊙9am-4:30pm, ranario to 8pm) Formerly known as the Ranario, or Frog Pond, this place added an insect house, a butterfly garden and canopy tour – hence, it's now a theme park. The frogs are still the highlight: about 25 species reside in transparent enclosures lining the winding indoor jungle paths. Sharp-eyed guides point out frogs, eggs and tadpoles with flashlights. Your ticket entitles you to two visits, so come back in the evening to see the nocturnal species.

Jardín de Orquídeas   Gardens

(Orchid Garden; ☎2645-5308; www.monteverdeorchidgarden.net; Santa Elena; adult/child US$10/free; ⊙8am-5pm) This sweet-smelling garden in Santa Elena has shady trails winding past more than 400 types of

Orchids

orchid organized into taxonomic groups. On your guided tour, you'll see such rarities as *Platystele jungermannioides,* the world's smallest orchid. If you have orchids at home, here's your chance to get tips from the experts on how to keep them beautiful and blooming.

Serpentarium ZOO

(Herpentario; ☏2645-6002; www.skyadventures.travel; Santa Elena; adult/student/child US$13/11/8; ⏲9am-8pm) A guide will show you around and introduce you to some 40 species of slithery snakes, plus a fair number of frogs, lizards, turtles and other cold-blooded critters. Your ticket entitles you to a return visit after dark, when all the nocturnal species come out. Guided tours leave every hour.

Bat Jungle ZOO

(☏2645-7701; www.batjungle.com; Monteverde; adult/child US$13/11; ⏲9am-7pm; ⏍) The so-called Bat Jungle in Monteverde is a small but informative exhibit, with good bilingual educational displays and a free-flying bat habitat housing almost 100 bats. Make a reservation for your 45-minute tour to learn about echolocation, bat-wing aerodynamics and other amazing flying-mammal facts.

Monteverde Friends School Cultural Centre

(www.mfschool.org; Monteverde; per person US$15; ⏲tours 8am Tue & Fri; ⏍) Here's a great way for children to learn about and interact with the local culture: spend some time at the schoolhouse. With advance reservation, visitors can sit in on morning assembly and tour the grounds. Kids are even invited to attend a class (and recess!) with an English-speaking buddy.

✪ ACTIVITIES

In addition to the two biggies anchoring this area at the north and south, Monteverde and Santa Elena are home to dozens of smaller private reserves (not to mention

🍴 Monteverde Cheese Factory

Until the upswing in ecotourism, Monteverde's number-one employer was the **Monteverde Cheese Factory** (La Lechería; ☏2645-7090; www.monteverdecheese factory.com; Monteverde; tours adult/child US$12/10; ⏲store 7:30am-5pm Mon-Sat, to 4pm Sun, tours 9am & 2pm Mon-Sat), which was started in 1953 by Monteverde's original Quaker settlers. Learn about the history of the Quakers in Costa Rica and their methods for producing and pasteurizing cheese on a two-hour tour of the factory (reservations required). You can also pop in any time to sample the creamy goodness. Bonus: now there's a Santa Elena outlet (p118), right next door to the Catholic church.

The Monteverde Cheese Factory is now the second-largest cheese producer in the country. It's no longer owned by the Quakers (it's now owned by the Mexican giant Sigma Alimentos), but the factory still uses their name and recipes, producing everything from a creamy Gouda to a very nice sharp, white cheddar, as well as other dairy products such as yogurt and, most importantly, ice cream. Don't miss the chance to sample Monte Rico, a Monteverde original.

the giant Children's Eternal Rainforest). The Monteverde and Santa Elena reserves are special – very special – because they are essentially the only cloud-forest reserves in

Monteverde & Santa Elena

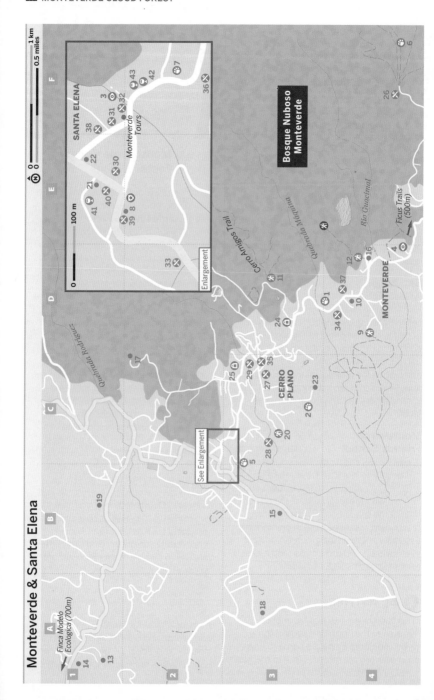

Monteverde & Santa Elena

the area. But if you want to immerse yourself in nature, get some exercise, spot some monkeys, admire a scenic vista, cool off in a waterfall, there are countless places to do so (most of which will be significantly less crowded than the Monteverde reserve).

Curi-Cancha Reserve
Hiking, Bird-Watching

(☑8356-1431, 2645-6915; www.curi-cancha.com; US$14, guided hike US$15, natural history tour US$45, bird tour US$60; ☺7am-3:30pm, guided hike 7:30am & 1:30pm) Bordering Monteverde but without the crowds, this lovely private reserve on the banks of the Río Cuecha is popular among birders. There are about 10km of well-marked trails, a hummingbird garden and a view of the continental divide. Make reservations for the guided hikes, including the early-morning bird walks and specialized three-hour natural history walks.

Bosque Eterno de los Niños
Hiking

(Children's Eternal Rainforest, BEN; ☑2645-5305; www.acmcr.org; adult/child US$12/free, guided night hike US$22/14, transportation per person US$4; ☺7:30am-5:30pm, night hike 5:30pm; 🖈)
🐾 What became of the efforts of a group of schoolchildren to save the rainforest? Only this enormous 220-sq-km reserve – the largest private reserve in the country. It is mostly inaccessible to tourists, with the exception of the well-marked 3.5km **Sendero Bajo del Tigre** (Jaguar Canyon Trail; ☑2645-5200; www.acmcr.org; adult/child US$12/free, night hike adult/student/child/transportation US$22/19/14/4; ☺8am-4pm, night hike 5:30pm; 🖈), which is actually a series of shorter trails. At the entrance there's an education center for children and a fabulous vista over the reserve.

Santa Elena Reserve

Though Monteverde gets all the attention, misty **Reserva Santa Elena** (☏2645-7107, 2645-5390; www.reservasanta elena.org; adult/student US$14/7, guided hike US$15; ☺7am-4pm) has plenty to recommend it. You can practically hear the epiphyte-draped canopy breathing in humid exhales as water drops onto the leaf litter and mud underfoot. The odd call of the three-wattled bellbird and the low crescendo of a howler monkey punctuate the higher-pitched bird chatter. While Monteverde Crowd...er... Cloud Forest entertains almost 200,000 visitors annually, Santa Elena sees fewer than 20,000 tourists each year, which means its dewy trails through mysteriously veiled forest are usually far quieter.

This cloud forest is slightly higher in elevation than Monteverde's, and as some of the forest is secondary growth, there are sunnier places for spotting birds and other animals throughout. There's a stable population of monkey and sloth, many of which can be seen on the road to the reserve.

At 310 hectares, the community-run Santa Elena is much smaller than the Monteverde forest reserve. More than 12km of well-marked trails are open for hiking, including four circular trails of varying difficulty and length. Guided hikes depart from the reserve office four times a day (reservations recommended).

Santuario Ecológico   Hiking
(Ecological Sanctuary; ☏2645-5869; www.santuarioecologico.com; Cerro Plano; adult/student/child US$17/14/11, morning tour US$35/31/29, night tour US$30/25/23; ☺7am-5:30pm, morning tour 7am, night tour 5:30pm) This smallish sanctuary is set on private property comprising premontane and secondary forest, coffee and banana plantations. Descend to an impressive 30m waterfall and cool off with a refreshing dip. These trails are not well trodden, so you're more likely to meet a coati or a sloth than another human being. Bird walks and night tours also available.

Cerro Amigos   Hiking
Take a hike up to the highest peak in the area (1842m) for good views of the surrounding rainforest and, on a clear day, Volcán Arenal, 20km away to the northeast. Behind Hotel Belmar in Cerro Plano, take the dirt road going downhill, then the next left. The trail ascends roughly 300m in 3km. Note that this trail does not connect to the trails in the Monteverde reserve.

🜛 TOURS

Finca Modelo Ecologica   Outdoors
(☏2645-5581; www.familiabrenestours.com; treetops/canyoning/combo US$40/70/100; ☺treetops 8am-4pm, canyoning 8am, 11am & 2pm) The Brenes family *finca* offers a number of unique and thrilling diversions. Their masterpiece is the two-hour canyoning tour, which descends six glorious waterfalls, the largest of which is 40m. No experience necessary, just an adventurous spirit. Tree-huggers can climb a 132ft ficus tree, using ropes and rappels to go up and down.

The *finca* is located 2km north of Santa Elena in the village of La Cruz, but transportation from your hotel is included in the price.

Hiking in Bosque Nuboso Monteverde (p104)

Sabine's Smiling Horses
Horseback Riding

(📞2645-6894; www.smilinghorses.com; Monteverde; 2hr/3hr/all-day ride per person US$45/65/105; ⊙tours 9am, 1pm & 3pm) Conversant in four languages (in addition to equine), Sabine will make sure you are comfortable on your horse, whether you're a novice rider or an experienced cowboy. Her longstanding operation in Monteverde offers a variety of treks, including a popular waterfall tour (three hours) and a magical full-moon tour (monthly). And yes, the horses really do smile.

Finca El Rodeo
Horseback Riding

(📞2645-6306; www.caballerizaelrodeo.com; Santa Elena; per person $40-60) Based at a local *finca,* this outfit offers tours on private trails through rainforest, coffee plantations and grasslands, with plenty of pauses to spot wildlife and admire the fantastic landscapes. The specialty is a sunset tour to a spot overlooking the Golfo de Nicoya. *¡Que hermoso!*

> *Monteverde is a bird-watching paradise*

Ficus Trails
Hiking

(📞2645-6474; www.ficustrails.com; adult/ student/child night hike US$25/20/15, natural history walk US$30/25/20, birding US$38) From the observation deck at this private reserve, you can see from the continental divide down to the San Luis falls, and out to the Golfo de Nicoya. The varied altitude means that it's home to a huge diversity of flora and fauna, some of which you can spot on guided daily bird walks and night hikes. The tour guides are attentive and patient, guaranteeing a worthwhile experience.

Take the road to San Luis and follow the signs.

Valle Escondido
Hiking

(Hidden Valley; 📞2645-6601; www.valleescondidopreserve.com; Cerro Plano; day use US$20, night tour adult/child US$25/15; ⊙7am-4pm,

★ Top 5 for Kids

Selvatura (p109)

Butterfly Garden (p110)

Monteverde Friends School (p111)

El Trapiche (p107)

Monteverde Theme Park (p110)

From left: Morpho butterfly, Butterfly Garden (p110);
Red-eyed tree frog (p276); Learning about butterflies at
the Butterfly Garden (p110)

night tour 5:30pm) Reserve in advance for the popular two-hour guided night tour, then come back the next day to explore the reserve on your own. Located behind Monteverde Inn in Cerro Plano, the well-marked trail winds through a deep canyon into an 11-hectare reserve, passing wonderful vistas and luscious waterfalls. During the day, Valle Escondido is quiet with few tourists, so it's recommended for birding and wildlife-watching.

Santa Maria Night Walk   Tour

(☎2645-6548; www.nightwalksantamarias.com; Santa Elena; per person US$25; ☉tour 5:30pm) Night walks have become so popular because 80% of the cloud-forest creatures are nocturnal. This one takes place on a private Santa Elena *finca*, with a 10-hectare swathe of primary and secondary forest. Expert guides point out all kinds of wildlife that are active in the evening, ranging from snakes and spiders to sloths and kinkajous. Flashlights are provided.

🛍 SHOPPING

Luna Azul   Jewelry

(☎2645-6638; www.facebook.com/lunaazul-monteverde; Cerro Plano; ☉9am-6pm) This supercute gallery and gift shop in Cerro Plano is packed to the gills with jewelry, clothing, soaps, sculpture and macramé, among other things. The jewelry in particular is stylish and stunning, crafted from silver, shell, crystals and turquoise.

Monteverde Art House   Handicrafts

(Casa de Arte; ☎2645-5275; www.monteverdearthouse.com; Cerro Plano; ☉9am-6:30pm) You'll find several rooms stuffed with colorful Costa Rican artistry here. The goods run the gamut, including jewelry, ceramic work, Boruca textiles and traditional handicrafts. There's a big variety, including some paintings and more contemporary work, but it's mostly at the the crafts end of the artsy-craftsy spectrum. Great for souvenirs. Find it in Cerro Plano.

Casem   Handicrafts

(Cooperativa de Artesanía Santa Elena
Monteverde; ✆2645-5190; www.casemcoop.
blogspot.com; ⊘8am-5pm) Begun in 1982 as
a women's cooperative representing eight
female artists, today Casem has expanded
to reportedly include almost 150 local
artisans (eight of whom are men). It's a
nice story, but a rather underwhelming
selection of stuff, featuring embroidered
clothing, painted handbags, polished
wooden tableware, and some bookmarks
and greeting cards.

🍴 EATING

Santa Elena and Monteverde offer high
quality but poor value in the kitchen. You'll
be delighted by the organic ingredients,
local flavors and international zest, but not
by the high price tags. Even the local *sodas*
and bakeries are more expensive than they
ought to be. Santa Elena has most of the
budget kitchens in the area, but there's
good eating throughout the Monteverde
swirl.

⊗ Santa Elena
Orchid Coffee   Cafe $

(✆2645-6850; mains US$4-12; ⊘7am-7pm;
🛜⏚) ✔ If you're feeling peckish, go straight
to this lovely cafe in Santa Elena, filled with
art and light. Take a seat on the front porch
and take a bite of heaven. It calls itself a
coffee shop, but there's a full menu of traditional and nontraditional breakfast items,
sweet and savory crepes, interesting and
unusual salads, and thoroughly satisfying
sandwiches. And coffee, too, but so much
more.

Taco Taco   Mexican $

(✆5108-0525; www.facebook.com/tacotaco-
monteverde; mains US$5-8; ⊘noon-8pm; 🛜)
Quick and convenient, this *taquería* (taco
bar) offers tasty Tex-Mex tacos, burritos
and quesadillas filled with shredded chick-
en, slow-roasted short rib, roasted veggies
and battered mahimahi. The only difficulty
is deciding (but you really can't go wrong).
The deck in front of Pensión Santa Elena
is perfect for people-watching, but the

Costa Rican *casado* (set meal)

seating supply is limited, especially if you want a shady spot.

Paz y Flora — Vegetarian $
([☎]2645-6782; www.pazyflorarestaurante.com; mains US$7-10; [♣][♿]) Good for the body, good for the soul and good for the earth. That's what Paz y Flora in Santa Elena strives for in its menu of vegetarian and vegan delights. It's a pretty comprehensive offering, with sandwiches, salads, pasta, rice and *rollitos*. It's all super fresh and deliciously satisfying. Look for the Buddha mosaic and you'll know you're in the right place.

Monteverde Cheese Factory Outlet — Ice Cream $
(ice cream $US2-4; [☉]10am-8pm) Now you don't have to trek all the way down to the Monteverde Cheese Factory to get the most delicious ice-cream in Costa Rica. Just pop into this ice cream parlor in central Santa Elena and order yourself a scoop of coffee. Mmmmmm is for Monteverde.

Sabor Tico — Soda $
([☎]2645-5827; www.restaurantesabortico.com; mains US$5-8; [☉]9am-9pm) [♥] Ticos and travelers alike rave about this local Santa Elena joint. Look for some tasty twists on the standard fare, such as *sopa da olla* (beef soup), *chorreada Tica* (fried corn cakes) and tamales (holiday fare, typically). The *gallos* (soft tortilla with delicious filling of your choice) are a perfect alternative to the more filling *casado* for lunch.

The original location is opposite the soccer field; there's a newer branch in the Centro Comercial.

Toro Tinto — Steak $$
([☎]2645-6252; www.facebook.com/torotinto.cr; [☉]noon-10pm) A Santa Elena newcomer, this Argentinean steakhouse lures in customers with soft lighting and cozy brick and wood interior. And it keeps them sated with steaks that are perfectly cut and grilled to order, not to mention unexpected specials and delicious desserts. The wine selection is good – mostly Chilean

and Argentine – but pricey. This place will warm your cloud-soaked soul.

Tree House Restaurant & Café
Cafe $$

(☑2645-5751; www.treehouse.cr; Santa Elena; mains US$7-18; ☺11am-10pm; 🛜) It's a fine line between hokey and happy. But this restaurant – built around a half-century-old *higuerón* (fig) tree – definitely makes us happy. There's a menu of well-prepared if overpriced standards, from *ceviche* (marinated seafood) to *sopa Azteca* (stew) to burgers. The service is spot-on, and the atmosphere is quite delightful. It's a lively space to have a bite, linger over wine and occasionally catch live music.

El Jardín
International $$$

(☑2645-5057; www.monteverdelodge.com; Monteverde Lodge, Santa Elena; lunch US$8-14, dinner US$16-22; ☺7am-10pm; 🛜) 🍴 Arguably the 'finest' dining in the area. The menu is wide ranging, always highlighting the local flavors. But these are not your typical *tipica:* beef tenderloin served on a sugarcane kebab, pan-fried trout topped with orange sauce. The setting – with windows to the trees – is lovely and service is superb. Romantics can opt for a private table in the garden.

Morpho's Restaurant
International $$$

(☑2645-7373; www.morphosrestaurant.com; mains US$8-20; ☺11am-9pm; P🍽) Dine among gushing waterfalls and fluttering butterflies at this downtown restaurant in Santa Elena. Some call it 'romantic,' others call it 'kitschy' – but nobody can dispute the excellent, sophisticated menu, which combines local ingredients with gourmet flair. The results are sure to please any palate.

❌ Cerro Plano & Monteverde

Cafe Colibri
Cafe $

(☑2645-7768; coffee drinks US$2; ☺8am-5pm) Just outside the reserve gates, the 'hummingbird cafe' is a top-notch stop to

Paving the Way

A 1983 feature article in *National Geographic* billed the Monteverde and Santa Elena area as the place to view one of Central America's most famous birds – the resplendent quetzal. Suddenly, hordes of tourists armed with tripods and telephoto lenses started braving Monteverde's notoriously awful access roads, which came as a huge shock to the then-established Quaker community. In an effort to stem the tourist flow, local communities lobbied to stop developers from paving the roads. It worked – for a while.

Eventually, the lobby to spur development bested the lobby to limit development.

In 2013, the transportation ministry announced that it would invest the necessary US$16 million to pave the 18km road from Guacimal to Santa Elena, which is the main access route to Monteverde. There was no sign of asphalt at the time of research, but this plan is moving forward and may be completed by the time you read this. Enjoy the smooth ride. Travel times will obviously be greatly reduced, but that's not the only change that road will bring.

With the paving of the main access road – expected to be completed in 2016 – this precious experiment in sustainable ecotourism will undergo a new set of trials.

JOHN COLETTI/GETTY IMAGES ©

refuel after a hike in the woods. The drinks will warm your body, but the humming of dozens of hummingbirds in the garden will delight your heart. An identification board shows the nine species that you're likely to see. Great photo ops.

Stella's Bakery
Bakery $

(🖉2645-5560; Monteverde; mains US$4-8; ⏱6am-10pm; 🛜🎛) A bakery for birders. Come in the morning for strong coffee and sweet pastries, or come later for sandwiches on homemade bread and rich, warming soup. Whenever you come, keep an eye on the bird feeder, which attracts tanagers, mot-mots and an emerald-green toucanet.

Whole Foods Market
Supermarket $

(Monteverde; ⏱7:30am-5:30pm) This is not the Whole Foods you might think it is, but you'll notice some similarities. This is a good but expensive place to pick up fresh produce, as well as spices and other imported ingredients you might not find in the big supermarket.

Café Caburé
Cafe $$$

(🖉2645-5020; www.cabure.net; Monteverde; lunch US$6-12, dinner US$14-20; ⏱9am-8pm Mon-Sat; 🅿🛜) This Argentine cafe above the Bat Jungle in Monteverde specializes in creative and delicious everything, from sandwiches on homemade bread and fresh salads, to more elaborate fare like sea bass in almond sauce or filet mignon with chimichurri. Save room for dessert because the chocolate treats are high art.

Quimera's
Tapas $$

(🖉2645-7037; Cerro Plano; tapas US$7-10) Come to this casual cafe in Cerro Plano for unexpected creations, like sea bass in ginger and rum, shrimp skewers in mango sauce, and roasted eggplant with smoked cheese and sun-dried tomatoes. The place promises 'Latin-infused tapas,' but the menu is actually infused with flavors and ingredients from all over the world, which is even better. Start yourself off with one of the house cocktails.

Pizzería Tramonti
Italian $$

(🖉2645-6120; www.tramonticr.com; Monteverde; mains US$10-16; ⏱11:30am-9:30pm Mon-Sat;

SAMANTHA MONTALVO/EYEEM/GETTY IMAGES ©

P ✎ ♿) Tramonti offers authentic Italian, specializing in fresh seafood, hearty pastas and wood-fired pizzas. There's a decent selection of wines from Italy and Argentina. With a greenery-filled dining room twinkling with lights, the ambiance is relaxed yet romantic.

Johnny's Pizzería   Pizza $$

(☎2645-5066; www.pizzeriadejohnny.com; Cerro Plano; mains US$11-24; ⊘11:30am-10pm; 🛜♿) Johnny's has been serving up wood-fired, thin-crust pizzas in Cerro Plano since 1993. Keep it simple with a margherita or let Johnny impress you with one of his creative combos (like the Monteverde, with prosciutto, green olives and home-grown organic leeks).

d'Sofia   Fusion $$$

(☎2645-7017; Cerro Plano; mains US$12-16; ⊘11:30am-9:30pm; 🛜) Sofia has established itself as one of the best places in town with its Nuevo Latino cuisine – a modern fusion of traditional Latin American cooking styles. Think plaintain-crusted sea bass, seafood chimichanga or beef tenderloin with roasted red pepper and cashew sauce.

The ambiance is enhanced by groovy music, picture windows, romantic candle lighting and potent cocktails.

🍸 DRINKING & NIGHTLIFE

Nightlife in these parts generally involves a guided hike and nocturnal critters, but since this misty green mountain draws artists and dreamers, there's a smattering of regular cultural offerings. When there's anything going on you'll see it heavily advertised around town. Especially during the dry season, you'll see some action at the bars in Santa Elena.

Bar Amigos   Bar

(☎2645-5071; www.baramigos.com; Santa Elena; ⊘noon-3am) With picture windows overlooking the mountainside, this Santa Elena mainstay evokes the atmosphere of a ski lodge. But, no, there are DJs, karaoke, billiards and sports on the screens. This is the one consistent place in the area to let loose, so there's usually a good, rowdy mix of Ticos and tourists. The food is also surprisingly good.

> ### ★ Top 5 for Foodies
> El Jardín (p119)
> d'Sofia (p121)
> Café Caburé (p120)
> Quimera's (p120)
> Whole Foods Market (p120)

From left: Pizza; Empanadas; Shrimp and mango kebabs

PINQOITA/GETTY IMAGES ©

DAVID LOFTUS/GETTY IMAGES ©

Monteverde
Beer House   Beer Garden
(☑8659-2054; www.facebook.com/monteverde-beerhouse; Santa Elena; 🛜) It's not a brewery – contrary to the sign – but they do offer a selection of local craft beers. There's a shady deck out back and smiling servers on hand, so it's a perfect atmosphere for kicking back after a day of adventures. The Middle Eastern food (mains US$6 to US$10) is hit or miss, but if you're hungry, go for the shakshuka.

La Taberna   Bar
(☑8379-9108; www.facebook.com/tabernatonight; ⊙4pm-2am) Known by many names in recent years, this Santa Elena drinking establishment will always be remembered as La Taberna. No matter what you call it, you'll find a friendly, divey outdoor bar, drink specials, pub fare and live music.

> *immerse yourself in nature, get some exercise, spot some monkeys*

ℹ️ INFORMATION

Monteverde Tours (Desafío Adventure Company; ☑2645-5874; www.monteverdetours.com) In partnership with Desafío Adventure Company, this tour agency and vacation planner can help you find the activity you are looking for. They can make arrangements for guided hikes, horseback riding, canopy tours, coffee tours and more, not to mention transportation like the taxi-boat-taxi to Arenal. It's a good resource if you're unsure how you want to spend your time.

Police (☑2645-6248) In Santa Elena.

ℹ️ GETTING THERE & AROUND

While most Costa Rican communities regularly request paved roads in their region, preservationists in Monteverde have done the opposite. All roads around here are shockingly rough. Even if you arrive on a newly paved road via Guacimal, you'll still want a 4WD to get around to the more remote lodges and reserves.

There are three roads from the Interamericana: coming from the south, the first well-

Heading to a canopy tour (p108)

DREAMPICTURES/SHANNON FAULK/GETTY IMAGES ©

signed turnoff is at Rancho Grande (18km north of the Puntarenas exit). The first stretch of this route (from Sardinal to Guacimal) was paved in 2011. The remaining 17km (from Guacimal to Santa Elena) is scheduled to be paved in 2016. At the time of research, it took about three hours to drive to San José, but that time will be reduced with the road improvements.

A second, shorter road goes via Juntas, but it's not paved except for the first few kilometers. Finally, if coming from the north, drivers can take the paved road from Cañas via Tilarán and then take the rough road from Tilarán to Santa Elena.

If you're coming from Arenal, consider taking the lakeside route through Tronadora and Río Chiquito, instead of going through Tilarán. The roads are rougher, but the panoramas of the lake, volcano and surrounding countryside are magnificent.

There are two gas stations open for business in the area.

VOLCÁN ARENAL

Volcán Arenal at a glance...

You know about the region's main attraction: that now-dormant volcano, surrounded by old lava fields, bubbling hot springs and a stunning lake. The volcano may be dormant, but plenty of adventure awaits you. There are trails to hike, waterfalls to rappel down, and sloths to spot. No matter your preferred method of exploring – hiking, biking, horseback riding, zip-lining – you can do it here. And when your body's had enough, you can ease into a volcano-heated pool to soak away your aches and pains.

Two Days at Arenal

On your first day, be brave (and crazy): start early to climb Cerro Chato, the ultimate hike in **Parque Nacional Volcán Arenal** (p128). Afterwards, head to the **hot springs** (p132) for a well deserved soak. On your second day, take a detour to El Castillo to visit the **Butterfly Conservatory** (p141) and have lunch at **La Ventanita** (p142).

Four Days at Arenal

If you have the luxury of a third day, return to the park to hike along old lava flows and spy on sloths. Travel on horseback or by mountain bike if you prefer. Your fourth day is free for a hike and swim at **Catarata Río Fortuna** (p134). Or, take a day trip to **Proyecto Asis** (p137) to support the animal sanctuary.

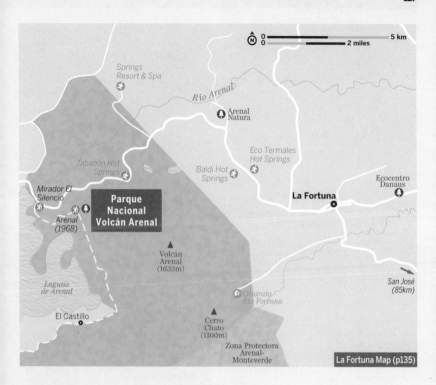

La Fortuna Map (p135)

Arriving in the Arenal Area

Whether you approach from the west or east, the drive into the Arenal area is spectacular. Coming from the west, the paved road hugs the northern bank of Laguna de Arenal. Approaching from the east, you'll have Volcán Platanar as the backdrop, as the road winds through this green, river-rich agrarian region. If the weather cooperates, the resolute peak of Arenal looms in front of you.

Where to Stay

La Fortuna is possibly Costa Rica's biggest tourist town, and there are some decent lodgings (especially budget options). Lodgings are also lined up along the roads heading out of La Fortuna west and south; essentially they have the national park as their backyard. Even lakefront properties around Laguna de Arenal are close enough to use as a base for exploring the region. Prices drop dramatically during the green season (May to November).

For a tiny place, El Castillo also has an impressive range of accommodations, from funky budget lodgings to charming B&Bs to expansive ecolodges.

Volcán Arenal

Parque Nacional Volcán Arenal

Volcán Arenal no longer lights up the night sky with molten lava, but it still provides a rugged terrain for hiking and a rich habitat for wildlife.

Great For...

ℹ Need to Know

☑2461-8499; adult/child US$15/5;
⊘8am-4pm

☑ **Don't Miss**

Swimming in the blue-green waters of the volcano lake atop Cerro Chato.

ESDELVAL/GETTY IMAGES ©

History

For most of modern history, Volcán Arenal was just another dormant volcano surrounded by fertile farmland. But for about 42 years – from its destructive explosion in 1968 until its sudden subsiding in 2010 – the volcano was an ever-active and awe-striking natural wonder, producing menacing ash columns, massive explosions and streams of glowing molten rock almost daily.

The fiery views are gone for now, but Arenal is still a worthy destination, thanks to the dense forest covering its lower slopes and foothills, and its picture-perfect conical shape up top (often shrouded in clouds, but still). The Parque Nacional Volcán Arenal is part of the Area de Conservación Arenal, which protects most of the Cordillera de Tilarán. This area is rugged and varied, rich with wildlife and laced with trails.

Hiking

Part of the Area de Conservación Arenal, the park is rugged and varied, with about 15km of well-marked trails that follow old lava flows. Hikers routinely spot sloths, coatis, howler monkeys, white-faced capuchins and even anteaters.

From the ranger station you can hike the Sendero Los Heliconias, a 1km circular track that passes by the site of the 1968 lava flow. A 1.5km-long path branches off this trail and leads to an overlook. The Sendero Las Coladas also branches off the Heliconias trail and wraps around the volcano for 2km past the 1993 lava flow before connecting with the Sendero Los Tucanes, which extends for another 3km through the rainforest at the base of the volcano. You'll get good views of the summit on the way back to the parking area.

Hiking in Parque Nacional Volcán Arenal

From the park headquarters (not the ranger station) is the 1.3km Sendero Los Miradores, which leads down to the shores of the volcanic lake and provides a good angle for volcano viewing. Also from park headquarters, the Old Lava Flow Trail is an interesting and strenuous lower elevation trail following the flow of the massive 1992 eruption. The 4km round trip takes two hours to complete. If you want to keep hiking, combine it with the Sendero El Ceibo, a scenic 1.8km trail through secondary forest.

There are additional trails departing from **Arenal Observatory Lodge** (www.

arenalobservatorylodge.com) and on a nearby private reserve.

Climbing Cerro Chato

The ultimate hike in the national park, the **Cerro Chato Trail** (day pass per person US$10) meanders through pasture before climbing steeply into patches of virgin growth, reaching into misty sky. The trail crests Cerro Chato, Arenal's dormant partner, and ends in a 1100m-high volcanic lake that is perfect for a dip. The hike is only 8km round trip, but it will take two to three hours each way.

The trail starts at the Arenal Observatory Lodge on the western side of the volcano, or there is an alternative, even more strenuous route that departs from La Catarata Rio Fortuna (p134) and approaches from the east. If you take the western route, be sure to enter the Observatory Lodge to get on the correct trail; bypass the dodgy operation that has set up shop just outside the gates.

Tours

In addition to hiking, it's also possible to explore the area on horseback or mountain bike.

Arenal Wilberth Stables (☑2479-7522; www.arenalwilberthstable.com; per person US$65; ☉7:30am, 11am & 2:30pm) Three-hour horseback-riding tours depart from these stables, at the foot for Arenal. The stables are opposite the entrance to the national park, but there's an office in town next to Arenal Resort Hostel.

Arenal 1968 (www.arenal1968.com; US$12, mountain bike rental US$45; ☉7am-10pm) Right next to the park entrance, you'll find a private trail network along the original 1968 lava flow. There's a lookout that, on a clear day, offers a perfect volcano view. Mountain bikes are available to ride on these trails. It's located 1.2km from the highway turnoff to the park, just before the ranger station.

> ✕ **Take a Break**
>
> There are no restaurants near the park, so pack a picnic from Rainforest Café (p137).

DENNIS K. JOHNSON/GETTY IMAGES ©

> ★ **Top Tip**
>
> The ranger station has trail maps available.

Tabacón Hot Springs

JOHN COLETTI/GETTY IMAGES ©

Hot Springs

Beneath La Fortuna the lava is still curdling and heating countless bubbling springs.

Great For...

☑ **Don't Miss**

Sitting in a hot tub with a cool cocktail and a marvelous volcano view.

Eco Termales Hot Springs

Everything from the natural circulation systems in the pools to the soft lighting is understated, luxurious and romantic at the gated, reservations-only **Eco Termales Hot Springs** (☎2479-8787; www.ecotermalesfortuna.cr; US$36; ☺10am, 1pm or 5pm; 👪) ✐ about 4.5km northwest of town. Lush greenery surrounds the walking paths that cut through these gorgeous grounds. Only 100 visitors are admitted at a time, to maintain the ambiance of serenity and seclusion.

Paradise Hot Springs

Low-key **Paradise Hot Springs** (www.paradisehotspringscr.com; adult/child US$23/15; ☺11am-9pm) has one lovely, large pool with a waterfall and several smaller, secluded

pools, surrounded by lush vegetation and tropical blooms. The pools vary in temperature (up to 40°C), and some have hydromassage. Paradise is much simpler than the other larger spring settings, but there are fewer people, and your experience is bound to be more relaxing and more romantic.

Springs Resort & Spa

If you're looking for a luxurious hot-spring experience, the **Springs Resort & Spa** (2401-3313, in USA 954-727-8333; www.thespringscostarica.com; 2-day pass US$60; 8am-10pm;) features 18 free-form pools with various temperatures, volcano views, landscaped gardens, waterfalls and swim-up bars, including a jungle bar

Need to Know

Towels and lockers are available at the hot springs facilities.

Take a Break

All of the hot springs facilities have restaurants and bars on site.

★ Top Tip

Near the entrance to Tabacón Resort, natural thermal pools are free for a soak.

with a waterslide. The whole scene is human-made, but it's lovely.

Tabacón Hot Springs

Some say it's cheesy and some say it's fun. We say it's both. At **Tabacón Hot Springs** (2519-1999; www.tabacon.com; day pass incl lunch or dinner adult/child US$85/30; 10am-10pm) , broad-leaf palms, rare orchids and other florid tropical blooms part to reveal a 40°C waterfall pouring over a fake cliff, concealing constructed caves complete with camouflaged cup holders. Lounged across each well-placed stonelike substance are overheated tourists of various shapes and sizes, relaxing.

Baldi Hot Springs

Big enough so that there's something for everyone, **Baldi** (2479-9917; www.baldihotsprings.cr; with/without buffet US$56/34; 10am-10pm;), about 4.5km northwest of town, has 25 thermal pools ranging in temperature from 32°C to a scalding 67°C. There are waterfalls and soaking pools for chill-seekers and 'Xtreme' slides for thrill-seekers, plus a good-size children's play area. At night, the thumping music and swim-up bars attract a young party crowd, but drinks are pricey!

La Fortuna

◎ SIGHTS

Catarata Río Fortuna   Waterfall

(US$12; ⊘8am-5pm) You can glimpse the sparkling 70m ribbon of clear water that pours through a sheer canyon of dark volcanic rock arrayed in bromeliads and ferns with minimal sweat equity. But it's worth the climb down and out to see it from the jungle floor. Though it's dangerous to dive beneath the thundering falls, a series of perfect swimming holes with spectacular views tiles the canyon in aquamarine. This is also the trailhead for the difficult hike to Cerro Chato (p131).

From the turnoff on the road to San Ramón, it's about 4km uphill to the falls. On the way up, you'll enjoy spectacular views of Cerro Chato as you hike through pastures and past the small hotels lining the road.

Arenal Natura   Park

(☑2479-1616; www.arenalnatura.com; day/night/bird tour US$29/39/49; ⊘8am-5:30pm; 👣) Located 6km west of La Fortuna, this is a well-manicured nature experience that includes frogs, turtles, snakes and crocs, all in their appointed places. The birdlife is also prodigious here. Excellent naturalist guides ensure that you don't miss anything hiding in the trees. Discounted rates for children and students.

Ecocentro Danaus   Nature Reserve

(☑2479-7019; www.ecocentrodanaus.com; admission with/without guide US$18/12, guided night tour US$35; ⊘8am-4pm Mon-Sat, 9am-3:30pm Sun, night tour 5:30pm; 👣) ✆ This center, 2km east of town, has a well-developed trail system that's good for birding, as well as spotting mammals such as sloth, coati and howler monkey. The price of admission also includes a visit to a butterfly garden, a ranarium featuring poison-dart frogs and a small lake containing caiman and turtles. Reserve in advance for the excellent night tour.

⊙ TOURS

Don Olivo Chocolate Tour   Ecotour

(☑6110-3556, 2469-1371; www.facebook.com/tourdechocolatedonolivo; tour US$25; ⊘8am, 10am, 1pm & 3pm; 👣) Let Don Olivo or his son show you around their family *finca* (farm), showing off their sugarcane, oranges and – of course – cocoa plants. The process of turning this funny fruit into the decadent dessert that we all know and love is truly fascinating. Bonus: lots of taste-testing along the way!

Alberto's Horse Tours   Horseback Riding

(☑2479-7711, 2479-9043; www.facebook.com/albertoshorses; per person US$85; ⊘8:30am-1:30pm) Alberto and his son lead popular horseback-riding trips to the Catarata de la Fortuna. It's a three- or four-hour trip, but you'll spend about an hour off your horse, when you hike down to the falls for a swim or a photo op. Beautiful setting, beautiful horses. Cash only.

Arenal Oasis   Bird-Watching, Night Walk

(☑2479-9526; www.arenaloasis.com; night/bird walks US$40/55; ⊘5:45pm) The Rojas Bonilla family has created this wild frog sanctuary, home to some 28 species of croaking critters. The frogs are just the beginning of this night walk, which continues into the rainforest to see what other nocturnal animals await. If you're more of a morning person, they also do a bird-watching tour. Reservations recommended. Located 3km from La Fortuna's centre; hotel pick-up costs US$10.

Bike Arenal   Cycling

(☑2479-7150; www.bikearenal.com; Av 319 A, Rte 702; rental per day/week US$25/150, half-/full-day tour US$85/135; ⊘7am-6pm) This outfit offers a variety of bike tours for all levels of rider, including a popular ride around the lake and a half-day ride to El Castillo. You can also do versions of these rides on your own. Make advance arrangements for rent-

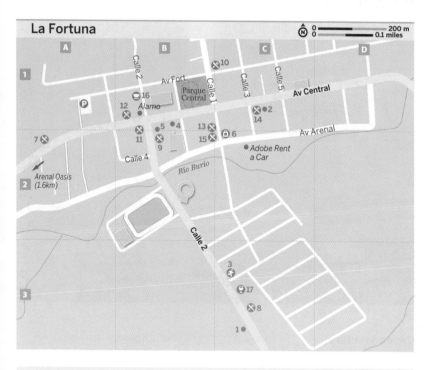

La Fortuna

al and an English-speaking bike mechanic will bring the bicycle to you.

PureTrek Canyoning   Canyoning
(☏2479-1313, US toll free 1-866-569-5723; www. puretrekcanyoning.com; 4hr incl transportation & lunch US$100; ☉7am-10pm; 🖐) 🖉 The reputable PureTrek leads guided rappels down three waterfalls, one of which is 50m high.

Also included: rock climbing and 'monkey drop,' which is actually a zip line with a rappel at the end of it. High marks for attention to safety and high-quality gear. They get some big groups, but they do a good job keeping things moving.

Check-in at PureTrek headquarters, located in a tree house 6km west of town.

GUIZIOU FRANCK/GETTY IMAGES ©

Catarata Río Fortuna (p134)

Canoa Aventura
Canoeing

(☏2479-8200; www.canoa-aventura.com; canoe trip US$67; ◷6:30am-9:30pm) ✦ This long-standing family-run company specializes in canoe and float trips led by bilingual naturalist guides. Most are geared toward wildlife- and bird-watching.

Jacamar Naturalist Tours
Hiking, Adventure Tour

(☏2479-9767; www.arenaltours.com; Av Central; ◷7am-9pm) Recommended for its variety of naturalist hikes, including Volcán Arenal, waterfall and hanging bridges. Customers rave about the guides' flexibility and attentiveness. Located on the ground level of Hotel Arenal Carmela.

Arenal Paraíso Canopy Tours
Canopy Tour

(☏2479-1100; www.arenalparaiso.com; tours US$45; ◷8am-5pm; 👶) A dozen cables zip across the canyon of the Río Arenal, giving a unique perspective on two waterfalls, as well as the rainforest canopy. Also includes admission to the resort's swimming pool

and 13 thermal pools, which are hidden among the rocks and greenery on the hillside.

Arenal Mundo Aventura
Adventure Tour, Hiking

(☏2479-9762; www.arenalmundoaventura.com; adult/child adventure tours US$67/51, hiking US$53/37; 👶) An all-in-one adventure park, this place offers various guided hikes, rappelling and horseback riding, as well as a canopy tour. It also hosts performances of indigenous Maleku dance and song. It is 2km south of La Fortuna, on the road to Chachagua.

Aventuras Arenal
Tour

(☏2479-9133; www.aventurasarenal.com; Av Central; kayaking US$60, hiking from US$60, horseback riding US$60-75; ◷7am-8pm) Around for over 25 years, Aventuras Arenal organizes a variety of local day tours on bike, boat and horseback. It also does trips further afield, including to Caño Negro and Río Celeste.

Canopy Los Cañones   Canopy Tour
(📞2479-1047; www.hotelloslagos.com; adult/child US$50/35) 🏊 Located at the Hotel Los Lagos, the Canopy Los Cañones has 12 cables over the rainforest, ranging from 50m to 500m long. The price includes admission to a frog farm, crocodile farm, butterfly farm, hot springs, natural pools and waterslides, which are all on the hotel grounds.

Ecoglide   Canopy Tour
(📞2479-7120; www.arenalecoglide.com; adult/child US$55/45; ⏰7am-4pm; 👪) Ecoglide is the biggest canopy game in town, featuring 13 cables, 15 platforms and a 'Tarzan' swing. The dual-cable safety system provides extra security and peace of mind.

🔒 SHOPPING

Hecho A Mano   Handicrafts
(Handmade Art Shop; 📞8611-0018; www.facebook.com/handmadeartshop; Calle 1; ⏰9am-10pm) There's no shortage of souvenirs for sale in La Fortuna. But this unique shop is something special, carrying an excellent selection of arts and crafts by local and national artists. You'll find representative pieces from Costa Rica's many subcultures, including Boruca masks, rasta handicrafts, lots of macrame and some lovely handmade jewelry.

**Neptune's House
of Hammocks**   Homewares
(📞2479-8269; ⏰8am-6pm) On the road to La Catarata de la Fortuna, it sells soft drinks and hammocks (US$50 to US$170). Take a breather and try one out.

✖ EATING

Unless you're eating exclusively at *sodas*, you'll find the restaurants in La Fortuna to be more expensive than in other parts of the country. But there are some excellent, innovative kitchens, including a few that are part of the farm-to-table movement. The restaurants are mostly clustered in town, but there are also places to eat on the road heading west.

 Community-Based Organization

It's an animal rescue center. It's a volunteer project. It's Spanish classes. Community-based organization **Proyecto Asis** (📞2475-9121; www.institutoasis.com; adult/child US$31/18, incl volunteering US$54/31; ⏰tours 8:30am & 1pm) 🏊 is doing a lot of good, and you can help. The introductory experience is a 1½-hour tour of the wildlife rescue center, but it's worth springing for the three-hour 'volunteering' experience, which includes hands-on interaction with the animals. It's pricey, but the cause is worthy.

Asis also offers homestays in the local community. It's located about 20km west of Quesada, past the village of Florencia. Reserve at least a day in advance.

Howler monkey (p277)
KRYSIA CAMPOS/GETTY IMAGES ©

Rainforest Café   Cafe $
(📞2479-7239; Calle 1 btwn Avs Central & Arenal; mains US$4-6; ⏰7am-8:30pm; 📶🍴) We know it's bad form to start with dessert, but the irresistible sweets at this popular spot are beautiful to behold and delicious to devour. The savory menu features tasty burritos, *casados,* sandwiches etc. There's also a full menu of hot and cold coffee, including some tempting specialty drinks (Mono Loco is coffee, banana, milk, chocolate, cinnamon).

There's a dash of urban-coffeehouse atmosphere here. Must be the writing in the milk foam.

 **Represa
Arenal**

Forget for a moment that there are always ecological issues associated with dams and revel in the fact that this one created a rather magnificent lake. In the absence of wind the glassy surface of Represa Arenal (Arenal Dam) reflects the volcano and the surrounding mountains teeming with cloud forest. Crowds congregate to admire the view and snap photos. (Unfortunately, there's no convenient place to stop, so you'll often encounter a minor traffic jam, especially at the dam's western end.)

Mistico Hanging Bridges (Puentes Cogantes de Arenal; www.misticopark.com; adult/child US$24/free, tours US$36-47; ⊙7:30am-4:30pm, tours 6am, 9am & 2pm) Unlike the fly-by view you'll get on a zip-line canopy tour, a walk along these hanging bridges allows you to explore the rainforest and canopy from six suspended bridges and 10 traditional bridges at a more natural and peaceful pace. The longest swaying bridge is 97m long and the highest is 25m above the earth. All are accessible from a single 3km trail.

La Roca Canyoneering (www.canyoneeringlaroca.com; tour US$95) Rappelling into river canyons, zip lines, hanging bridges, a Tarzan swing, swimming and snacks are packed into this adrenaline-pumping half-day tour. Make sure you bring a change of clothes, as you will get wet. La Roca is 4km from the dam; it also has an office at **Sunset Tours** (www.sunsettour.net; Calle 2; ⊙6:30am-9pm) in La Fortuna.

Mistico Hanging Bridges
ALEX ROBINSON/GETTY IMAGES ©

La Central — Cafe $

(⊘2479-8080; cnr Calle 2 & Av Central; breakfast US$3, mains US$4-8; ⊙8am-6pm Wed-Mon; 🛜🍴) A breezy terrace, filled with greenery and art, this is a perfect stop for breakfast or lunch. The place touts natural healthy food, and you'll find lots of vegetarian options – fresh, hearty salads, a tasty veggie burger, and a Middle Eastern spread with hummus and baba ganoush. Come later in the day for fresh fruit-juice cocktails and occasional live music acts.

Soda Viquez — Soda $

(⊘2479-7133; cnr Calle 1 & Av Arenal; mains US$6-10; ⊙7am-10pm; 🍴) Travelers adore the 'local flavor' that's served up at Soda Viquez (in all senses of the expression). It's a super-friendly spot, offering tasty *tipica*, especially *casados*, rice dishes and fresh fruit *batidos*. Reasonable prices, ample portions.

Chifa La Familia Feliz — Fusion $$

(⊘8469-6327; Calle 2; mains US$8-12; ⊙11am-10pm; 🛜🍴👪) If you're looking for a change of taste – a real change from *casados* and pizza – check this out. In case you didn't know, *Chifa* means 'Chinese food' in Peruvian–Spanish. So what we have here is Peruvian Chinese food, which is something special indeed. The chef goes out of his way to welcome and satisfy all comers.

Anch'io Ristorante & Pizzeria — Italian $$

(⊘2479-7024; Av Central; mains US$10-18; ⊙noon-10pm; 🅿🛜👪) If you have a hankering for pizza, you can't do better than Anch'io, where the crust is crispy thin, the toppings are plentiful, and the pie is cooked in a wood-fired oven. Start yourself off with a traditional antipasto. Accompany with cold beer or a bottle of red. Add super service and pleasant patio seating. And you've got yourself a winner.

Lava Lounge — International $$

(⊘2479-7365; www.lavaloungecostarica.com; Av Central btwn Calles 4 & 2; mains US$8-12; ⊙7am-10:30pm; 🅿🛜🍴) This hip, open-air restaurant is a relief when you just can't abide another *casado*. There is pizza and pasta, wraps and salads, with loads of vegetarian options. Both food and service are variable, but the picnic tables and *palapa* roof create a cool, rustic vibe. Add colorful cocktails and occasional live reggae music, and the place is pretty irresistible.

Café Mediterraneo   Italian $$

(2479-7497; Calle 2; mains US$8-12; 11am-10pm) It's worth the jaunt out of town to eat at this delightful osteria, which cooks up in the homemade pasta dishes and wood-fired pizza. Customers rave about the personable service and decadent desserts. Nutella pizza? *Sì, grazie!*

Kappa Sushi   Sushi $$

(Calle 1 & Ave Fort; sushi & rolls US$7-10; noon-10pm;) When you're surrounded by mountains and cattle farms, who's thinking of sushi? Well, think of it. The fish is fresh (you're not *that* far from the ocean) and the preparations are innovative. The dragon roll (shrimp tempura, avocado and eel sauce) is a favorite. Sit at an outside table and enjoy the view of Arenal while you feast on raw fish – or go for the veg options.

Benedictus
Steakhouse   Steak $$$

(2479-1912; www.facebook.com/benedictussteakhouse; mains US$14-30; noon-10pm) Turn off the highway and drive about 1km up a steep, rough dirt road to arrive at this spectacularly situated steak house (tricky to find in the dark, so arrive before the sun goes down). You'll be rewarded with a gorgeous view, followed by an amazing meal. In addition to the meats, there is heavenly homemade bread, fantastic *ceviche* (marinated seafood) and tantalizing desserts.

The steaks come from free-range cattle that graze on grass in the pastures below the restaurant. They also raise lambs, chickens and pigs. Veggies come from the organic greenhouse. Farm to table direct. Speaking of tables, there are only a few of them, so make sure you reserve.

Restaurant
Don Rufino   International $$$

(2479-9997; www.donrufino.com; cnr Av Central & Calle 3; mains US$16-40; 11am-11pm) The vibe is trendy and the service is hopping at this indoor-outdoor grill. The

Costa Rican breakfast

Top 5 for Wildlife

Arenal Oasis (p134)

Arenal Natura (p134)

Canoa Aventura (p136)

Jacamar Naturalist Tours (p136)

Ecocentro Danaus (p134)

From left: Horseback riding near Arenal Observatory Lodge (p131); Hanging bridge in Parque Nacional Volcán Arenal; Guided tour in Parque Nacional Volcán Arenal

highlight of the menu is the perfectly pre-pared grilled meats. If you're cutting back, go for Grandma's BBQ chicken (seasoned with chocolate, wrapped in a banana leaf) or the chef's special tuna (seasoned with ginger oil, served with rice noodles, tamarind sauce and cashew nuts).

🍷 DRINKING & NIGHTLIFE

Down to Earth Coffee

(📞2479-8568; www.godowntoearth.org; Calle 2; ⊗8am-8pm) This place is all about the coffee, which is brewed from single-origin beans from the owner's farm in the Dota Tarrazu Valley. There's no food here, just coffee – smooth, strong and revitalizing. Drink it, or buy some beans to take home. Sure, it's kind of pricey, but so is Starbucks.

El Establo Bar

(📞2479-7675; Calle 2; ⊗5pm-2am Wed-Sat) La Fortuna's raucous *sendero* bar with an attached disco fronts the bull ring and at-tracts an ever-enthusiastic local following. The age demographic here ranges from 18 to 88. That's almost always a good thing.

Vagabondo Reggae Bar Bar

(📞2479-8087; Av Central; ⊗8pm-2am) Chill out with cheap beers and good vibes at this super-relaxed reggae bar, located about 2km west of town. Behind the lion's face, you'll find a dimly lit bar, populated by both Ticos and tourists, playing pool and (maybe) dancing.

ℹ️ GETTING THERE & AWAY

The fastest route between Monteverde-Santa Elena and La Fortuna is the taxi-boat-taxi combo (formerly known as jeep-boat-jeep, which sounds sexy but it was the same thing). It is actually a minivan with the requisite yellow *'turismo'* tattoo, which takes you to Laguna de Arenal, meeting a boat that crosses the lake, where a 4WD taxi on the other side continues to Monteverde. It's a terrific transportation option that can be arranged through almost any hotel or tour operator (US$25 to US$35, four hours).

This is increasingly becoming the primary transportation between La Fortuna and Monte-verde as it's incredibly scenic and reasonably priced.

GUZIOU FRANCK/GETTY IMAGES ©

❶ GETTING AROUND

La Fortuna is easy to access by public transportation, but nearby attractions such as the hot springs, Parque Nacional Volcán Arenal and Laguna de Arenal demand internal combustion (or a tour operator). You can also rent a car in town.

Adobe Rent a Car (☑2479-7202; www.adobecar. com; Av Arenal; ☉8am-5pm)

Alamo (☑2479-9090; www.alamocostarica.com; cnr Av Central & Calle 2; ☉7:30am-5:30pm)

El Castillo

◉ SIGHTS

El Castillo-Arenal Butterfly Conservatory   Wildlife Reserve

(☑2479-1149; www.butterflyconservatory.org; adult/student US$16/11; ☉8am-4pm) This is more than just a butterfly conservatory (although it has one of the largest butterfly exhibitions in Costa Rica). Altogether there are six domed habitats, a ranarium, an insect museum, a medicinal herb garden, and an hour's worth of trails through a botanic garden and along the river. The birding is

also excellent at this peaceful place, which has wonderful volcano views.

Arenal EcoZoo   Zoo

(El Serpentario; ☑2479-1059; www.arenalecozoo. com; adult/child US$20/16; ☉8am-7pm) This snake house offers a hands-on animal experience, as in, handling and milking a venomous snake. The EcoZoo is also home to a red-tailed boa (one of the largest snakes in the world), as well as frogs, amphibious lizards, iguanas, turtles, scorpions, tarantulas and butterflies. Come at feeding time if you want to see snakes devouring bugs, frogs and other snakes!

❺ TOURS

La Gavilana   Tour

(☑2479-1747, 8433-7902; night hike US$45, waterfall tour US$90, Big Forest hike US$130) The adventurous folks at La Gavilana Herbs & Art offer a two-day 'extreme hike' of the Big Forest trail between El Castillo and San Gerardo (near Santa Elena). Traversing old-growth forests and raging rivers, hikers overnight at the rustic

Welcome to El Castillo

The tiny mountain village of El Castillo is a beautiful, bucolic alternative to La Fortuna, if you don't mind the treacherous roads. This picturesque locale has easy access to Parque Nacional Volcán Arenal and amazing, up-close views of the looming mountain – with none of the traffic or tourist madness of its bigger neighbor.

There is a tight-knit expat community, some of whom have opened appealing lodges and top-notch restaurants. There are hiking trails and swimming holes, and even a few worthy attractions – a butterfly house and an eco-zoo. The only thing El Castillo doesn't have is pavement. And maybe that's a good thing.

Mountain Lodge, El Castillo
JOHN COLETTI/GETTY IMAGES ©

Rancho Maximo in San Gerardo. Dinner and breakfast are provided. La Gavilana offers a few additional adventures, including an extended night hike and one-day waterfall tour.

Rancho Adventure Tours
Adventure Tour

(☏8302-7318; www.ranchomargot.com; farm tour US$35, other tours US$55) Rancho Margot has a good selection of guided tours, including horseback riding on the southern side of Laguna de Arenal, kayaking on the lake, and touring the ranch to learn about the workings of a sustainable farm.

Sky Adventures
Canopy Tour

(☏2479-4100; www.skyadventures.travel; adult/child SkyTrek US$77/53, Sky Tram US$44/37, Sky Walk US$37/26, Sky Limit US$77/53; ⊙7:30am-4pm) El Castillo's entry in the canopy-tour category has zip lines (Sky Trek), a floating gondola (Sky Tram) and a series of hanging bridges (Sky Walk). It's safe and well run, and visitors tend to leave smiling. A unique combo, Sky River Drift combines zip-lining with tree-climbing (and jumping) and river tubing. There's also mountain biking on the property.

🗙 EATING

Your eating options are pretty limited in El Castillo, but there are some good ones – enough to keep you fed for several days at least. In addition to the few places in the village, several lodgings on the outskirts have recommended restaurants. Of course, you have many more choices in La Fortuna, but you'll have to traverse 9km of bumpy gravel roads to get there.

La Ventanita
Cafe $

(☏2479-1735; mains US$3-5; ⊙10:30am-9pm; ☏) *La ventanita* refers to the 'little window' at Kelly's house where you place your order. Soon enough, you'll be devouring the best burrito or *chifrijo* (rice and pinto beans with fried pork and capped with fresh tomato salsa and corn chips) that you've ever had, along with a nutritious and delicious *batido* (smoothie). It's typical fare with a twist – pulled pork and bacon burritos, for example. Kelly is a wealth of information about the area, so ask away.

La Gavilana Herbs & Art
Bakery $

(☏2479-1747; www.facebook.com/LaGavilana-HerbsandArt; items US$2-6; ⊙8am-5pm Mon-Fri, 9am-2pm Sat) Meet Thomas and Hannah. He's Czech and makes the hot sauce and vinegar; she's American and bakes the cookies and breads. Their place is decked with paintings (by Hannah), while the grounds contain a food forest (by Thomas), filled with medicinal herbs and fruit trees.

Sky Tram canopy tour, Sky Adventures

The whole place is filled with love, beauty and creativity. It's 100m uphill from Essence Arenal hostel.

Fusion Grill Fusion **$$**

(☏2479-1949; www.fusiongrillrestaurant. com; mains US$8-15; ☺7am-10pm) Set in an open-air dining room with an incredible vista of the volcano, Fusion Grill shows off a little swank (at least, more than other restaurants in El Castillo). Chef Benedictus is rightly proud of his *ceviche,* but he has a full, solid menu, featuring steaks and seafood and phenomenal desserts.

🍷 DRINKING & NIGHTLIFE

There's only one place to go out drinking in El Castillo, but it's worth a visit. You have more options in La Fortuna, but keep in mind that it's a tricky business getting back here after dark.

Howlers Bar & Grill Bar

(☏2479-1785; www.facebook.com/howlersbarandgrill; ☺noon-10pm Tue-Sun) This lakefront bar is a fun choice for a night out drinking in El Castillo. (Good thing, as it's your only choice.) The American-style pub grub is excellent, as is the cold draught beer. It's a popular place for the expat community to congregate, guaranteeing an upbeat, *pura vida* vibe.

ℹ️ GETTING THERE & AWAY

El Castillo is located 8km past the entrance to Parque Nacional Volcán Arenal. It's a rough gravel road, and it only gets worse once you get to the village. A 4WD is required in the rainy season and recommended year-round.

There is no public transportation, but a **private shuttle bus** (☏8887-9141) runs from the MegaSuper in La Fortuna (one hour, US$10). The bus departs Rancho Margot at 6am, 10am and 4pm, returning from La Fortuna at 7am, 12:30pm and 5:15pm. The schedule is subject to change; reservations are required anyway so it's best to call ahead.

MONTEZUMA

Montezuma at a glance...

Montezuma is an immediately endearing beach town that demands you abandon the car to stroll, swim and, if you can stroll a little further, surf. The warm and wild ocean and that ever-audible jungle has helped this rocky nook cultivate an inviting, boho vibe. Tourist offerings such as canopy tours do a brisk trade here, but you'll also bump up against Montezuma's artsy-rootsy beach culture in yoga classes, volunteer corps, veggie-friendly dining rooms and neo-Rastas hawking uplifting herbs.

Two Days in Montezuma

On your first day, make the trek to **Montezuma Waterfalls** (p150) for thrilling jumps and cooling dips. Have lunch at **Cocina Clandestina** (p154), then head to **Playa Montezuma** (p152) for an afternoon of swimming and sunbathing. Spend day two exploring the trails at **Reserva Natural Absoluta Cabo Blanco** (p148), saving time to relax and relish the gorgeous wilderness beach.

Four Days in Montezuma

Learn to surf! Sign up for a lesson with **Young Vision Surf School** (p153) and learn to ride the waves at **Playa Grande** (p152). That night, treat yourself to a delectable beachside dinner at **Playa de los Artistas** (p156). On your last day, get an early start on the beach hike to **Playa Cocolito** (p159), where you can luxuriate in some of the most magnificent scenery around.

Golfo de Nicoya

Carmona

Jicaral   Lepanto

Puntarenas

Isla San Lucas

Santa Marta

Cangrejal

Playa Naranjo

Islita

Bejuco

Jabilla

San Francisco de Coyote

Paquera

Curú

Isla Tortuga

Pochote

Playa Tambor

Tambor

Golfo de Nicoya

Cóbano

Montezuma

Montezuma Waterfalls

Santa Teresa

Cabuya

Reserva Natural Absoluta Cabo Blanco

Montezuma Map (p153)

Arriving in Montezuma

The easiest way to reach Montezuma is to abandon your own vehicle and hop on a boat shuttle from Jacó. It's also manageable by bus and ferry, or car, though it's not an easy trip, due to horrendous roads in the southern Península de Nicoya.

Where to Stay

Montezuma is a hub of the southern Península de Nicoya, so you'll find a great range of accommodation options catering to all budgets. But there are *cabinas* and other more interesting accommodations sprinkled along the roads into town and in its tiny neighboring village, Cabuya. It's a tiny little *pueblo*, so you'll obviously find a greater choice back in Montezuma.

There's also a sprinkling of guesthouses and boutique hotels above Montezuma, off the road to Cóbano, some of which are highly recommended, but are only suitable if you have wheels.

ROB FRANCIS/GETTY IMAGES ©

Reserva Natural Absoluta Cabo Blanco

At the tip of the Península de Nicoya, the unique park is covered by evergreen forests, bisected by a hiking trail and flanked by empty white-sand beaches and offshore islands

Great For...

☑ **Don't Miss**

Picnicking and swimming at a deserted beach at the tip of the peninsula.

The Reserve

Just 11km south of Montezuma is Costa Rica's oldest protected wilderness area. Cabo Blanco comprises 12 sq km of land and 17 sq km of surrounding ocean, and includes the entire southern tip of the Península de Nicoya. The moist microclimate on the tip of the peninsula fosters the growth of evergreen forests, which are unique when compared with the dry tropical forests typical of Nicoya. The park also encompasses a number of pristine white-sand beaches and offshore islands that are favored nesting areas for various bird species.

Hiking trail, Cabo Blanco

ADRIAN HEPWORTH/ALAMY STOCK PHOTO

Montezuma

Santa Teresa

Cabuya

Reserva Natural Absoluta Cabo Blanco

ℹ Need to Know

☎2642-0093; adult/child US$12/2; ⊙8am-4pm Wed-Sun

✕ Take a Break

Pack a picnic with sandwiches from Panadería Cabuya (p159).

★ Top Tip

Cabo Blanco is called an 'absolute' nature reserve because visitors were originally not permitted (prior to the late 1980s).

Armadillos, pizotes (coatis), peccaries and anteaters are also occasionally sighted.

Beaches

The wide, sandy pebble beach at the end of the Sendero Sueco is magnificent. It's backed by jungle, sheltered by two rugged headlands, including one that stretches out into a rock reef with island views just offshore. The water is striped turquoise at low tide, but the cool currents still make for a refreshing dip. Visibility isn't always great for snorkeling, but you may want to bring a mask anyway. Driftwood is smooth, weathered and piled haphazardly here and there. There are even picnic tables and a grill, if you care to get ambitious. Simply put, it is a postcard, and should be required for visitors to the southern peninsula. Leave the beach by 2pm to get out before the park closes.

Hiking

From the ranger station, the **Sendero Sueco** (Swedish Trail) leads 4.5km down to a wilderness beach at the tip of the peninsula, while the **Sendero Danes** (Danish Trail) is a spur that branches from Sendero Sueco and reconnects 1km later. So, you can make this small 2km loop and stay in the woods, or take on the considerably more difficult, but much more rewarding, hike to the cape, heading down one way and taking the other path back up. Be advised that the trails can get very muddy (especially in the rainy season) and are fairly steep in certain parts – plan for about two hours in each direction.

Monkeys, squirrels, sloths, deer, agoutis and raccoon abound at Cabo Blanco.

TRAVELSTOCK44/GETTY IMAGES ©

Montezuma Waterfalls

A river hike leads to a waterfall with a delicious swimming hole. Further along the trail, a second set of falls offers a good clean 10m leap into deep water.

Great For...

☑ Don't Miss

That agonizing, heart-thumping moment when you have to let go of the rope.

Head south past Hotel La Cascada, where you'll find a parking area. Then take the trail to the right just after the bridge. You'll want proper hiking footwear.

Waterfall Trail

The first waterfall has a lusciously inviting swimming hole, where you'll want to cool off from the hike. Remember that it's shallow and rocky and not suitable for diving.

From here, if you continue on the well-marked trail that leads around and up, you will come to a second set of falls. This is where you'll find a good clean leap into the deep water below. At 10m high, they are also the tallest of the three falls. To reach the jumping point, continue on the trail up the side of the hill until you reach the

Canopy tour, Montezuma

Montezuma

Montezuma Waterfalls

Río Montezuma

PACIFIC OCEAN

❶ Need to Know

parking US$2

✕ Take a Break

Recover from your adventure with gourmet tacos and craft beer at Cocina Clandestina (p154).

★ Top Tip
Hit the trail early and you may have the falls to yourself.

Canopy Tour

Tour company **Sun Trails** (Montezuma Waterfall Canopy Tour; ☏2642-0808; www.montezumatraveladventures.com; tours US$45; ⊙9am-3pm) operates a 2½-hour canopy tour. After you've flown down nine zip lines, you'll hike down – rather than up – to the waterfalls. Bring your swimsuit, so you can jump off the rocks and cool off. Book at the Sun Trails office in town.

Butterfly Garden

About 1km south of town, alongside the waterfall trail, you can take a tour through this lush *mariposario* (butterfly garden) and nursery at **Montezuma Gardens** (☏2642-1317; www.montezumagardens.com; US$4; ⊙8am-4pm), where the mysterious metamorphoses occur. You'll learn about the life cycles and benefits of a dozen local species, of which you'll see many colorful varieties.

diving area. Do not attempt to scale the falls. The rocks are slippery and several travelers have met their death in this way.

From this point, the trail continues up the hill to the third and last set of falls. These are not suitable for jumping, but daring souls can swing out on the rope and drop right into the deeper part of the swimming hole.

Playing it Safe

⚬ Don't attempt to jump into the lower pool, which is rocky and shallow.

⚬ Don't attempt to scale the waterfall.

⚬ Don't jump into the third upper pool without the aid of the swing.

⚬ Don't mix weed and waterfalls. (But you already knew that.)

Montezuma

◎ SIGHTS

Picture-perfect white-sand beaches are strung along the coast, separated by small rocky headlands, offering great beach-combing and ideal tide-pool contemplation. Unfortunately, there are strong riptides, so inquire locally before going for a swim.

Playa Montezuma   Beach
The best beach close to town is just north of Cocolores restaurant, where the sand is powdery and sheltered from big swells. This is your glorious sun-soaked crash pad. The water's shade of teal is immediately nourishing, the temperature is perfect and fish are abundant. At the north end of the beach, look for the trail that leads to a cove known as Piedra Colorada. A small waterfall

> *Picture-perfect white-sand beaches are strung along the coast*

forms a freshwater pool, which is a perfect swimming spot.

Playa Grande   Beach
About 7km north of town, Playa Grande is the best surf beach in the area. It's a 3km-plus stretch of waves and sand, which never gets too crowded as it requires a 30-minute hike to get here. But what a hike it is, wandering along between the turquoise waters of the Pacific and the lush greenery of the Montezuma Biological Reserve.

✪ ACTIVITIES

Montezuma Yoga   Yoga
(☏2642-1311, 8704-1632; www.montezuma yoga.com; per person US$14; ⊙classes 8:30am & 6pm daily) Anusara-inspired instruction, which pairs Iyengar alignment princi-ples with a Vinyasa flow, is available in a gorgeous studio kissed by ocean breezes, sheltered by a peaked tin roof and serenaded by the sounds of nature. The

Playa Montezuma

CHRISTER FREDRIKSSON/GETTY IMAGES ©

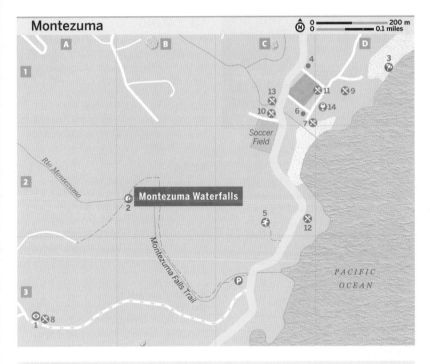

Montezuma

Sunday night candlelight class is a close-to-heaven experience. On the grounds of Hotel Los Mangos.

Young Vision Surf School   Surfing
(☑8669-6835; www.youngvisionsurf.com; 2hr lessons US$45) Manny and Alvaro get rave reviews for their knowledge, enthusiasm and patience with new surfers of all ages. Daily lessons take place on Playa Grande,

with no more than three people in the class. Surfboard, rash guard and fresh fruit are included. They also offer week-long camps for families, surfer chicks and yogis.

La Escuela del Sol   Course
(☑8884-8444; www.laescueladelsol.com) Based at the Hotel El Tajalin, this eclectic educational vortex offers Spanish, surf,

 The Wessburg Legacy

The reserve at Cabo Blanco was originally established by a Danish–Swedish couple, the late Karen Mogensen and Olof Nicolas Wessberg, who settled in Montezuma in the 1950s and were among the first conservationists in Costa Rica. In 1960 the couple was distraught when they discovered that sections of Cabo Blanco had been clear-cut. At the time, the Costa Rican government was primarily focused on the agricultural development of the country, and had not yet formulated its modern-day conservation policy. Karen and Nicolas, as he was known, were instrumental in convincing the government to establish a national park system, which eventually led to the creation of the Cabo Blanco reserve in 1963.

The couple continued to fight for increased conservation of ecologically rich areas. Tragically, Olof was murdered in 1975 during a campaign in the Península de Osa. Karen continued their work until her death in 1994, and today they are buried in the Reserva Absoluta Nicolás Wessberg, the site of their original homestead.

Commemorative plaque for Mogensen and Wessberg

yoga, fire dance and scuba instruction. In other words, there is no excuse to leave Montezuma without a bilingual, underwater, surf warrior, dreadlocked hippie soul.

 EATING

Montezuma is experiencing the same food revolution that is taking place on other parts of the peninsula. Local ingredients are meeting international chefs, with magnificent results. Montezuma is also good for traditional Tico fare, often with ocean-side service. Most of the restaurants are clustered around the central park and along the beach.

Kalibó   Cafe $
(②2642-4545; mains US$3-8; ◎6am-9pm; ✉) A tiny place with an open kitchen and half a dozen tables, across from the bus stop. This perfect breakfast stop does homemade pastries, fresh fruit smoothies and strong local coffee, and also serves salads, sandwiches and proper meals. It's a charmer.

Bar Restaurante
Moctezuma   Mediterranean $$
(②2642-0058; mains US$9-23; ◎7:30am-11pm; 🛜🍴) The long menu has just about everything, especially when it comes to seafood. Look for steamed mussels, broiled octopus, fish carpaccio and grilled shrimp, not to mention basics like burgers and *casados*. You're bound to find something you like, and you can't beat the prime beachfront location.

Soda Monte Sol   Soda $
(②8849-4962; mains US$5-14; ◎7am-9pm) A cute, colorful *soda* that does all the *típica* dishes, tasty and affordable *casados*, pastas, burgers and a variety of juices and smoothies. All is served at a leisurely pace in a humble dining room touched with grace. Great people-watching spot.

Cocina
Clandestina   Latin American $$
(②8315-8003; www.facebook.com/clandestinamontezuma; mains US$8-12; ◎noon-9pm Tue-Sat; 🛜✏️🍴) The secret is out. The hottest new restaurant in Montezuma is this awesome, artistic place in the trees

Souvenir stall, Playa Montezuma (p152)

at the butterfly gardens (p151). Look for innovative takes on Central American standards, such as daily changing taco specials and delectable chicken mole enchiladas. Vegetarians are joyfully accommodated with yam and lentil cakes or *chilles rellenos*. The beverage of choice is Butterfly Beer, brewed on site.

Cocolores International $$

(☑2642-0348; mains US$9-22; ☺5-10pm Tue-Sun) Set on a beachside terrace lit with lanterns, Cocolores is one of Montezuma's top spots for an upscale dinner. The wide-ranging menu includes curries, pasta, fajitas and steaks, all prepared and served with careful attention to delicious details. Prices aren't cheap, but it's worth it.

Tierra y Fuega Italian $$

(☑2642-1593; mains US$8-15; ☺5-10pm; P✹≋) Take a taxi (or drive in the dark!) up to this Italian gem in the hills above Montezuma. This Italian outpost looks as though it's straight out of the Tuscan countryside, complete with brick ovens

bump up against Montezuma's artsy-rootsy beach culture

warming the kitchen and chickens roasting over the fire. The menu is mostly pizza and pasta, but the flavors are divine – not surprising given the ingredients are all imported from Italy or grown on site.

Puggo's Middle Eastern $$

(☑2642-0325; mains US$10-20; ☺noon-11pm) A locally beloved restaurant decorated like a bedouin tent, Puggo's specializes in Middle Eastern cuisine, including falafel, hummus, kebabs and aromatic fish, which they dress in imported spices and herbs and roast whole. Cap it off with a strong cup of Turkish coffee.

Orgánico Vegetarian $$

(☑2642-1322; mains US$8-12; ☺8am-9pm; ✹) When they say 'pure food made with love,' they mean it – this healthy cafe turns out vegetarian and vegan dishes such as

CHRISTER FREDRIKSSON/GETTY IMAGES ©

 Puntarenas–Paquera Ferry

The road from Paquera to Cóbano is paved, but the rest of the southern peninsula is not. Be forewarned: you're in for a bumpy ride, especially if you are coming from other parts of the peninsula. Ferries carry cars and passengers across the Golfo de Nicoya (from Puntarenas to Paquera) so you can save yourself some driving there if you're coming from the mainland.

In Puntarenas, car and passenger ferries bound for Paquera depart several times a day from the **northwestern dock** (Av 3 btwn Calles 31 & 33). If you are driving and will be taking the car ferry, arrive at the dock early to get in line. The vehicle section tends to fill up quickly and you may not make it on. In addition, make sure that you have purchased your ticket from the walk-up ticket window before driving onto the ferry. You will not be admitted onto the boat if you don't already have a ticket.

Naviera Tambor (☏2661-2084; www.navieratambor.com; adult/child US$1.60/1, bike/car US$4.40/23) has daily departures to Paquera (for transfer to Montezuma and Mal País) at 5am, 9am, 11am, 2pm, 5pm and 8:30pm.

From Paquera to Puntarenas, Naviera Tambor leaves daily at 5:30am, 9am, 11am, 2pm, 5pm and 8pm. The trip to Puntarenas takes about an hour.

spicy Thai burgers, a *sopa azteca* with tofu, smoothies and more (as well as meaty options too). Avocado ice cream is something everyone should try. There's live music almost nightly, including a wildly popular open mike on Monday nights.

Playa de los Artistas International $$$
(☏2642-0920; www.playamontezuma.net/playadelosartistas.htm; mains US$9-18; ☺5-9pm Mon-Fri, noon-9pm Sat) Most romantic dinner ever. If you're lucky, you'll snag one of the tree-trunk tables under the palms. The international menu with Mediterranean influences changes daily, though you can always count on fresh seafood roasted in the wood oven. The service is flawless, the cooking is innovative, and the setting is downright dreamy. Cash only (back to reality).

🍷 DRINKING & NIGHTLIFE

If you want to party hardy, there's exactly one place in town to do it. (On the upside, that one place is hopping almost any night of the week – at least during the high season.)

Chico's Bar Bar
(☺11am-2am) When it comes to nightlife, Chico's is the main (only?) game in town, which means that everybody ends up here eventually – old, young, Ticos, tourists, rowdy, dowdy – especially on Thursday nights, which is reggae night. Snag a table on the back patio for a lovely view of the beach and beyond.

ℹ️ INFORMATION

The only ATM in town is a BCR *cajero* located across from Chico's Bar. The nearest full-service bank is in Cóbano. For money exchange, tour operators in town will take US dollars, euros or travelers checks.

Clockwise from top: Beach house; Lizard; Meal at Playa de los Artistas

Agouti

ⓘ GETTING THERE & AWAY

Zuma Tours (📞2642-0024; www.zumatours. net) operates a fast water shuttle connecting Montezuma to Jacó in an hour. At US$40 or so, it's not cheap, but it'll save you a day's worth of travel. From Montezuma, boats depart at 9:30am daily, and the price includes van transfer from the beach to the Jacó bus terminal. From Jacó, the departure to Montezuma is at 11am. During the high season, they may run an additional shuttle, departing Montezuma at 1:30pm and departing Jacó at 3pm. Book in advance from any tour operator. Also, dress appropriately; you will get wet.

ⓘ GETTING AROUND

Although the road from Paquera to Cóbano is paved, the stretch between Cóbano and Montezuma is not, and it can be brutal. During the rainy season you will need a 4WD. In the village itself, parking can be a problem, though it's easy enough to walk everywhere.

Cabuya

◎ SIGHTS

This tiny, bucolic village unfurls along a rugged dirt road about 7km south of Montezuma. Don't miss the amazing Cabuya ficus tree, which claims to be the largest strangler fig in Costa Rica, measuring 40m high and 22m in diameter!

The beach here is rocky and not great for swimming or surfing. But you're just a short walk from Playa los Cedros, a great surf spot that is halfway between Montezuma and Cabuya.

Alternatively, at low tide you can walk across the natural bridge to Isla Cabuya, which has a small sandy beach and good snorkeling spots, as well as an evocative island cemetery. Keep an eye on the tides or you'll have to swim back!

MARK KOSTICH/GETTY IMAGES ©

⊗ EATING

Cabuya proudly claims a *soda*, a bakery and a pizzeria – as does any proper Tico village. If none of those suit your fancy, you can always drive 7km north to Montezuma for an excellent selection of eateries.

Panadería Cabuya   Cafe $

(⌕2642-1184; www.cabuyabeach.com; mains US$3-17; ⊙6:30am-8pm Mon-Sat, to 6pm Sun; 🛜) A local landmark. Set on a tropical patio, this inviting cafe serves up a stellar menu including fresh bread, pastries and strong coffee for breakfast, as well as soups and sandwiches for later in the day. If you have a thing for tall, dark and handsome, you should meet the chocolate cake.

Café Coyote   Pizza $

(⌕2642-0354; www.cabuyabeach.com; mains US$5-11; ⊙8am-10pm; 🛜) Jenny can help you with just about anything you need, from calling a taxi to organizing an adventure outing, pouring you a cold *cerveza* or making you a tasty pizza (her specialty). She also offers delicious breakfast options and other meals to sate your appetite at any time of day.

Soda Marvin   Soda $

(mains US$4-10; ⊙7am-9pm; 🛜🍴) Here's your local family-run *soda*, offering all your Tico favorites. Non-meat-eaters will be surprised and delighted by the excellent vegetarian *casado*, but there's also seafood pasta, fish fajitas, filling breakfasts and the ever-important, strong, dark coffee.

Playa Cocolito

Here's your chance to see a waterfall crashing down a cliff, straight onto the rocks and into the ocean. And yes, it is as spectacular as it sounds. El Chorro Waterfall is the *pièce de résistance* of Playa Cocolito, which is itself pretty irresistible.

It's a hot, two-hour, 12km hike from Montezuma: leave at sunrise to spot plenty of wildlife along the way. Alternatively, this is a popular destination for horseback riding. In any case, be sure to bring water and snacks as there are no facilities here.

The waters here are a dreamy, iridescent azure, with pink rocky cliffs creating two inviting swimming areas. It's far enough from the action that you are likely to have the place to yourself.

❶ GETTING THERE & AWAY

Driving from Montezuma, it's a straight shot 7km down the coast to the village of Cabuya. Buses make this run – en route to Cabo Blanco – four times a day in either direction.

PLAYA
SÁMARA

Playa Sámara at a glance...

Is Sámara the black hole of happiness? That's what more than one expat has said after stopping here on vacation and never leaving. The crescent-shaped strip of pale-gray sand spans two rocky headlands, where the sea is calm and beautiful. It's not spectacular, just safe, mellow, reasonably developed, easily navigable on foot and accessible by public transportation. Not surprisingly, it's popular with vacationing Ticos, foreign families and backpackers, who enjoy Sámara's palpable ease and tranquillity. But be careful: the longer you stay, the less you'll want to leave. If you've got some extra time and a 4WD, explore the hidden beaches north of Sámara, such as Playas Barrigona and Buenavista.

Two Days in Sámara

Unlike many places in Costa Rica, in Sámara, you don't need to feel obligated to do anything. It's perfectly acceptable to spend two days sitting on the beach, swimming in the surf and eating tacos at **Lo Que Hay** (p164). Should things get monotonous, change location to Playa Carrillo (p170).

Four Days in Sámara

If you have not yet been to **Roots Bakery** (p169), go there for breakfast. Inquire at **Samara Info Center** (p171) to schedule a **turtle tour** (p166) to Playa Ostional. Return to the beach. By day four, you may be wondering what else goes on around here, in which case you should take a hike with **Samara Trails** (p168) to find out. And then... back to the beach.

0 — 5 km
0 — 2 miles

Nicoya (15km)

Río Nosara

Playa Ostial

Nosara

Refugio Nacional
Playa Nosara de Vida Silvestre
Ostional

Turtle Tours

Playa Pelada

Playa Guiones

Garza

*Bahía
Garza*

Sámara

Playa
Carrillo

Playa Sámara

Carrillo

Beach Bars

PACIFIC OCEAN

Arriving in Sámara

Playa Sámara lies about 35km south-west of Nicoya on a paved road. No flights were operating out of the Sámara airport (PLD) at the time of research.

Where to Stay

There are plenty of excellent places to stay right in Playa Sámara. Benefits include being close to the beach and the bars. If you prefer to be further away from civilization, you'll find some lovely options north of town along the beach and south of town in Playa Carrillo – though you'll want a car (or at least a bi-cycle). All price ranges are represented.

Beachside beers

HOLGER LEUE/GETTY IMAGES ©

Beach Bars

Many restaurants and bars have prime beachfront property, which guarantees a good experience no matter what you're eating or drinking.

Great For...

☑ **Don't Miss**

Watching the fiery orb drop into the sea.

It's not exactly a party town, but Sámara sees some action at night. All of the beach bars get busy starting around sunset. Try some of the following spots, most of which serve food as well as drinks.

Lo Que Hay

(☎2656-0811; www.loquehaybeachbar.com; tacos US$2, mains US$5-10; ☺7am-late) This rocking beachside *taqueria* (taco bar) and pub offers six delectable taco fillings: fish, chorizo, chicken, beef, pork, veggie. The grilled avocados stuffed with *pico de gallo* are choice. Even *sin* tacos, a good time will be had, as the bar crowd sips into the wee small hours.

Drinking at a beachside bar

BERNARD/IMAGEBROKER/AGEFOTOSTOCK ©

the beach. If you care to linger, there are lounge chairs on the sand, lockers and beach volleyball.

La Vela Latina

(☎2656-2286; ⏰11am-midnight; 🛜) Here's your sunset happy hour spot. Settle into a comfy chair on the sand and order a bucket of icy beers or a perfectly blended cocktail at this beach bar. There's also a menu of sophisticated *bocas* (appetizers) and American-style pub grub.

Bar Olas

(☎2656-0319; ⏰11am-2:30am) If you'd like to settle in for an evening of beers with the locals, check out Bar Olas on the north end of the beach. This archetypal seafront dive makes almost no effort (even the beer should be colder), but they're open early, serve late and drinks are cheap.

La Dolce Vita

(☎2656-3371; www.facebook.com/ladolcevita. samara; US$8-15) Life is sweet when you're sitting under a giant *palapa* on the sand, drinking a smoothie and watching the surfers. This is a popular spot for pizza and sundowners, thanks to affable Italian owners and a prime beachfront locale.

Gusto

(☎2656-0252; mains US$10-17; ⏰9am-11pm; 🅿🛜) Good food, great location. Service is lacking, but you're not in any hurry, right? Enjoy pastas, salads and seafood, as well as phenomenal smoothies and creative cocktails, all while watching the action on

RON LEVINE/GETTY IMAGES ©

Turtle Tours

About 40km northwest of Sámara, Playa Ostional hosts a monthly arrival of olive ridley sea turtles, which come ashore to nest en masse.

The 248-hectare Refugio Nacional de Fauna Silvestre Ostional extends from Punta India in the north to Playa Guiones in the south, and includes the beaches of Playa Nosara and Playa Ostional. It was created in 1992 to protect the *arribadas* (mass nestings) of the olive ridley sea turtles, which occur from from July to December (peaking in September and October).

Protecting the Olive Ridley

The olive ridley is one of the smallest species of sea turtle, typically weighing around 45kg. Although they are endangered, there are a few beaches in the world where ridleys nest in large groups that can number in the thousands. Scientists believe that this behavior is an attempt to overwhelm predators.

Great For...

☑ **Don't Miss**

Arriving during the rainy season to catch the mass arrivals of nesting turtles.

Olive ridley sea turtle hatchlings

ⓘ Need to Know

Refugio Nacional de Fauna Silvestre Ostional (☑2683-0400; www.sinac.go.cr/AC/ACT/RVSOstional; adult/child US$12/2, turtle tours incl admission US$20)

✕ Take a Break

You'll find an open-air snack shack on the main drag in Ostional, opposite the guiding office.

★ Top Tip

Flash photography is not permitted, but turtle tours start around 4pm, when it's still light out.

Prior to the creation of the park, coastal residents used to harvest and sell eggs indiscriminately (raw turtle eggs increase sexual vigor, or so they say). In recent years, however, an imaginative conservation plan has been put into place. Residents of Ostional are allowed to harvest eggs from the first laying, as these eggs are often trampled by subsequent waves of nesting turtles anyway. By allowing this limited harvesting, the community maintains its economic livelihood, and the villagers in turn act as park rangers to prevent poachers from infringing on their enterprise.

Turtle Tours

Mass arrivals of nesting turtles occur during the rainy season every three or four weeks (usually on dark nights preceding a new moon) and last about four nights. It's possible to see turtles in lesser numbers almost any night during nesting season. In the dry season, a fitting consolation prize is the small number of leatherback and green turtles that also nest here.

Many tour operators in the region offer tours to Ostional, which includes transportation and English-speaking guide. Make arrangements through the Sámara Info Center (p171). Or, you can arrange with local guides to visit independently, although you'll have to drive yourself, and your guide is unlikely to speak English.

Asociación de Guías Locales (☑2682-0428; www.facebook.com/Asociacion.Guias.Ostional; turtle tours per person US$8) You can't miss the local guides' office in Ostional, located on the main road just south of the plaza. During *arribada*, the guides lead 30-minute tours on the beach starting around 4pm and continuing until after dark. Early risers can also go for a tour shortly before sunrise. Check the website for details.

Sámara

ACTIVITIES

No matter what you like to do at the beach, you can probably do it at Playa Sámara. Expert surfers might get bored by Sámara's inconsistent waves, but beginners will have a blast. Otherwise, there's hiking, horseback riding and sea kayaking, as well as snorkeling out around Isla la Chora. Take a break from the beach to explore the forested hillsides on foot or by zip line.

Pato Surf School   Surfing

(☏8761-4638; www.patossurfingsamara.com; board rental per day US$15, lessons US$30-40) Set right on the beach, Pato offers inexpensive and quality board rental, as well as beginner surf instruction. Pay for a lesson and get free board rental for five days! Also on offer: stand-up paddle rental and lessons; kayak rental and tours; and snorkel gear. Plus, massage on the beach and occasional beach yoga. What else do you want?

C&C Surf School   Surfing

(☏8599-1874; www.cncsurfschool.com; board rentals per day US$15, lessons group/private US$40/60; ☺8am-8pm) A great choice, offering lessons for individuals, pairs and small groups. Especially recommended for beginners. Owner Adolfo Gómez is a champion longboarder who has represented Costa Rica in the Central American Surfing Games.

TOURS

Samara Trails   Hiking

(☏2656-0920; samaratrails.com; adult/child US$40/30; ☺7am & 3pm, with reservation) This hike departs from the office across from WingNuts, then follows a 6km route through a mango plantation and into the Werner Sauter Biological Reserve, a private reserve located in the hills above Sámara. In two hours, your naturalist guide covers the history of the area and the ecology of the dry tropical forest.

Birds, bugs and monkeys are usually sighted. Great views along the way (including a sunset, if you take the afternoon tour).

Wingnuts   Canopy Tour

(☏2656-0153; www.wingnutscanopy.com; adult/child US$60/45; ☺tours 8am, 9am, noon & 1pm) One entrepreneurial family found a way to preserve their beautiful, wild patch of dry tropical forest: by setting up a small-scale canopy tour. Family-owned and professionally run, this 10-platform operation is unique for its personal approach, as groups max out at 10 people. The price includes transportation from your hotel in Sámara.

Flying Crocodile   Scenic Flights

(☏2656-8048; www.flying-crocodile.com; per person US$110) About 6km north of Sámara in Playa Buenavista, the Flying Crocodile offers ultralight flights over the nearby beaches and mangroves. On site there is also a pretty cool hotel, set on jungly grounds and populated by wildlife.

Leo Tours   Adventure Tour

(☏8995-6820; leotourssamara.com; kayak-snorkel per person US$40) Leo has kayaks, he has fishing rods, he has snorkel gear and he even has a boat. That means he'll take you out for any kind of water fun you crave, from sea kayaking to sport fishing. A favorite tour is kayaking out to Isla Chora, where you can relax, hunt for iguanas (as in try to find them) and snorkel around the island.

Look for Leo on the beach in front of Gusto (p165).

SHOPPING

Sámara has a more creative vibe than most beach towns on the peninsula. You'll find a handful of galleries selling handcrafted jewelry and exquisite items, as well as vendors hawking their wares at stands along the main road.

Surf school, Playa Sámara

Cocotales   Jewelry
(📞8807-7056; ⊘9am-7:30pm) Carlos Caicedo travels around South America to procure gorgeous semiprecious stones, which he crafts into fine jewelry right here in the back of his shop. There are also plenty of clever creations from recycled materials. But his most unique and eye-catching pieces are crafted from cocoa beans (grown locally, of course).

Marea Surf Shop Cafe'   Sports
(📞2656-1181; www.facebook.com/mareasurf-shopcafe2013; ⊘7am-7pm) Part cafe, part downtown surf shop, it doesn't rent gear but it does have top-quality rash guards, board shorts and boards for the buying. Bonus: the shopkeeper steams a fine espresso.

EATING

You won't find the most creative cooking you've ever eaten in Playa Sámara, but you uwon't go hungry. Burger joints, BBQ grills,

> *No matter what you like to do at the beach, you can probably do it at Playa Sámara.*

taquerias and pizzerias all do their thing and do it well. With two totally meat-free restaurants, vegetarians have more options here than they do in most American cities. Many restaurants and bars have prime beachfront property, which guarantees a good experience no matter what you're eating.

Roots Bakery   Bakery $
(📞8924-2770; www.facebook.com/rootsbak-erycafeEnSamara; items US$3-5; ⊘7am-4pm; 🛜) The carrot cake is really good; and the spinach quiche is better. But the cinnamon buns are otherworldly – so rich and gooey and sweet and chewy that you might have to do penance after you eat one. Required eating. Roots is on the main drag, opposite the turnoff to Carrillo.

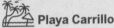 **Playa Carrillo**

About 4km southeast of Sámara, Carrillo is a wide, crescent-shaped beach with clean white sand, cracked granite headlands and a jungle backdrop. On weekends and holidays, the palm-fringed boulevard is lined with cars and the beach crowded with Tico families. At other times, it's practically deserted. The little town is on a hillside above the beach and attracts a trickle of sunbathers and surfers working their way down the coast.

Ahora Sí Vegetarian $

(☎2656-0741; www.ahorasi.isamara.co; mains US$5-11; ☺8am-10pm; 🅿🛜🍴) A Venetian-owned vegetarian restaurant and all-natural cocktail bar. They do smoothies with coconut milk; gnocchi with nutmeg, sage and smoked cheese; soy burgers and yucca fries; wok stir-fries; and thin-crust pizzas. All served on a lovingly decorated tiled patio.

Luv Burger Vegetarian, Burgers $

(☎2656-3348; www.luvburger.com; mains US$5-8; ☺8am-5pm; 🍴) 'Luv' is the operative word here. Feel it, veggies. There are burgers, but they are not made of meat. Neither are the sandwiches, salads or *casados* (set meals). It's all veggie, all the time, from vegan pancakes for breakfast to guilt-free ice cream for dessert. Even the coffee drinks

are made only with soy or almond milk. See how delicious animal-free can be.

Sámara Organics – Mercado Organico Market $$

(☎2656-3046; www.samaraorganics.com; drinks US$2-5; ☺7am-8pm) It's not cheap, but self-caterers (and anybody with a dietary restriction) will appreciate this cafe and market, well-stocked with organic produce and delicious prepared foods. Come get your healthy food fix.

El Lagarto BBQ $$

(☎2656-0750; www.ellagartobbq.com; mains US$11-20; ☺3-11pm; 🛜) Grilled meats are the big draw at this beachfront alfresco restaurant, studded with old trees. Watching the chefs work their magic on the giant wood-fired oven is part of the fun. The surf and turf is highly recommended, as are the cocktails.

Casa Esmeralda Soda $$

(☎2656-0489; www.facebook.com/casaesmeralda.samara; mains US$9-18; ☺noon-9:30pm Mon-Sat) A favorite with locals, this is a dressed-up *soda* with tablecloths, faux-dobe walls and excellent food. The menu ranges from the expected (*arroz con pollo*) to the exotic (Italian octopus appetizer), all of which is fantastic. When the place gets busy, as it does, be prepared to wait.

🍷 DRINKING & NIGHTLIFE

Flying Taco Bar

(☎8409-5376; ☺noon-2am; 🛜) This joint is a laid-back, Tex-Mex beach bar. It's open for lunch – and the grub is recommended – but it's more fun to come at night, when you can also listen to live music, sing karaoke, play poker and drink margaritas (don't skip the tacos though).

Bar Arriba Sports Bar

(☎2656-1052; www.facebook.com/SamarArriba; ☺5:30pm-2am) The requisite sports bar in this surf town is Bar Arriba, located upstairs on the main drag. The place shows international sporting matches on its flat screens, so they're bound to be showing your game. The food is surprisingly satisfying: try the yucca fries (pub grub with a Central American twist).

 INFORMATION

Samara Info Center (☑2656-2424; www. samarainfocenter.com; ⊙9am-9pm) Located on the beach near Lo Que Hay, the Info Center is run by the amiable Brenda and Christopher. It's basically a tour consolidator, but they can help with accommodations, restaurant recommendations, transportation and simply answering questions about Sámara and Carrillo. And they book tours.

❶ GETTING THERE & AWAY

Playa Sámara is a two-hour drive from Liberia and a four-hour drive from San José. The **Sámara Info Center** (p171) offers shuttles several times a day to/from La Fortuna, Liberia and Monteverde, as well as San José. **Interbus** (p291) also runs a daily shuttle from San José.

MANUEL ANTONIO

Manuel Antonio at a glance...

The air is heavy with humidity, scented with thick vegetation and alive with the call of birds and monkeys – this is the tropics. The reason to come here is the Parque Nacional Manuel Antonio, among the most picturesque tropical coast in Costa Rica. If you get bored with cooing at the baby monkeys scurrying in the canopy and scanning for birds and sloths, the turquoise waves and perfect sand provide endless entertainment. Despite the area's overdevelopment, the rainforested hills and the blissful beaches make the park a stunning destination worthy of the tourist hype.

One Day in Manuel Antonio

Spend your first day at the **Parque Nacional Manuel Antonio** (p176), hiking the well-trodden trails and lounging on the picture-perfect beaches. Keep a lookout for monkeys, sloths and other wildlife (p180). At the end of the day, head to **Lush Tapas & Lounge** (p189) for cocktails, tapas and splendid sunset views.

Two Days in Manuel Antonio

Spend your second day taking an adventure tour, whether a paddleboarding outing with **Paddle 9** (p182), a guided coastal hike with **Unique Tours** (p182) or a canopy tour with **Amigos del Río** (p188). Stop for a recovery drink at **Ronny's Place** (p191) before heading to Quepos for a scrumptious seafood dinner at **Gabriella's** (p185).

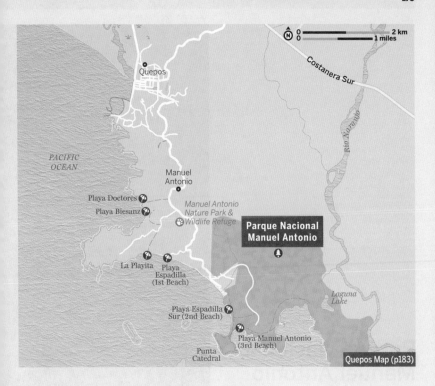

Quepos Map (p183)

Arriving in Manuel Antonio

Both **NatureAir** (p187) and **Sansa** (p187) service Quepos. Prices vary according to season and availability, though you can pay a little less than US$75 for a flight from San José or Liberia. Flights are packed during the high season, so book (and pay) for your ticket well ahead of time and reconfirm often. The airport is 5km out of town.

Where to Stay

The village of Manuel Antonio is the closest base for exploring the national park, though the selection of sleeping options is more varied in Quepos or on the Quepos–Manuel Antonio stretch of road. The Quepos–Manuel Antonio road is skewed toward ultra-top-end hotels, but plenty of noteworthy midrange and budget options are hidden along the way. Many sleeping options along the Quepos–Manuel Antonio road require a taxi or a long walk to reach the park.

Staying in Quepos offers a cheaper alternative. It can also be more convenient, as all the banks, supermarkets and bus stops are in Quepos.

Red-eyed tree frog (p276)

Parque Nacional Manuel Antonio

A place of swaying palms and playful monkeys, sparkling blue water and a riot of tropical birds, Parque Nacional Manuel Antonio is the country's smallest (19.83 sq km) and most popular national park.

Great For...

ⓘ Need to Know

2777-0644; park entrance US$16; ⊙7am-4pm Tue-Sun

★ **Top Tip**
Get here early (7am) and head for the park's furthest reaches to avoid the crowds.

Parque Nacional Manuel Antonio is a truly lovely place; the clearly marked trail system winds through rainforest-backed white-sand beaches and rocky headlands, the wildlife (iguanas, sloths, monkeys) is plentiful, and the views across the bay to the pristine outer islands are gorgeous.

The downside? The crowds. Visitors are confined to around 6.8 sq km of the park (the rest is set aside for ranger patrols battling poaching) and the place gets packed when mid-morning tour buses roll in.

Beaches

There are four beautiful beaches – three within the park and one just outside the park entrance. The beaches are often numbered – most people call Playa Espadilla (outside the park) '1st beach,' Playa Espadilla Sur '2nd beach,' Playa Manuel Antonio '3rd beach,' Playa Puerto Escondido '4th beach' and Playa Playitas '5th beach.' Some people begin counting at Espadilla Sur, which is the first beach in the park, so it can be a bit confusing trying to figure out which beach people may be talking about. Regardless, they're all equally pristine; check conditions with the rangers to see which ones are safe for swimming.

Playa Espadilla Sur North of Punta Catedral; swimming here can be dangerous. The beach is a half-hour hike from the park entrance.

Punta Catedral Geography fun fact: this isthmus, which is the centerpiece of the park, is called a *tombolo* and was formed by the accumulation of sand between the mainland and the peninsula beyond, which was once an island. At its end, the isthmus widens into a rocky peninsula, with thick for-

Hiking trails, Parque Nacional Manuel Antonio

est in the middle, encircled by Sendero Punta Catedral. Along this land bridge are the park's two amazing beaches, Playa Manuel Antonio, on the ocean side, and the slightly less visited (and occasionally rough) Playa Espadilla Sur, which faces Manuel Antonio village. With their turquoise waters, shaded hideouts and continual aerial show of brown pelicans, these beaches are dreamy.

Playa Manuel Antonio With its turquoise waters, this lovely beach fronts a deep bay, sheltered by the Punta Catedral on the west side and a promontory on the east. This is the best beach for swimming, but it also gets the most crowded, so get here early.

> ☑ **Don't Miss**
>
> The pre-Columbian turtle trap, built out of rocks, at the western end of Playa Manuel Antonio.

CHRISTER FREDRIKSSON/GETTY IMAGES ©

Hiking

Parque Manuel Antonio has an official road, Sendero El Perezoso, that's paved and wheelchair-accessible and connects the entrance to the network of seven short trails. None of them are strenuous, all are well-marked and heavily traversed, though there are some quiet corners near the ends of the trails. Off-trail hiking is not permitted. A new (as yet nameless) trail was added in 2015, its boardwalk parallel to the Sendero Principal; it provides a quieter alternative to the crowds along the main stretch.

Sendero Principal The longest trail in the park (2.2km) fringes Playa Espadilla Sur in Manuel Antonio village.

Sendero Punta Catedral This 1.4km loop takes in the whole of Punta Catedral, passing through dense vegetation and with glorious views of the Pacific. The blink-and-you'll-miss-it 200m Sendero La Tampa cuts across part of the loop.

Sendero El Mirador Heading into the forest from the east side of Playa Manuel Antonio, this 1.3km trail climbs to a bluff overlooking Puerto Escondido and Punta Serrucho beyond. Rangers reportedly limit the number of hikers on this trail to 45.

Sendero Playas Gemelas & Puerto Escondido The second-longest trail in the park (1.6km) is steep and slippery during the wet months and leads to quiet Playa Puerto Escondido through dense forest and across a creek.

Advance Planning

The average daily temperature is 27°C (80°F) and average annual rainfall is 3875mm. The dry season is not entirely dry, merely less wet, so you should be prepared for rain (although it can also be dry for days on end).

> ★ **Top Tip**
>
> Make sure you carry plenty of water, sun protection and insect repellent. Pack lunch if you're spending the day.

Squirrel monkey (p277)

SAM CAMP/GETTY IMAGES ©

Wildlife Watching

Capuchin monkeys scurry across idyllic beaches, brown pelicans dive-bomb clear waters and sloths spy on hikers on the trail, in this tiny park that's packed with life.

Great For...

☑ Don't Miss

Howlers crossing the 'monkey bridges' that were erected along the road between Quepos and Manuel Antonio.

Mammals

White-faced capuchins are very used to people, and normally troops feed and interact within a short distance of visitors; they can be encountered anywhere along the main access road and around Playa Manuel Antonio. The capuchins are the worst culprits for snatching bags, so watch your stuff.

You'll probably also hear mantled howler monkeys soon after sunrise. Like capuchins, they can be seen virtually anywhere inside the park and even along the road to Quepos – watch for them crossing the monkey bridges that were erected by several local conservation groups.

Coatis can be seen darting across various paths and can get aggressive on the

Iguana

FFENNEMA/GETTY IMAGES ©

ℹ️ Need to Know

A wildlife guide costs US$20 per person for a two-hour tour. Ask to see the guide's ICT license before hiring.

✕ Take a Break

Order a sandwich to-go from El Patio de Café Milagro (p189) and take it for your picnic.

★ Top Tip

Lenny Montenegro (☏8875-0437) is a recommended wildlife and bird guide.

beach if you're eating. Three-toed and two-toed sloths are also common in the park. Guides are extremely helpful in spotting sloths, as they tend not to move around all that much.

However, the movements of the park's star animal and Central America's rarest primate, namely the Central American squirrel monkey, are far less predictable. These adorable monkeys are more retiring than capuchins, and though they are occasionally seen near the park entrance in the early morning, they usually melt into the forest well before opening time. With luck, however, a troop could be encountered during a morning's walk, and they often reappear in beachside trees and on the fringes of Manuel Antonio village in the early evening.

Marine Animals

Offshore, keep your eyes peeled for pan-tropical spotted and bottle-nosed dolphins, as well as humpback whales passing by on their regular migration routes. Other possibilities include orcas (killer whales), false killers and rough-toothed dolphins.

Reptiles

Big lizards are also a featured sighting at Manuel Antonio – it's hard to miss the large ctenosaurs and green iguanas that bask along the beach at Playa Manuel Antonio and in the vegetation behind Playa Espadilla Sur. To spot the well-camouflaged basilisk, listen for the rustle of leaves along the edges of the trails, especially near the lagoon.

Birds

Manuel Antonio is not usually on the serious birdwatchers' trail of Costa Rica, though the list of birds here is respectable. The usual suspects include the blue-gray and palm tanagers, great-tailed grackles, bananaquits, blue dacnises and at least 15 species of hummingbird. Among the regional endemics you should look out for are the fiery-billed aracaris, black-hooded antshrikes, Baird's trogons, black-bellied whistling ducks, yellow-crowned night herons, brown pelicans, magnificent frigate birds, brown boobies, spotted sandpipers, green herons and ringed kingfishers.

Quepos

Located just 7km from the entrance to Manuel Antonio, the small, busy town of Quepos serves as the gateway to the national park, as well as a convenient port of call for travelers in need of goods and services. Although the Manuel Antonio area was rapidly and irreversibly transformed following the ecotourism boom, Quepos has largely retained an authentic Tico feel.

TOURS

There are numerous reputable tour operators in the Quepos area, who specialize in everything from white-water rafting on nearby rivers and mangrove kayaking to newly introduced paddleboarding tours and waterfall tours of the Pacific coast.

Paddle 9 — Adventure Tour
(☏2777-7436; www.paddle9sup.com; tours US$60-150) These new kids on the block are a young, passionate, safety-conscious team who've introduced stand-up paddleboarding (SUP) to Quepos (the tour leader's a pro) and who delight in showing visitors around the Pacific coast. Apart from their three-hour mangrove or ocean paddleboarding tours, their most popular outing is a seven-hour tour that involves swimming in various waterfalls, with a paddleboarding intro.

Unique Tours — Adventure Tour
(☏8396-0679, 2777-1119; www.costaricaunique-tours.com) This established local operator organizes entertaining rafting tours of the Río Savegre, ocean and mangrove kayaking outings and more. But what makes them unique is that they're the only operator to do coastal hikes to Parque Nacional Manuel Antonio. Prices vary depending on group size.

Oceans Unlimited — Diving
(☏2777-3171; www.scubadivingcostarica.com; 2-tank dive US$110) ✏ This shop takes its diving very seriously, and runs most of its excursions out to Isla Larga and Isla del Caño, which is south in Bahía Drake (connected via a two-hour bus trip). It also has a range of specialized PADI certifications, and regular environmental-awareness projects that make it stand out from the pack.

Oceans Unlimited is located 400m up the road to Parque Nacional Manuel Antonio.

H2O Adventures — Adventure Sports
(Ríos Tropicales; ☏2777-4092; www.h2ocr.com) The venerable Costa Rican rafting company Ríos Tropicales has a hugely popular franchise in Quepos called H2O Adventures, which organizes rafting outings on the Naranjo, El Chorro and Savegre rivers, as well as kayaking and tubing outings. Rates for Class II to IV rapids are US$70.

Manuel Antonio Surf School — Surfing
(MASS; ☏2777-4842, 2777-1955; www.manuelantoniosurfschool.com; group lesson US$65) Manuel Antonio Surf School offers friendly, safe and fun small-group lessons daily, lasting for three hours and with a three-to-one student-instructor ratio. It has a stand about 500m up the Manuel Antonio road south of Quepos.

Titi Canopy Tours — Adventure Tour
(☏2777-3130; www.titicanopytour.com; Costanera Sur; day/night tours US$70/80; ◷tours 7:30am, 9:30am, 11:30am, 1:30pm, 3:30pm & 5:30pm) Offering zip-lining adventures during the day and night, this outfit has friendly, professional guides and a convenient location just outside of central Quepos (150m south of the hospital). Tour rates include drinks, snacks and local transportation; group discounts are available.

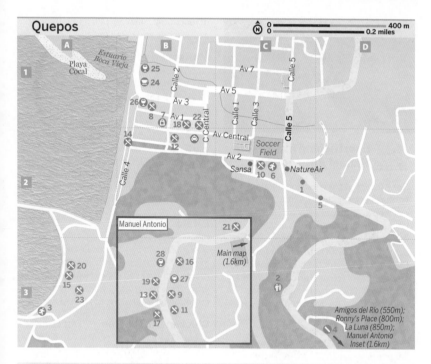

Quepos

⊙ Activities, Courses & Tours
1 H2O Adventures	C2
2 Manuel Antonio Surf School	C3
3 Marina Pez Vela	A3
4 Oceans Unlimited	D3
5 Paddle 9	D2
6 Quepos Sailfishing Charters	C2

ⓐ Shopping
7 Jaime Peligro Books & Adventures	B1

⊗ Eating
8 Brooklyn Bakery	B1
9 Café Milagro	B3
10 Chicken On The Run	C2
11 El Patio de Café Milagro	B3
12 Escalofrío	B2
13 Falafel Bar	B3
14 Farmers Market	B2

15 Gabriella's	A3
16 Kapi Kapi Restaurant	B3
L'Italo	(see 12)
17 Lush Tapas & Lounge	B3
18 Mercado Central	B1
19 Restaurante Barba Roja	B3
20 Runaway Grill	A3
21 Sancho's	C2
22 Soda Come Bien	B1
23 Z Gastrobar	A3

⊙ Drinking & Nightlife
24 Café Milagro	B1
25 Cuban Republik Disco Lounge	B1
Dos Locos	(see 12)
26 El Gran Escape	B1
27 Karma Lounge	B3
28 Salsipuedes	B3

⊗ EATING

One benefit of staying in Quepos proper is the accessibility of a wide range of dining opportunities. The **Mercado Central** (Central Market; Av 1; meals from US$4; ⊙hours vary) is packed with produce vendors and good *sodas* too numerous to list, so follow your nose and the locals. Self-caterers should also check out the **farmers' market** (Calle 4;

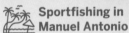
Sportfishing in Manuel Antonio

Sportfishing is big here, and offshore ventures are said to be best from December to April, when sailfish are being hooked. By and large this is a high-dollar activity and you can expect to pay upwards of US$1000 to hire a boat for the day. If you want to shop around a bit, visit the office of **Marina Pez Vela** (☏2774-9000; www.marinapezvela.com), 500m south of the town center, which can connect you with captains of boats best suited to your needs.

Quepos-based **Quepos Sailfishing Charters** (☏2777-2025, toll free in USA 800-603-0015; www.queposfishing.com) gets good reviews from sportfishers and offers charters on fleets of variously sized boats, whether you're after sailfish, marlin, dorado or wahoo. Rates vary significantly depending on season, number of people and size of boat. It also offers packages that include accommodations and transfers.

Marlin
ANDREW CASTELLANO/GETTY IMAGES ©

⊙4pm Fri-noon Sat) near the waterfront, where you can buy directly from farmers, bakers and other food producers.

Brooklyn Bakery   Bakery $
(Av 3; bagels US$1.50, mains US$5-8; ⊙7:30am-6pm Mon-Sat; 🛜🖉) Real New York–style bagels and lox! (A real rarity in Costa Rica). Rye bread! Iced coffee! This adorable little bakery bakes its fresh wares every morning, as well as serving light bites throughout the day and delicious specials

at lunchtime, such as Italian meatball sandwiches and oxtail ravioli.

Marisquería Jiuberth   Seafood $
(☏2777-1292; mains from US$7; ⊙11am-10pm) Run by a hardworking fisherman's family, this local institution with brightly tiled floors serves some of the best seafood in town, yet is practically unknown to visitors because it's tucked out of the way. Whether you have the catch of the day, or the moreish, satisfying fish soup, the portions are wonderfully generous and the service attentive. Follow unpaved Calle 2 out of town.

L'Italo   Deli $
(☏2777-4129; Calle 2; sandwiches US$5-7; ⊙9am-6pm Mon-Sat) This deli makes excellent sandwiches with imported Italian meats and cheeses, served with a side of ill grace from the grumpy waiter, but perfect for toting on excursions to Manuel Antonio.

Chicken On The Run   Fast Food $
(mains US$4-16; ⊙8am-9pm Mon-Sat) If it's crispy fried chicken you're craving, this is the best little joint in town. Grab a wing or breast to go, or bring some friends for a sitdown meal of an entire roast chicken with all the trimmings. *Casados* are a bargain, too.

Soda Come Bien   Cafeteria $
(☏2777-2550; Av 1; mains US$3.50-8; ⊙6am-5pm Mon-Sat, to 11am Sun) The daily rotation of delicious cafeteria options might include fish in tomato sauce, *olla de carne* (beef soup with rice) or chicken soup, but everything is fresh, the ladies behind the counter are friendly and the burly portions are a dream come true for hungry shoestringers. Or, pick up a fresh *empanada* before or after a long bus ride.

Z Gastrobar   Fusion $$$
(☏2777-6948; Marina Pez Vela; mains US$15-25; ⊙7:30am-10pm; 🅿🛜) Bright, open to the breeze from all sides ,and with colorful cushions strewn on its comfy couches, this is a terrific spot for lingering with a coffee and dessert, or over a lunch of

Ceviche

dorado *ceviche* (marinated seafood) in coconut milk or an imaginative salad. The arty presentation matches the terrific flavors and the service is excellent.

Runaway Grill American $$

(☏2519-9095; Marina Pez Vela; mains US$12-25; ☺noon-11pm; P❄🛜) An all-round crowd pleaser, Runaway Grill's menu spans steaks, wraps, salads, tacos, burgers, sandwiches and more. Portions are sizable and come with a sea view, the mint lemonades are refreshing and enormous, and the service is friendly (though they struggle sometimes when the place is packed).

Escalofrío Italian $$

(☏2777-1902; Av Central; mains US$10-22; ☺2:30-10:30pm Tue-Sun; ❄🛜) Gelato lovers should make a point of stopping here, to choose from more than 20 flavors of the heavenly stuff. This spacious alfresco restaurant may also be the only game in town on Sunday night during slow season, a godsend especially if you enjoy thin-crust wood-fired pizza.

Gabriella's Seafood $$$

(☏2519-9300; Marina Pez Vela; mains US$25-35; ☺5-11pm; P❄🛜) A serious contender for the region's best restaurant, Gabriella's does many things well. The veranda catches the sunset, and the service is attentive, but the food is the real star, with a great emphasis on fresh fish and seafood. We're particularly big fans of the seared tuna with chipotle sauce and the spicy sausage and shrimp pasta. In a word: terrific.

🍷 DRINKING & NIGHTLIFE

Café Milagro Cafe

(☏2777-1707; www.cafemilagro.com; Calle 4; ☺7am-5pm Mon-Sat) Café Milagro sources its coffee beans from all over Costa Rica and produces a variety of estate, single-origin and blended roasts to suit any coffee fiend's palate, with 1% of its profits going to environmental causes via international nonprofit 1% for the Planet. Unlike its other, bigger branch en route to Manuel Antonio, this is takeout coffee only; no meals (drinks cost US$3.50 to US$7).

Blue morpho butterflies (p277)

> the views across the bay
> to the pristine outer islands
> are gorgeous

Cuban Republik
Disco Lounge   Club

(☎8345-9922; cover charge US$4; ⊙9pm-3am Thu-Sun) Cuban Republik hosts the most reliable party in central Quepos, and it has some kind of drink special nearly every night if you arrive early (before 10:30pm or 11pm). Later, the DJs get loud, the drinks get more pricey. Women get in for free before 11pm on Friday night and it's a nice, mixed Tico and gringo scene (cover charge is US$4).

El Gran Escape   Bar

(☎2777-0395; Av 3; ⊙6am-11pm; 🛜) This long-standing pub has relocated back to central Quepos from Marina Pez Vela. Expect sports on the big screen, delicious (though pricey) burgers and prompt bar staff.

Dos Locos   Bar

(☎2777-1526; Av Central; ⊙7am-11pm Mon-Sat, 11am-10pm Sun) This popular pseudo-Mexican restaurant is the regular watering hole for the local expat community, and serves as a venue for the occasional live band. Opening onto the central cross-streets of town, it's fun for people-watching (and cheap Imperials). There's an English-language trivia night every Thursday. Added bonus: breakfast is served all day.

ℹ️ INFORMATION

The best source of books for travelers within miles is **Jaime Peligro Books & Adventures** (☎2777-7106; www.queposbooks.com; Calle 2; ⊙9:30am-5:30pm Mon-Sat), which has a complete selection of local guides, literature in a number of languages and tons of local information.

Look out for *Quepolandia*, a free English-language monthly magazine that can be found at many of the town's businesses.

ℹ GETTING THERE & AWAY

Both **NatureAir** (www.natureair.com) and **Sansa** (www.sansa.com) service Quepos. Prices vary according to season and availability, though you can pay a little less than US$75 for a flight from San José or Liberia. Flights are packed in the high season, so book your ticket well ahead. The airport is 5km out of town, and taxis make the trip for a few thousand colones.

ℹ GETTING AROUND

A number of international car-rental companies, such as **Budget** (☑2774-0140; www.budget. co.cr; Quepos Airport; ⏰8am-5pm Mon-Sat, to 4pm Sun), operate in Quepos; reserve ahead and reconfirm to guarantee availability.

Colectivo taxis run between Quepos and Manuel Antonio (US$1 for a short hop). A private taxi will cost a few thousand colones. Catch one at the **taxi stand** (Av Central) south of the market. The trip between Quepos and the park should cost about US$15.

Manuel Antonio

◎ SIGHTS

Manuel Antonio Nature Park & Wildlife Refuge
Wildlife Reserve

(☑2777-0850; adult/child US$15/8; ⏰8am-4pm; 👶) This private rainforest preserve and butterfly garden breeds about three-dozen species of butterfly – a delicate population compared to the menagerie of lizards, reptiles and frogs that inspire gleeful squeals from the little ones. A jungle night tour (5:30pm to 7:30pm, US$39/29 per adult/child) showcases the colorful local frogs and their songs, while day tours (US$15/8 per adult/child) introduce you either to the fluttering or the slithering denizens (or both; joint tickets US$25).

La Playita
Beach

At the far western end of Playa Espadilla, beyond a rocky headland (wear sandals), is one of Costa Rica's most famous gay

Monkey Business

There are a number of stands on the beach that cater to hungry tourists, though everything is exuberantly over-priced and of dubious quality. Plus, all the food scraps have negatively impacted the monkey population. Before you offer a monkey your scraps, consider the following risks to their health:

○ Monkeys are susceptible to bacteria transmitted from human hands.

○ Irregular feeding will lead to aggressive behavior as well as create a dangerous dependency (picnickers in Manuel Antonio suffer downright intimidating mobs of them sometimes).

○ Bananas are not their preferred food, and can cause serious digestive problems.

○ Increased exposure to humans facilitates illegal poaching as well as attacks from dogs.

○ It goes without saying: don't feed the monkeys. And, if you do happen to come across someone doing so, take the initiative and ask them politely to stop.

White-faced capuchin (p277)
HBRIZARD/GETTY IMAGES ©

beaches, a particular draw for young men. The beach is inaccessible one hour before and after the high tide, so time your walk well. Also, don't be fooled – you do not need to pay to use the beaches, as they're outside the park.

 X Marks the Spot

Locals have long believed that a treasure worth billions and billions of dollars lies somewhere in the Quepos and Manuel Antonio area, waiting to be discovered. The legend was popularized by English pirate John Clipperton, who befriended the coastal Quepoa during his years of sailing to and from the South Pacific.

Clipperton's belief stemmed from a rumor that in 1670 a number of Spanish ships laden with treasure escaped from Panama City moments before it was burned to the ground by Captain Henry Morgan. Since the ships were probably off-loaded quickly to avoid being raided at sea, a likely destination was the San Bernadino de Quepo Mission, which had strong loyalty to the Spanish crown.

John Clipperton died in 1722 without ever discovering the legendary treasure, and the mission closed permanently in 1746, as most of the Quepoa had succumbed to European diseases. Although the ruins of the mission were discovered in 1974, they were virtually destroyed and had long since been looted. However, if the treasure was indeed as large as it's described in lore, it is possible that a few gold doubloons could still be lying somewhere, waiting to be unearthed.

Playa Manuel Antonio (p178)

 TOURS

Amigos del Río Adventure Tour
(☏2777-0082; www.adradventurepark.com; tours US$135) Pack all of your canopy-tour jungle fantasies into one day on Amigos del Río's 10-in-One Adventure, featuring ziplining, a Tarzan swing, rappelling down a waterfall and more. The seven-hour adventure tour includes a free transfer from the Quepos and Manuel Antonio area as well as breakfast and lunch. Amigos del Río is also a reliable outfit for white-water-rafting trips.

 EATING

The road to Manuel Antonio plays host to some of the best restaurants in the area, and many hotels along this road also have good restaurants open to the public. As with sleeping venues, eating and drinking establishments along this stretch are skewed toward the upmarket. Reservations are recommended on weekends and holidays and during the busy dry season.

Falafel Bar Mediterranean $
(☏2777-4135; mains US$5-9; ⊙11am-7pm; 🅟🍴) Adding to the diversity of cuisine to be found along the road, this falafel spot dishes up authentic Israeli favorites. You'll also find plenty of vegetarian options, including couscous, fresh salads, stuffed grape leaves, fab fruit smoothies and even french fries for the picky little ones.

Sancho's Mexican $
(☏2777-0340; mains from US$5; ⊙8am-10pm; 🅟) A great view from the open-air terrace, potent house margaritas, excellent fish tacos and humongous chile verde burritos are just some of the draws at this friendly gringo-run joint. A place to knock back a few beers with friends in a convivial, chilled-out atmosphere, rather than woo your date.

Café Milagro Cafe $$
(☏2777-0794; www.cafemilagro.com; mains US$8-23; ⊙7am-9:30pm; 🅟🍴) With a menu full of vibrant, refreshing delectables – like gazpacho, salads tossed with mango and

chayote squash in passion-fruit dressing, fish tacos with chunky guacamole, or banana-macadamia pancakes – this appealing cafe is worth a stop morning, noon or night. Like its sister cafe in Quepos, it also serves a mean cuppa joe.

El Patio de Café Milagro   Fusion $$

(🕿2777-2272; www.cafemilagro.com; mains from US$7; ⏰7am-10pm) This is a fine stop for fancy coffee drinks, and even better for decadent breakfasts (banana pancakes with macadamia nuts), sandwiches (mango mahimahi wrap) and sophisticated interpretations of Tico fare for dinner (Creole pork). The patio itself is a lovely setting surrounded by tropical gardens; you can also order your sandwich packed for a picnic in the park.

Lush Tapas & Lounge   Fusion $$

(🕿2777-3939; Plaza Vista II; tapas US$10-12; ⏰3pm-late Mon-Sat; 🛜🍸) On the 2nd floor of Plaza Vista II, the tables and chairs of this new tapas bar face the sunset and there are few better places to be at that time of day, cocktail in hand. There's a succinct tapas menu to complement your drink, with interesting flavor combinations and meticulous presentation. The mini-pulled-pork burgers and fish-and-mango *ceviche* stand out.

Agua Azul   International $$

(🕿2777-5280; www.cafeaguaazul.com; meals US$10-25; ⏰11am-10pm Thu-Tue; 🛜) Perched on the 2nd floor with uninterrupted ocean views, Agua Azul is a killer lunch spot on this stretch of road – perfect for early-morning park visitors who are heading back to their hotel. The breezy, unpretentious open-air restaurant, renowned for its 'big-ass burger,' also serves up the likes of fajitas, panko-crusted tuna and smoked-trout salad.

Claro Que Sí   Seafood $$

(🕿2777-0777; Hotel Sí Como No; meals US$9-22; ⏰11am-8pm; 🛜🍴) ✔ A casual restaurant that passes on pretension without sacrificing quality, Claro Que Sí proudly serves organic and locally sourced food items that are in line with the philosophy of its parent hotel, Sí Como No. Guilt-free meats and fish are expertly complemented with fresh produce, resulting in flavorful dishes typical of both the Pacific and Caribbean coasts.

Manuel Antonio street life

La Luna
International $$

(☎2777-9797; www.gaiahr.com; Gaia Hotel; mains US$8-24; ⊘6am-11pm; 🛜🍴) Unpretentious and friendly, La Luna makes a lovely spot for a special-occasion dinner, with a spectacular backdrop of jungle and ocean. An international menu offers everything from spicy tuna and mango tacos to mahimahi *ceviche* to lobster tails, with a Tico-style twist – such as grouper baked *en papillote*, with plantain puree and coconut milk. Separate vegetarian menu available.

Restaurante Barba Roja
Seafood $$

(☎2777-0331; www.barbarojarestaurant.com; meals US$9-22; ⊘10am-10pm Tue-Sun) A Manuel Antonio area institution, the Barba Roja is both a lively bar and a seafood-and-steak spot with a respectable sushi menu and weekly specials (Friday is smoked-rib night). The terrace affords fantastic ocean views, best enjoyed with a local Libertas y La Segua craft brew (pints are US$6) or Mexican-style *michelada*.

Kapi Kapi Restaurant
Fusion $$$

(☎2777-5049; www.restaurantekapikapi.com; meals US$16-40; ⊘4-10pm; ❄🛜🍴) While there is some stiff competition for the title of best restaurant in the area, this Californian creation certainly raises the bar. The menu at Kapi Kapi (a traditional greeting of the indigenous Maleku) spans the globe from America to Asia. Pan-Asian-style seafood features prominently; macadamia-nut-crusted-mahimahi, lobster ravioli and sugar-cane-skewered prawns are all standouts.

🍸 DRINKING & NIGHTLIFE

Bars in several accommodations aside, there's no nightlife in Manuel Antonio village to speak of, though there are several clubs and bars along the road to Quepos.

El Avión
Bar

(☎2777-3378; ⊘11:30am-late; 🛜) Constructed around a 1954 Fairchild C-123 plane, allegedly purchased by the US government in the '80s for the Nicaraguan Contras but never used, this striking bar-restaurant

El Avión

is a great spot for a beer and stellar sunset-watching. Skip the food, though.

In 2000 the enterprising owners of El Avión purchased the plane for the surprisingly reasonable sum of US$3000 (it never made it out of its hangar in San José because of the Iran-Contra scandal that embroiled Oliver North and his cohorts), and proceeded to cart it piece by piece to Manuel Antonio. It now sits on the side of the main road.

Ronny's Place   Bar
(☏2777-5120; www.ronnysplace.com; ◷noon-10pm) The insane views of two pristine bays and jungle on all sides make it worth a detour (just for a drink – don't bother eating here). While plenty of places on this stretch of road boast similar views, the off-the-beaten-path location makes it feel like a secret find. Look for the well-marked dirt road off the main drag.

Salsipuedes   Bar
(☏2777-5019; ◷7am-10pm Wed-Mon) With fantastic views at sunset, Salsipuedes ('leave if you can') is a great place for tapas (US$7 to US$9) and beer – or for the more adventurous, cocktails made with *guaro* (a local firewater made with sugarcane). Leave if you can after a few of those! Quesadillas, *ceviche* and white bean and chicken stew are some of the tapas on offer.

❶ INFORMATION

La Buena Nota (☏2777-1002; ◷8am-6pm), at the northern end of Manuel Antonio village, serves as an informal tourist information center.

❶ GETTING THERE & AWAY

Driving the winding 7km road between Quepos and Manuel Antonio village on any day but Monday means spending time in traffic jams and potentially exorbitant parking fees.

Note that the road to Manuel Antonio is very narrow and congested, so it's suggested that you leave your car at your hotel and take an

LGBT Manuel Antonio

For jet-setting gay and lesbian travelers the world over, Manuel Antonio has long been regarded as a dream destination. Homosexuality has been decriminalized in Costa Rica since the 1970s – a rarity in all-too-often machismo-fueled, conservative Central America – and a well-established gay scene blossomed in Manuel Antonio soon after. Gay and lesbian travelers will find that it's unlike any other destination in the country.

It's not hard to understand why Manuel Antonio first started attracting gay travelers. Not only is the area stunningly beautiful but it's also long attracted liberal-minded individuals. There is a burgeoning artist community and a sophisticated restaurant scene; check out www.gaymanuelantonio.com for a full list of gay and gay-friendly accommodations, events, restaurants and bars.

During the day, the epicenter of gay Manuel Antonio is the famous La Playita (p187), a beach with a long history of nude sunbathing for gay men. Alas, the days when you could sun in the buff are gone, but La Playita is still widely regarded as a playful pick-up scene for gay men.

The Manuel Antonio area has always been proud to host one of the most sophisticated and cosmopolitan restaurant scenes on the central Pacific coast. A few venues have particularly good gay-oriented events. **Karma Lounge** (☏2777-7230; www.facebook.com/karmaloungema; ◷6pm-midnight Tue-Sun) is a friendly spot with an excellent happy hour and Lush (p189) serves imaginative tapas coupled with sunset views.

early-morning bus to the park entrance instead, then simply walk in.

Local buses (US$0.50, 20 minutes, every 30 minutes) and shared taxis connect Manuel Antonio village with Quepos.

PENÍNSULA DE OSA

Península de Osa at a glance...

The steamy coastal jungles of the Península de Osa encompass some of the country's least-explored land. Scarlet macaw appearances are the norm. Besides the easily spotted birds, monkeys, sloths and coatis roaming the region's abundant parks and reserves, in Parque Nacional Corcovado there's also the rare chance to spy tapir. Meanwhile, the rugged coasts captivate with abandoned wilderness beaches and world-class surf. This is the land for intrepid travelers yearning for something truly wild.

Two Days in Osa

Hire a guide for a day of hiking and **wildlife-watching** (p200) in Parque Nacional Corcovado or explore the **Agujitas-Corcovado coastal trail** (p207) along Bahía Drake. Spend your second day watching cetaceans with **Divine Dolphin** (p208) or scuba diving with **Drake Divers** (p208), or just swimming and snorkeling at the local beaches.

Four Days in Osa

You'll spend two days hiking across **Parque Nacional Corcovado** (p196) and tallying up the animal sightings. On day three, return to Jiménez for a celebratory breakfast at **Restaurante Monka** (p204), then retreat to **Playa Platanares** (p202) for recovery. Your fourth day is free to spend waterfall rappelling with **Psycho Tours** (p202) or learning about the cultivation of chocolate at **Finca Köbö** (p207).

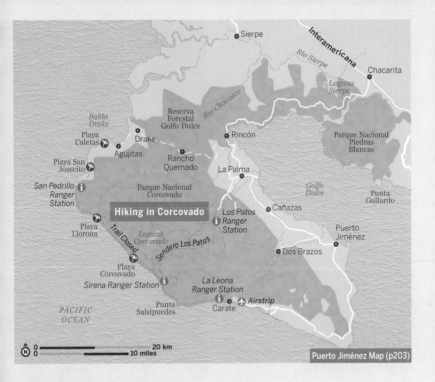

Hiking in Corcovado

Puerto Jiménez Map (p203)

Arriving in Osa

Getting to Osa demands one of two things: lots of patience or an airplane. Given the reasonable cost of flights, flying is a good option for exploring the peninsula, especially if your time is limited. If you choose to drive, you'll need a 4WD and plenty of confidence: many roads in Osa are extremely poor and there are river crossings involved.

Where to Stay

Jiménez has the best range of accommodations in the area, many geared toward Corcovado-bound backpackers. Top-end options tend to be located on the outskirts of town. Some of the best wilderness lodges are found in Bahía Drake, as well as Cabo Matapalo and Carate. This area is off the grid, so some places do not have electricity around the clock or hot water; top-end lodges have their own generators. Dos Brazos is emerging as the next ecotourism hotspot, with remote lodges and get-away-from-it-all rural hostels and guesthouses.

Hiking from La Leona to Sirena (p198)

Hiking in Corcovado

Corcovado's amazing biodiversity as well as the park's demanding, multiday hiking trails attract a stream of visitors who descend from Bahía Drake and Puerto Jiménez to experience a bona fide jungle adventure.

Great For...

ⓘ Need to Know

Área de Conservación Osa (ACOSA; Osa Conservation Area Headquarters); ☏2735-5036; Corcovado park fee per person per day US$15; ⊙8am-noon & 1-4pm Mon-Fri

☑ **Don't Miss**

The chance to see a rare Baird's tapir in its natural habitat near Sirena station.

Hiking Trails

There are three main trails in the park that are open to visitors, as well as shorter trails around the ranger stations. Trails are primitive and the hiking is hot, humid and insect-ridden, but the challenge of the trek and the interaction with wildlife at Corcovado are thrilling. Carry plenty of food, water and insect repellent.

The most popular route traverses the park from Los Patos to Sirena, then exits the park at La Leona (or vice versa). This allows hikers to begin and end their journey in or near Puerto Jiménez, offering easy access to La Leona and Los Patos.

A new El Tigre trail loop has been added; it starts in Dos Brazos and dips into the park but doesn't join up with the rest of the trail network (you still have to pay the full park fee to hike it, though).

La Leona to Sirena

The largely flat 16km hike (five to seven hours) follows the shoreline through coastal forest and along deserted beaches. Take plenty of water, a hat and sunscreen. It involves one major river crossing at Río Claro, just south of Sirena, and there's an excellent chance of seeing monkeys, tapirs and scarlet macaws en route. La Leona is an additional 3.5km to Carate. A new trail running parallel to this trail allows you to avoid the sizzling tramp along the beach.

Sirena to Los Patos

This trail goes 18km through the heart of Corcovado, passing through primary and secondary forest, and is relatively flat for the first 12km. After you wade through two river tributaries before reaching the Laguna Corcovado, the route undulates steeply for

Stream crossing in Parque Nacional Corcovado

the remaining 6km. It's less punishing to do this trek in the opposite direction.

Sendero El Tigre

Part of this new 8km loop trail passes through Parque Nacional Corcovado, so a guide is mandatory. It's a fairly rugged trail, part of which passes through an ancient indigenous burial ground; be prepared to spend most of a day hiking. It's doable as a day trip yet gives a good taste of the park.

Tour Guides

All visitors to Corcovado must be accompanied by an ICT-certified guide. Besides their intimate knowledge of the trails, local guides

SAM CAMP/GETTY IMAGES ©

> ★ **Top Tip**
>
> Hiking is best in the dry season (December to April), but it's still muddy.

are amazingly informed about flora and fauna, including the best places to spot various species. Most guides also carry telescopes, allowing for up-close views of wildlife. Operators include the following:

Osa Wild (☑8709-1083, 8376-1152, 2735-5848; www.osawildtravel.com; Rte 245, downtown Puerto Jiménez; tours from US$30, 1-day Corcovado tour US$85; ☺8:30am-noon & 2:30-7pm) 🌿 Osa Wild is a resource for travelers to connect with community-oriented initiatives that go to the heart of the real Osa through homestays, farm tours and sustainable cultural exchanges. They also offer kayaking tours and guided trips through Corcovado.

Osa Aventura (☑8372-6135, 2735-5670; www. osaaventura.com) 🌿 Run by Mike Boston, a biologist with a real passion for nature, Osa Aventura aims to introduce travelers to the beauty of rainforest life and to raise awareness of the need for preservation.

Surcos Tours (☑8603-2387, 2227-1484; www. surcostours.com) 🌿 A trio of excellent guides make Surcos the best company tours into Osa that focus on wildlife and birdwatching. Tours vary from day hikes in Corcovado and Matapalo to multiday experiences in Corcovado. Arrangements for tours are made through their website.

Carlos González (clgonzalez08@gmail.com; birdwatching tours from US$70) Highly recommended birdwatching guide with many years' experience, who can tailor excursions to suit your needs. He also conducts excellent mangrove tours.

Corcovado Info Center (☑2775-0916, 8846-4734; www.corcovadoinfocenter.com; whale-watching/Corcovado day tours US$110/90) Leading tours into Corcovado and Isla del Caño, all guides with this outfit are local, bilingual and ICT-certified. They're at the beach end of the main road in Aguijitas.

> 🍴 **Take a Break**
>
> Make reservations in advance to camp and eat at Sirena Ranger station (per person US$6).

Scarlet macaws (p274)

SAM CAMP/GETTY IMAGES ©

Wildlife Watching

This bastion of biological diversity is home to half of Costa Rica's species, including the largest population of scarlet macaws, as well as countless other endangered species.

Great For...

☑ **Don't Miss**

The hard-to-spot silky anteater frequents the beachside forests between the Río Claro and Sirena station.

The best wildlife-watching in Corcovado is around Sirena, but the coastal trails have two advantages: they are more open, and the constant crashing of waves covers the sound of noisy walkers. White-faced capuchin, red-tailed squirrel, collared peccary, white-nosed coati, tapir and northern tamandua are regularly seen on all of these trails.

Coastal Trails

Besides the park trail between Sirena and La Leona ranger stations, there is an additional coastal trail that runs 17km – mostly *outside* the park – from Bahía Drake to San Pedrillo station. These coastal trails produce an endless pageant of birds. Sightings of scarlet macaws are guaranteed, as the

White-faced capuchins (p277)

PANORAMIC IMAGES/GETTY IMAGES ©

❶ Need to Know

All visitors to Corcovado must be accompanied by an ICT-certified guide (see p199).

✕ Take a Break

Make arrangements in advance to camp and eat at Sirena Ranger Station (per person US$6).

★ Top Tip

Corcovado is the only national park in Costa Rica that has all four of the country's primate species.

tropical almond trees lining the coast are a favorite food. The sections along the beach shelter mangrove black hawk by the dozens and numerous waterbird species.

Los Patos–Sirena Trail

The Los Patos–Sirena trail attracts lowland rainforest birds such as great curassow, chestnut-mandibled toucan, fiery-billed aracari and rufous piha. Encounters with mixed flocks are common.

All of the typical mammals get spotted here, but Los Patos is better for primates. Indeed, the Los Platos–Sirena trail is the best place to see the country's most endangered monkey, the Central American squirrel monkey. It's also excellent for other herbivores, particularly red brocket and both species of peccary.

Sirena Station

For wildlife-watchers frustrated at the difficulty of seeing rainforest mammals, a stay at Sirena ranger station (p199) is a must. Baird's tapirs are practically assured – a statement that can be made at few other places in the world. This endangered and distant relative of the rhinoceros is frequently spotted grazing along the airstrip after dusk. Agouti and tayra are also common.

Jaguars are spotted extremely rarely, as their population in the Osa is suspected to be in the single digits. Ocelot represents your best chance for observing a cat, but again, don't get your hopes up. At night look for kinkajou and crab-eating skunk (especially at the mouth of the Río Sirena).

You might see any or all of the four monkey species, especially the more common species – Spider monkey, mantled howler and white-faced capuchin.

The Río Sirena is a popular spot for the American crocodile, three-toed sloth and bull shark.

Puerto Jiménez

Sliced in half by the swampy, overgrown Quebrada Cacao, and flanked on one side by the emerald waters of the Golfo Dulce, the vaguely Wild West outpost of Puerto Jiménez is shared equally by local residents and wildlife. While walking through the dusty streets of Jiménez (as it's known to locals), it's not unusual to spot scarlet macaws roosting on the soccer field, or white-faced capuchins traversing the tree-tops adjacent to the main street.

On the edge of Parque Nacional Corcovado, Jiménez is the preferred jumping-off point for travelers heading to the famed Sirena ranger station, and a great place to organize an expedition, stock up on supplies, eat a hot meal and get a good night's rest before hitting the trails.

Despite the region's largest and most diverse offering of hotels, restaurants and other tourist services, this is very much a close-knit Tico community at its core.

◎ SIGHTS

Playa Platanares   Beach
About 5km east of town, the long, secluded – and often deserted – Playa Platanares is excellent for swimming, sunning and recovering from too much adventure. The nearby mangroves of Río Platanares are a paradise for kayaking and birdwatching. Take the road that runs parallel to the airstrip.

Herrera Gardens & Conservation Project   Gardens
(☑2735-5267; US$7, 2hr guided tour US$40; ☺6am-5pm) ✦ The Herrera Gardens & Conservation Project is a 250-acre reserve with beautiful botanical gardens. This innovative, long-term reforestation project offers an ecologically and economically sustainable alternative to cattle-grazing. Visitors can explore the 5km of garden trails or 15km of well-marked forest trails, where you're likely to see capuchin monkeys and macaws. It's located 400m east of the airstrip.

Guided tours focus on birding, botany or even tree climbing. Jagua Arts & Craftssells map and arranges tours.

🎯 ACTIVITIES

Surfers head to Cabo Matapalo, which juts into the Pacific at the southernmost tip of the Península de Osa. The turn-off is about 17km south of Puerto Jiménez.

Playa Matapalo   Surfing
There are three excellent right point breaks off this beach, not far from Encanta La Vida. If there's a south or west swell this is the best time to hit the waves.

Playa Pan Dulce   Surfing
Good for beginners and intermediate surfers, Pan Dulce gets some nice longboard waves most days. You can also go swimming here, but be careful of rip tides.

🌀 TOURS

Psycho Tours   Adventure Tour
(Everyday Adventures; ☑8353-8619; www.psychotours.com; tours US$45-120) Witty, energetic naturalist Andy Pruter runs Psycho Tours, which offers high-adrenaline adventures in Cabo Matapalo. His signature tour is tree climbing (US$65 per person): scaling a 60m ficus tree, aptly named 'Cathedral.' Also popular – and definitely adrenaline inducing – is waterfall rappelling (US$95) down cascades ranging from 15m to 30m. The best one? The tree-climbing/waterfall combo tour (US$130).

For the tamer of heart, excellent three- to four-hour guided nature walks (US$55) tap into the extensive knowledge of Andy and his staff members.

Aventuras Tropicales   Adventure Tour
(☑2735-5195; www.aventurastropicales.com) Aventuras Tropicales is a professional, Tico-run operation that offers all sorts of active adventures. Some of its most popular excursions include kayaking tours

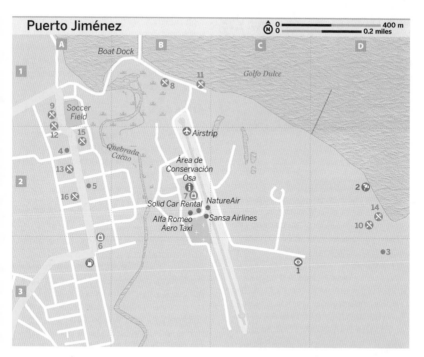

Puerto Jiménez

of the mangroves, which cost $45 per person, and their 'intense adventure' day trip (US$90). Located 2km east on the road to Platanares.

Osa Corcovado   Adventure Tour
(☑8632-8150; www.soldeosa.com; Hwy 245; ☺8am-noon & 2-5pm) Newish operator offering anything from three-day Corcovado hikes to kayaking in the mangroves, sunset

kayak dolphin-watching tours on the Golfo Dulce (US$45) and Matapalo day hikes.

ⓐ SHOPPING

Jagua Arts & Crafts   Arts, Crafts
(☑2735-5267; ☺6:30am-5pm) A terrific, well-stocked crafts shop, featuring local art and jewelry, a wonderful collection of

Caminos de Osa

Developed in response to the overcrowding of Parque Nacional Corcovado by a cooperation of private, public, academic and non-profit sectors, the **Caminos de Osa** (Osa Trails; www.caminosdeosa.com), when completed, will take visitors along three different routes bisecting the Osa Peninsula. Passing close to the park, they'll allow visitors to commune with wildlife and introduce them to the rural communities that call Osa home.

The **Oro trail** will skirt Corcovado and pass through the former gold-mining villages of Rancho Quemado and Dos Brazos. Visitors will be able to participate in rural activities from gold-panning to horseriding, before finishing in Carate.

Passing through the Sierpe mangroves by boat, the **Agua trail** will deposit visitors at San Pedrillo ranger station, also bordering Corcovado, from where they'll be able to hike into Bahía Drake and take the boat back to Sierpe.

Finally, the **Selva trail** will explore the southeastern part of the peninsula, connecting Dos Brazos to Puerto Jiménez and La Palma.

The trails were still in the making at the time of research, but the Caminos de Osa are actively working together with the communities of Dos Brazos, Rancho Quemado and La Palma, which visitors can easily visit now, with their rural tourism infrastructure developed and the communities eager to share their way of life with visitors.

Jungle paths
INGALLS PHOTOGRAPHY/GETTY IMAGES ©

high-quality, colorful Boruca masks and black-and-ochre Guaitil pottery, as well as woven goods by the Emberá and Wounaan people. Kuna weavings technically belong across the border in Panama, but they make excellent gifts.

Artes de Osa
Arts, Crafts

(☑2735-5317; ⊙7am-7pm) This locally run souvenir shop has interesting handmade carvings, furniture and other handicrafts, all made by Costa Rican artisans.

✪ EATING

Jardín Dulce
French $

(mains US$6-8; ⊙7am-9pm Tue-Sat; 🛜✎) Just across from the soccer field, this delightful garden cafe that doubles as a florist is French-run and serves delicious homemade food. Half the dishes are vegetarian, but you'll also find the likes of quiche lorraine, *croque monsieur* and Lebanese-style chicken. Whatever you do, don't skip the homemade sweets: the fame of their truffles has spread far and wide.

Restaurante Monka
Costa Rican $

(☑2735-5051; mains US$5-6; ⊙6am-10pm; 🛜✎) Bright, airy and the best breakfast spot in town, Monka does excellent smoothies and extensive breakfast platters, from American-style, involving bacon and pancakes, to Mexican-style *huevos rancheros*. The rest of the day you can fill up on good, inexpensive *casados* (set meals). Several breakfast options and *casados* are vegetarian.

Los Delfines
Costa Rican $

(☑2735-5083; meals US$6-14; ⊙10am-10pm) At the end of the beach road that passes the waterfront walk, Los Delfines is the perfect toes-in-the-sand spot for a late *gallo pinto* breakfast or a beer and delish *ceviche* (marinated seafood) after sunning on the crescent of beach just beyond.

Soda Valeria
Costa Rican $

(mains US$4-8; ⊙10am-8pm Mon-Sat) Clean, cute and smack-dab in the middle of town, this *soda* is a dream – the kind of place you

MARK/HARISS/GETTY IMAGES ©

Tent-making bats

know is good because the local government workers all pile in at lunch. The heaping, fresh *casados* change daily and are delivered with fresh, homemade tortillas and sides of fresh fruit. Considerate, quick service is an extra boon.

Restaurant Carolina Costa Rican $
(☏2735-5185; dishes US$3-8; ⊙6am-10pm; 🖥) This local favorite on the main drag still attracts its share of expats, nature guides, tourists and locals. Expect Tico standards, fresh-fruit drinks, extensive breakfasts, good coffee and cold beers that go down pretty easily on a hot day.

La Perla de Osa International $$
(☏8829-5865; mains US$10-17; ⊙11am-8:30pm; P🖥🗡) On the grounds of Iguana Lodge, this jungle-fringed restaurant-bar is locally (and justifiably) famous for its cocktails, accompanied by such delectable nibbles as pulled-pork tacos, grilled Asian-style tuna and shrimp plates. Skip the spicy gazpacho, though. Very popular with locals on weekends.

There are vegetarian soups, salads and meat-free pasta mains.

**Restaurante
Agua Dulce** International $$
(www.aguadulceresort.com; Agua Dulce Beach Resort; mains from US$8; ⊙7am-10pm; 🖥🗡) This breezy restaurant, on the premises of Agua Dulce Beach Resort on Playa Platanares, is a trusty spot for imaginative pasta dishes, grilled fish and ample breakfasts, although the service is positively languid. There are various vegetarian pasta dishes and salads.

Pizzamail.it Pizza $$
(pizzas US$10-20; ⊙4-10:30pm; 🖥🗡) While this pizzeria's name sounds more like a website, all doubts will be cast aside when a server at Pizzamail.it brings out the pie: a thin-crust, wood-fired piece of Italy in the middle of the jungle. From its small patio diners can watch squawking macaws in the trees over the soccer pitch. Several pizza options are meat-free. *Bellissimo!*

MATTEO COLOMBO/GETTY IMAGES ©

Bahía Drake beach

> *Bahía Drake is a veritable
> Lost World*

Il Giardino   Italian $$
(☏2735-5129; www.ilgiardinoitalianrestaurant.
com; meals US$11-16; ⏱noon-10pm) While the
possibly overextended menu touts steaks
and sushi as offerings, Il Giardino shines
when it sticks to Italian specialties – home-
made pasta with smoked salmon, gnocchi
and pizza. Our kingdom for a pepper grind-
er, though. Both service and cuisine can be
somewhat inconsistent, but it has a reliably
romantic, candle-lit waterfront ambience.

❶ INFORMATION

Área de Conservación Osa (ACOSA; Osa
Conservation Area Headquarters; ☏2735-5036;
Corcovado park fee per person per day US$15;
⏱8am-noon & 1-4pm Mon-Fri) Information
about Parque Nacional Corcovado, Isla del
Caño, Parque Nacional Marino Ballena and
Golfito parks and reserves.

❶ GETTING THERE & AWAY

The airstrip is to the east of town. NatureAir
(p292) and Sansa (p292) have flights to/from
San José (50 minutes, up to four daily); one-way
flights are approximately US$130. NatureAir also
does the puddle jumper to Golfito (10 minutes,
daily).

Alfa Romeo Aero Taxi (www.alfaromeoair.com)
has light aircraft (for three and five passengers)
for charter flights to Golfito, Carate, Drake,
Sirena, Palmar Sur, Quepos and Limón.

Puerto Jiménez is now connected to the
rest of the country by a beautifully paved road.
You can rent a vehicle from **Solid Car Rental**
(☏2735-5777; www.solidcarrental.com). If you're
driving to Carate or Matapalo, you'll need a 4WD;
be sure to fill up at the gas station in Jiménez.

❶ GETTING AROUND

If you're driving to Carate (the entrance to
Corcovado), you'll need a 4WD, even in the dry
season, as there are several streams to ford, as
well as river.

Assuming you don't have valuables in sight, you can leave your car at the *pulpería* (per night US$5) or at any of the tented camps along the road (with prior arrangements), and hike to La Leona station (1½ hours).

The *colectivo* (US$9) departs Puerto Jiménez for Carate at 5:30am and 1:30pm, returning at 8:15am and 3:45pm. Note that it often fills up on its return trip to Puerto Jiménez, especially during the dry season. Arrive at least 30 minutes ahead of time or you might find yourself stranded. Alternatively, catch a taxi from Puerto Jiménez (US$90).

Bahía Drake

One of Costa Rica's most isolated destinations, Bahía Drake (*drah-kay*) is a veritable Lost World, bordered by Parque Nacional Corcovado to the south. In the rainforest canopy, howlers greet the rising sun with their haunting bellows, while pairs of macaws soar between the treetops, filling the air with their cacophonous squawking. Offshore in the bay itself, pods of migrating dolphins flit through turquoise waters near the beautiful Isla del Caño marine reserve.

⊙ SIGHTS

Playa Cocalito   Beach
Just west of Punta Agujitas, a short detour off the main trail leads to the picturesque Playa Cocalito, a secluded cove perfect for sunning, swimming and body surfing.

Playa Caletas   Beach
This is one of the recommended spots for snorkeling. It is situated just in front of the Corcovado Adventures Tent Camp.

Playa San Josecito   Beach
South of Río Claro, Playa San Josecito is the longest stretch of white-sand beach on this side of the Península de Osa. It is popular with swimmers, snorkelers and sunbathers, though you'll only find it crowded at lunchtime since it's the favorite

¶◯¶ Chocolate Farm

About 8km south of La Palma, **Finca Köbö** (🕾8398-7604; www.fincakobo.com; 3hr tour US$32; 🅿) 🍽 is a chocolate-lover's dream come true (in fact köbö means 'dream' in Ngöbere). The 20-hectare finca (farm) is dedicated to the organic cultivation of fruits and vegetables and – the product of choice – cacao. Tours in English give a comprehensive overview of the life cycle of cacao plants and the production of chocolate (with degustation!). More than half of the territory is dedicated to protecting and reforesting natural ecosystems.

Tasting cacao at Finca Köbö
AGE FOTOSTOCK/ALAMY STOCK PHOTO ©

post-snorkeling picnic spot for tour companies coming back from Isla del Caño. Watch out for capuchin monkeys!

🏃 ACTIVITIES

Agujitas–Corcovado Trail   Hiking
This 17km public trail follows the coastline from Agujitas to the San Pedrillo ranger station for the entire spectacular stretch, and it's excellent for wildlife-spotting (particularly early in the morning), beach-hopping and canoe tours with Río Claro Tours (p208). Tour operators can drop you off by boat at a point of your choosing and you can walk back to Agujitas.

Snorkel & Scuba
Drake Bay

Isla del Caño (admission US$10, diving charge US$4, incl in tour price) is one of Costa Rica's top spots for diving, with attractions including intricate rock and coral formations and an amazing array of underwater life. Divers report that the schools of fish swimming overhead are often so dense that they block the sunlight from filtering down.

Bajo del Diablo (Devil's Rock), one of the best dive sites in the bay, is an astonishing formation of submerged mountains that attracts an incredible variety of fish species, including jack, snapper, barracuda, puffer, parrotfish, moray eel and shark.

A two-tank dive runs from US$120 to US$150 depending on the site. Several upscale lodges have on-site dive centers, and there are several dive centers in Agujitas.

Operators include the following:

Drake Divers (✆2775-1818; www.drakediverscr.com; ☉7am-7pm) This outfit specializes in diving at Isla del Caño, charging US$135/180 for two-/three-tank dives. Snorkelers are welcome to come along (US$80). The equipment is not the newest and the boat is not a purpose-built diving boat, but the divemasters are experienced.

Osa Divers (✆8994-9309; www.osadivers.com) Competitively priced, recommended diving outfit whisking divers (and snorkelers) off for underwater adventures around Isla del Caño. Snorkeling tours cost US$80; two-/three-tank dives are US$120/160. Equipment could be newer, though, and the divemasters don't have too much patience with novices.

Río Agujitas
Kayaking

The idyllic Río Agujitas attracts a huge variety of birdlife and lots of reptiles. The river conveniently empties out into the bay, which is surrounded by hidden coves and sandy beaches ideal for exploring in a sea kayak, best done at high tide. Some accommodations have kayaks and canoes for rent; or else kayaks can be rented along Agujitas beach (around US$15 per hour).

 ## TOURS

Divine Dolphin
Wildlife Watching

(www.divinedolphin.com; adult/under 11yr US$115/75) Sierra Goodman is the experienced original tour operator who introduced whale-watching to Drake Bay and she's also deeply involved in conservation projects. Half-day tours depart at 8am and the on-board hydrophone lets you hear the whale and dolphin sounds.

Pacheco Tours
Wildlife Watching

(✆8906-2002; www.pachecotours.com) Very competent all-rounder organizing snorkeling tours to Isla del Caño, day trips to Corcovado, day-long tours combining jungle trekking with waterfall swimming (US$55), and whale-watching excursions.

Tracie the Bug Lady
Wildlife Watching

(✆8701-7356, 8701-7462; www.thenighttour.com; tours US$40; ☉7:30-10pm) Tracie the 'Bug Lady' has created quite a name for herself with this fascinating nighttime walk in the jungle that takes in bugs, reptiles and birds. Tracie is a walking encyclopedia on bug facts – one of her fields of research is the military use of insects! Her Tico naturalist-photographer husband Gian also leads the night tours; reserve in advance.

Río Claro Tours
Canoeing

(per person US$15) A 20-minute hike toward Agujitas from Playa San Josecito, a hermit called Ricardo ('Clavito') lives by the Río Claro and runs hugely entertaining canoeing tours that start with a rope-swing plunge and continue to some waterfalls with refreshing plunge pools. Various tour operators can drop you off by boat, leaving you to walk back to Agujitas afterwards.

Original Canopy Tour
Tour

(☎8371-1598, 2291-4465; www.jinetesdeosa.com/canopy_tour.htm; US$35; ☺8am-4pm) At Hotel Jinetes de Osa, the Original Canopy Tour has nine platforms, six cables and one 20m observation deck from where you can get a new perspective on the rainforest. Tours take two to three hours.

✖ EATING

There are several local restaurants in the heart of Agujitas, as well as two supermarkets. Some accommodations, particularly the more remote ones, offer full board.

Gringo Curt's
International $$

(☎6198-5899; mains US$10; ☺noon-9pm) Gringo Curt offers just three things: fish tacos, noodles tossed with vegetables (and sometimes garnished with catch-of-the-day) and superfresh fish steamed in a banana leaf (serves two). This one-man operation is hugely popular with visitors, and the portions are very generous. Curt's a great source of local info, too, and runs nature tours along with Tico Esteban.

Drake's Kitchen
Costa Rican $

(☎2775-1405; mains from US$7; ☺noon-9pm; P) Excellent, small local restaurant along the main dirt road from Aguitas to the airstrip. The *casados*, such as catch-of-the-day with fried plantains and avocado, are clearly prepared by a capable chef, the fresh juices are stellar and the ambiance mellow.

Restaurante Mar y Bosque
Costa Rican $

(☎8313-1366; mains US$5-16; ☺5:30am-9pm; ☏) This restaurant up the hill in Aguitas has a spacious terrace from where it's possible to catch a cool breeze and spot pairs of scarlet macaws passing overhead. Serving typical Tico cuisine and an array of desserts, it even has free wi-fi.

Margarita's Marisquería
Seafood $$

(☎2775-1905; mains US$7-12; ☺11:30am-9:30pm) Right near the beach, this open-air eatery serves up mostly fishy delights, from garlic shrimp spaghetti and *ceviche* to generous helpings of freshly grilled

Buttress roots of a kapok tree, Parque Nacional Corcovado (p196)

MICHAEL FISCHER/IMAGEBROKER/AGEFOTOSTOCK ©

fish, fish tacos and *arroz con mariscos* (seafood-fried rice). The food is great, but the service lives by Zen time and it's best to double-check the bill.

ⓘ GETTING THERE & AWAY

AIR

Departing from San José, **NatureAir** (www.natureair.com) and **Sansa** (www.flysansa.com) have daily flights to the Drake airstrip, which is 2km north of Agujitas. Prices vary according to season and availability, though you can expect to pay around US$105 one-way.

Alfa Romeo Aero Taxi (www.afaromeoair.com) offers charter flights connecting Drake to Puerto Jiménez (US$430), Carate (US$450) and Sirena (US$420). Flights are best booked at the airport in person; if there are several of you, one-way fares are typically less than US$100.

> *Boats travel along the river through the rainforest and the mangrove estuary.*

BOAT

Alternatively, Sansa (p292) has daily flights from San José to the Palmar airstrip. Prices vary according to season and availability, though you can expect to pay around US$108 to/from San José.

An exhilarating boat ride from nearby Sierpe is one of the true thrills of visiting the area. Boats travel along the river through the rainforest and the mangrove estuary. Captains then pilot boats through tidal currents and surf the river mouth into the ocean. All of the hotels offer boat transfers between Sierpe and Bahía Drake with prior arrangements. Most hotels in Drake have beach landings, so wear appropriate footwear.

If you have not made advance arrangements with your lodge for a pick-up, two *colectivo* boats depart daily from Sierpe at 11:30am and 4:30pm, and from Bahía Drake back to Sierpe at 7:15am (US$15) and 2:30pm (US$20).

ⓘ GETTING AROUND

Once you reach Bahía Drake, the only want to get around is on foot or by boat.

Río Sierpe, Parque Nacional Corcovado

JUAN CARLOS MUÑOZ/AGEFOTOSTOCK ©

Sierpe

This sleepy village on the Río Sierpe is the gateway to Bahía Drake, and if you've made a reservation with any of the jungle lodges further down the coast, you will be picked up here by boat. Mangrove cruises can also be arranged here.

SIGHTS

Sitio Arqueológico
Finca 6   Archaeological Site
(🖉2100-6000; finca6@museocostarica.go.cr; 4km north of Sierpe; admission US$6; ⊘8am-4pm Tue-Sun) This site offers the best opportunity to view the mysterious pre-Columbian spheres created by the Diquís civilization between 300 BC and 1500 AD, in their originally discovered locale, near culturally significant mounds 20m and 30m in diameter. Walking around you can really appreciate their size and perfect sphericity.

The on-site museum screens a terrific video on the spheres' significance and purpose. The museum displays other fascinating artifacts discovered here, such as stone sculptures unique to the Diquís and *metates* (grain-grinding stones).

EATING

There are three restaurants in this tiny town, two of them by the waterfront.

Kokopelli   International $
(🖉2788-1259; mains US$6-12; ⊘9am-1pm Mon, 7am-9pm Tue-Sun; 🅿🛜) The nicest of Sierpe's three restaurants, Kokopelli serves large portions from a somewhat eclectic menu of *ceviche*, cheeseburgers, quesadillas and more. Sure, it's aimed at the mangrove tour crowd, but the offerings are fresh and tasty and it's the only place for miles around with an espresso machine. Check out the gift shop next door that sells Boruca masks.

Sir Francis Drake Slept Here

The bay is named for Sir Francis Drake himself, who visited this area in March 1579, during his circumnavigation in the *Golden Hind*. History has it that he stopped on the nearby Isla del Caño, but locals speculate that he probably landed on the continent as well. A monument at Punta Agujitas, located on the grounds of the Drake Bay Wilderness Resort, states as much.

Bahía Drake
PITAMITZ SERGIO/HEMIS.FR/GETTY IMAGES ©

ℹ INFORMATION

La Perla del Sur (🖉2788-1082, 2788-1071; info@perladelsur.net; ⊘8am-5pm; 🛜) This info center and open-air restaurant next to the boat dock is the hub of Sierpe – arrange your long-term parking (US$6 per night), book a tour and take advantage of the free wi-fi before catching your boat to Drake. The food is hit and miss, though.

ℹ GETTING THERE & AWAY

Scheduled flights and charters fly into Palmar Sur, 14km north of Sierpe. If you are heading to Bahía Drake, most upmarket lodges will arrange the boat transfer. Should things go awry or if you're traveling independently, there's no shortage of water taxis milling about – be prepared to negotiate a fair price. Regularly scheduled *colectivo* boats depart Sierpe for Drake at 11:30am (US$15) and 4:30pm (US$20).

PARQUE NACIONAL CERRO CHIRRIPÓ

Parque Nacional Cerro Chirripó at a glance...

Costa Rica's mountainous spine runs the length of the country in four mountain ranges, of which the Cordillera de Talamanca is the longest and most remote. The cordillera's highlight and the focus of the high-altitude Parque Nacional Chirripó is Costa Rica's highest peak, Cerro Chirripó (3820m). Above 3400m, the landscape is páramo, comprising scrubby trees and grasslands. The bare páramo contrasts with the lush cloud forest, which dominates the hillsides between 2500m and 3400m.

Two Days in Chirripó

What do you know? You have two days – the exact amount of time that it takes to **climb Cerro Chirripó** (p216) – how perfect! Be sure to arrive early enough to check in at the ranger station the day before you hike.

Four Days in Chirripó

You have the luxury of spending two nights at Crestones Base Lodge, allowing two days to climb, plus an extra day to explore the trails around the summit and/or lodge. Your fourth day is a recovery day: take advantage of the amenities offered by some of the area accommodations (hot tub, anyone?).

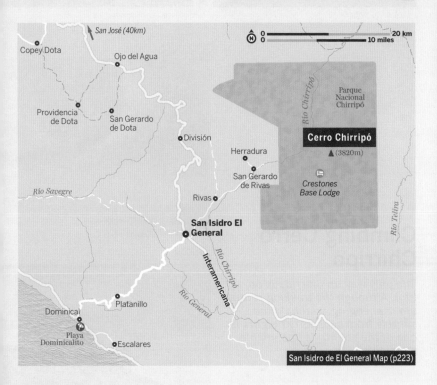

San José (40km)
Copey Dota
Ojo del Agua
Providencia de Dota
San Gerardo de Dota
División
Herradura
San Gerardo de Rivas
Rivas
Río Savegre
San Isidro El General
Río Chirripó
Interamericana
Río General
Platanillo
Dominical
Playa Dominicalito
Escalares

Parque Nacional Chirripó
Cerro Chirripó
▲ (3820m)
Crestones Base Lodge
Río Chirripó
Río Talila

0   20 km
0   10 miles

San Isidro de El General Map (p223)

Arriving at Chirripó

Traveling south from San José, the road to Chirripó passes through gorgeous countryside of redolent coffee plantations and cool, misty cloud forest. It's one of the most beautiful drives in the country, with gorgeous vistas revealed after every switchback. It's also one of the most dangerous, due to frequent mist and dangerous maneuvers by local drivers.

Where to Stay

Even though San Isidro is the regional hub, few travelers stay there, moving on to San Gerardo de Rivas if they're hikers. Many accommodations in the Rivas area are geared toward backpackers in search of adventure, although there are a few upscale mountain lodges and boutique hotels.

Note that many accommodations close when Chirripó closes, during the last half of May and all of October.

The view from Cerro Chirripó

Climbing Cerro Chirripó

The only way up Chirripó is on foot. Although the trekking routes are challenging, watching the sunrise from such lofty heights is one of the country's undeniable highlights.

Great For...

Cerro Chirripó

Río Chirripó

Río Talira

San Gerardo de Rivas

Parque Nacional Chirripó

ⓘ Need to Know

☎ 2742-5083; park fee per day US$20; ⊙ closed Oct & 2nd half of May

☑ **Don't Miss**

Watching the sun rise over Costa Rica from the country's highest peak.

MAX ILV/EYEEM/GETTY IMAGES ©

Getting Started

The park entrance is at San Gerardo de Rivas, which lies 1219m above sea level; the altitude at the summit is 3820m, which makes it 2.6km straight up! A well-marked 19.6km trail leads all the way to the top, with trail markers every kilometer, and no technical climbing is required. It would be nearly impossible to get lost.

Altitude sickness can be an issue as you get higher up. Watch out for nausea, shortness of breath, headaches and exhaustion. If you start feeling unwell, rest for a little while; if the symptoms persist, descend immediately.

Advance Planning

o The only way to secure a park permit and reservation at Crestones Base Lodge from abroad is through a third party such as **Jane & Fraser Tyrell booking service** (⌨2556-8664, UK 0800 612 8718, US & Canada 888-434-0076; chirripo@costaricarios.com).

o You must check in at the ranger station (p222) the day before you hike, to register your permit and confirm your reservation.

Timing

It takes about seven hours for a reasonably fit person to cover the 14.5km from the start of the trail to the Crestones Base Lodge. From the lodge it's another 5.1km to the summit, which takes around 1½ hours one way.

A minimum of two days is recommended to climb from the ranger station in San Gerardo to the summit and back, although this leaves no time for exploration. During peak season you're allowed to book a maximum of two nights at the lodge, which

A bridge in Parque Nacional Cerro Chirripó

gives you an extra day to explore the trails around the summit and/or the Base Lodge.

The Route

Most hikers start the hike between 5am or 6am, or earlier.

The first 6km or so are mostly uphill, over uneven, rocky ground, with some relatively flat stretches. You pass through dense cloud forest, so keep an eye out for quetzals.

Then there's a gentle descent toward the shelter at Llano Bonito (7.5km), which is a good place for a break. Here you can stock up on drinking water, use the flushing toilets and buy snacks and even aspirin.

> ★ **Top Tip**
>
> You *must* register your permit with the ranger office the day before you hike.

ESPIIX/ALAMY STOCK PHOTO ©

This place is intended for emergency use, not overnight stays, however.

Just beyond begins the Cuesta de los Arrepentidos ('Hill of the Repentants') and boy, will you repent! It's a steep uphill slog until you reach the top of Monte Sin Fe ('Mountain Without Faith'), a preliminary crest that reaches 3200m at around Km 10. By then you're on exposed ground, flanked by stunted tree growth, with gorgeous mountain views around you.

The trail then descends gently for around 1.5km. The last section is an interminable, steep ascent before you see the green roofs of the Crestones Base Lodge just downhill from you; breathe a sigh of relief before descending to 3400m. Most hikers reach the lodge around lunchtime and spend the rest of the day recuperating.

From here, the hike to the summit is 5.1km on relatively flatter terrain (although the last 100m is very steep). Carry a warm jacket, rain gear, water, snacks and a flashlight just in case, but leave anything you don't need at the lodge. From the summit on a clear day, the vista stretches to both the Caribbean Sea and the Pacific Ocean. The deep-blue lakes and the plush-green hills carpet the Valle de las Morenas in the foreground. Most hikers leave for the summit around 3am to arrive in time to watch the sunrise – a spectacular experience.

Seasons & Weather

The dry season (from late December to April) is the most popular time to visit Chirripó. February and March are the driest months with the clearest skies. The park is closed in May and October.

In any season, temperatures can drop below freezing at night, so warm clothes (including hat and gloves) and rainwear are necessary. Wear sturdy boots and bring good second-skin blister plasters.

> ✕ **Take a Break**
>
> Advance reservations are required to eat and sleep at **Crestones Base Lodge** (dm US$39; ☎).

San Gerardo de Rivas

If you have plans to climb Chirripó, you're in the right place – the tiny, tranquil, spread-out town of San Gerardo de Rivas is at the doorstep of the national park. This is a place to get supplies, a good night's rest and a hot shower before and after the trek.

◎ SIGHTS

Cloudbridge Nature Reserve
Nature Reserve

(📋in USA 917-494-5408; www.cloudbridge. org; admission by donation; ⊙sunrise-sunset) About 2km past the trailhead to Cerro Chirripó you will find the entrance to the mystical, magical Cloudbridge Nature Reserve. Covering 182 hectares on the side of Cerro Chirripó, this private reserve is an ongoing reforestation and preservation project spearheaded by New Yorkers Ian and Genevieve Giddy. A network of trails traverses the property, which is easy to explore independently. Even if you don't get far past the entrance, you'll find two waterfalls, including the magnificent Catarata Pacifica.

The trails range from the gentle Sendero Catarata Pacifica, leading to the waterfalls, to the steep uphill Sendero Montaña that joins the main trail up Cerro Chirripó.

Volunteer reforestation and conservation opportunities are listed on the reserve's website.

Talamanca Reserve
Nature Reserve

(www.talamancareserve.com) With over 4000 acres of primary and secondary cloud forest, this private reserve has numerous hiking trails, the longest being a seven-hour trek, and another leading to its 10 waterfalls. Talamanca is doing its best to promote itself as an alternative to Parque Nacional Chirripó, and nonguests are welcome to hike their trails for a day fee of US$25. ATV tours are available both to guests and nonguests.

From left: Yellow mushrooms; Red and white mushrooms; Oyster mushrooms; Parasitic plant

🏃 ACTIVITIES

Cocolisos Truchero   Fishing, Food

(📞2742-5023; ⏰8am-6pm Sat & Sun, & by appointment) Down the left fork road just before the Quebrada Chispa bridge, uphill from the ranger station, is this lovely family-run trout farm. Catch your own fish from the trout pools or take in the celebrated orchid collection. Naturally, the fish are the best part; matronly Garita puts together a homemade feast of trout and home-cooked sides for US$7.

Thermal Hot Springs   Hot Spring

(Aguas Termales; 📞2742-5210; www.sangerardocostarica.com; Herradura; US$6; ⏰7am-5:30pm) Between the ranger station and upper San Gerardo lies a bridge; before the bridge, a road forks to the left. Take this and walk for about 1km on a paved road, then turn right and take the suspension bridge over the river. A switchback trail leads for 1km to a house with a *soda*, the entrance to the hot springs – two pools popular with soaking locals.

🍴 EATING

Hotels and most guesthouses offer meals, or else a guest kitchen. There are a couple of eateries near the soccer field.

Restaurante Rios   Pizza $

(mains from US$8; ⏰11am-9pm; 🍴) Not far from the soccer field, this new place serves surprisingly good pizzas; we particularly like the one topped with imported meats. Generous portions, and several pizza options are meat-free.

Roca Dura   International $

(mains from US$6; ⏰11am-10pm) The most happenin' place in town, right by the soccer field. The standard dishes won't set your tastebuds alight, but their French fries are excellent and it's a terrific place for people-watching.

ℹ️ INFORMATION

Consorcio Aguas Eternas (Consortium Office; 📞2742-5097; infochirriposervicios@gmail.com; ⏰8am-noon & 1:30-4:30pm) **Right by the**

Can't Get Enough?

Costa Rica Trekking Adventures
(☎2771-4582; www.chirripo.com) offers hard-core adventurers an alternative Chirripó ascent. This guided three- or five-day loop trek begins in the nearby village of Herradura and spends a day or two traversing cloud forest and páramo on the slopes of Fila Urán. Hikers ascend Cerro Urán (3600m) before the final ascent of Chirripó and then descend through San Gerardo.

soccer field, this is the office responsible for the Crestones Base Lodge bookings. If you've had a third party reserve your space for you, you still need to check in here the day before your hike; otherwise, you may only reserve your space via phone or email with a prior reservation code from the park ranger's office.

Ranger Station (Sinac; ☎2742-5348; ⏰6:30am-noon & 1-4:30pm) The Chirripó ranger station is 1km below the soccer field, at the entrance to San Gerardo de Rivas. You must stop by the day before to confirm your permit. If you haven't booked your park permit in advance, there's a very slim chance of next-day availability.

 GETTING THERE & AWAY

The road to San Gerardo de Rivas winds its way 22km up the valley of the Río Chirripó from San Isidro.

Driving from San Isidro, head south on the Interamericana and cross Río San Isidro south of town. About 500m further on, cross the unsigned Río Jilguero and take the first, steep turn up to the left, about 300m beyond the Jilguero. Note that this turnoff is not marked (if you miss the turn, it is signed from the northbound side).

The ranger station is about 18km up this road from the Interamericana. The road passes through Rivas village and is paved as far as the entrance to San Gerardo de Rivas now. It is

passable for ordinary cars, but a 4WD is recommended if you are driving to Albergue Urán or to Cloudbridge Nature Reserve, as the unpaved road is steep and hideous.

 GETTING AROUND

From opposite the ranger station, in front of Cabinas El Bosque, there is free transportation to the trailhead at 5am. Also, several hotels offer early-morning trailhead transportation for their guests.

San Isidro de El General

With a population of around 45,000, San Isidro de El General is the fastest-growing urban area outside the capital. Little more than a sprawling, utilitarian market town at the crossroads between some of Costa Rica's prime destinations, it's a place where few travelers choose to linger.

'El General' (often referred to as Pérez Zeledón, the name of the municipality) is the region's largest population center and major transportation hub. If you're traveling to the southern Pacific beaches or Chirripó, a brief stop is inevitable.

 SIGHTS

Cathedral   Cathedral
(Calle 3) Love it or hate it, San Isidro's modernist, concrete cathedral dominates the main square and is the town's most interesting architectural feature. That says it all, really. Look out for the surprisingly beautiful stained-glass windows.

 TOURS

Aratinga Tours   Birdwatching
(☎2574-2319; www.aratinga-tours.com) ✈ Pieter Westra runs this highly recommended company, and the Belgian expat is fluent in English, Spanish and many dialects of bird. The website provides an excellent introduction to birdwatching in Costa Rica. All-inclusive two-week tours start at around US$2260, and custom trips can also be arranged.

San Isidro de El General

Refugio de Aves Los Cusingos   Birdwatching

(☏2738-2070; www.cct.or.cr; adult/child US$13/6; ⏰7am-4pm Mon-Sat, 7am-1pm Sun) This small birding reserve was donated to Costa Rica by Alexander Skutch, co-author of *Birds of Costa Rica*. Expert birding guides are available (US$10) to help you make the most of the birding trails. It's south of San Isidro in Quizzara, on the opposite side of the Río General, signposted off the road to Santa Elena/Quizarra valley. Call ahead.

Along with spotting numerous species of birds, you may also see capuchin monkeys thanks to the joining of the biological corridors across part of the Cordillera de Talamanca. On the property you can also see some impressive pre-Columbian petroglyphs, as well as Alexander Skutch's home, maintained as it was the day he died.

◈ EATING

Central San Isidro is loaded with inexpensive local eateries – travelers really counting their colones should head for inexpensive *casados* (set meals) in the Mercado Central – as well as a couple of more upmarket options. Some travelers may be thrilled to see the only golden arches of a certain fast-food chain in the region.

Parque Nacional Cerro Chirripó

> *deep-blue lakes and the plush-green hills carpet the Valle de las Morenas*

Urban Farm Cafe — International $

(☏2771-2442; Calle Central; mains US$5-7; ⊘7am-7pm Mon-Sat; 🛜🍴) With its 'from farm to table' motto, this delightful cafe single-handedly pushes San Isidro's dining scene up a big notch. Breakfast options range from 'Hawaiian-style' macadamia pancakes with banana, to veggie omelettes and bacon wraps, while their lunchtime wraps and salads are just overflowing with fresh vegetables. Wash it down with a delectable fruit smoothie.

Farmers' Market — Market $

(off Calle 3) The largest *feria* in the region, this farmers market starts early Thursday morning and usually winds down by early afternoon on Friday; organic produce, prepared foods and goods are bountiful.

Kafe de la Casa — Cafe $$

(☏2770-4816; Av 3 btwn Calles 2 & 4; meals US$7-14; ⊘7am-8pm Mon-Sat, 7am-3pm Sun; 🛜🍴) Set in an old Tico house, this bohemian cafe features eclectic artwork, an open kitchen and breezy garden seating. The menu has excellent breakfasts, light lunches, gourmet dinners and plenty of coffee drinks. Veggie options include salads and sandwiches.

La Casa del Marisco — Seafood $$

(☏8366-1880, 2772-2862; Calle Central; mains US$5-12; ⊘10am-10pm Mon-Sat) Since this unpretentious seafood spot is usually slammed at lunchtime, it's best to come during off hours for its several daily varieties of *ceviche* (marinated seafood), fresh fish or shrimp prepared as you like it (plus pastas, burgers, salads and soups). The crowd of local clientele not-so-subtly hints at the choice sustenance served here.

Bazookas International $$

(www.bazookasrestaurant.com; Interamericana; mains US$5-15; ⊙7am-10pm; P 🛜) Toward the north exit from San Isidro and brightened up by colorful Boruca masks, this diner caters to hungry travelers with a good mix of Tico dishes (decent *gallo pinto*), vast breakfast platters involving bacon, eggs and pancakes, and more robust dinner mains, such as the tender rack of ribs the size of a cow, and slabs of steak.

Supermercados Coopeagri Supermarket $

(📞2785-0227; Av 6 btwn Calles Central & 2; ⊙7am-9pm Mon-Sat, 8am-4pm Sun) Self-caterers can shop at this large, reasonably well-stocked supermarket.

GETTING THERE & AWAY

There are flights between San José and San Isidro with **Sansa** (www.flysansa.com) on Sunday, Tuesday and Friday, from US$70 one way.

GETTING AROUND

A 4WD taxi to San Gerardo de Rivas will cost around US$30. To arrange one, it's best to inquire through your accommodations.

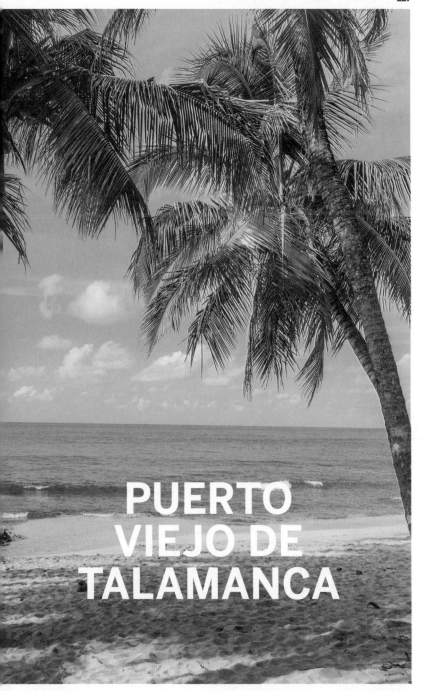

PUERTO VIEJO DE TALAMANCA

Puerto Viejo de Talamanca at a glance...

There was a time when the only travelers to the little seaside settlement were intrepid surfers. That is no longer the case; this party town is bustling with tourist activity. The scene can get downright hedonistic, attracting dedicated revelers who marinate in ganja and guaro. Nonetheless, Puerto Viejo manages to hold on to an easy charm. Stray from the main commercial strip and you might find yourself on a sleepy road, savoring a spicy Caribbean stew in the company of local families. Chill a little. Party a little. Surf a little. You've come to just the right place.

Two Days in Puerto Viejo de Talamanca

When in Puerto Viejo, go **surfing** (p230)! Remember that Salsa Brava is for experts only; otherwise, head to Playa Cocles. After riding the waves, enjoy a seafood feast at **Laszlo's** (p238). On day two, explore **Regama** (p232) with an early-morning hike, followed by lunch at the **Cool & Calm Cafe** (p242), and an afternoon of swimming and snorkeling at Manzanillo beach.

Four Days in Puerto Viejo de Talamanca

Rent a bicycle and spend a day beach-hopping from Playa Cocles to Playa Chiquita to Punta Uva, with a stop at the **Jaguar Centro de Rescate** (p234). Have dinner at one of Punta Uva's phenomenal restaurants, such as **La Pecora Nera** (p237) or **Selvin's** (p237). Your final day is free for the **Chocolate Forest Experience** (p234). How's that for dessert?

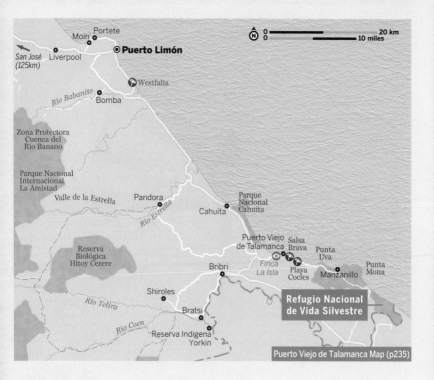

Arriving in Puerto Viejo de Talamanca

It's about a four-hour drive from San José to Puerto Viejo de Talamanca, on paved (but not always well-maintained) roads. Shuttle companies like **Grayline** (p73) and **Interbus** (p291) make this run, as do the public buses.

Where to Stay

Puerto Viejo has a little bit of everything. All budget spots have private hot-water bathrooms unless otherwise stated. Note that rates are generally discounted slightly when paid in cash.

Southeast of town, there is a stretch of beaches that features some of the most charming and romantic accommodations in the country. There are a few (as in, three) places to stay in Manzanillo village, ranging from budget *cabinas* to upscale bungalows.

Surfing at Playa Cocles

ADRIAN HEPWORTH/ALAMY STOCK PHOTO ©

Surfing

This town was built on waves – specifically, the infamous 'Salsa Brava' that breaks on the sharp, shallow reef offshore. But there are other, more forgiving places to surf, even for beginners.

Where to Surf

Breaking on the reef that hugs the village is the famed Salsa Brava, a shallow break that is also one of the country's most infamous waves. It's a tricky ride – if you lose it, the waves will plow you straight into the reef – and definitely not for beginners. Salsa Brava offers both rights and lefts, although the right is usually faster. Conditions are best with an easterly swell.

For a softer landing, try the beach break at Playa Cocles – where the waves are almost as impressive and the landing far less damaging. Cocles is about 2km east of town. Conditions are usually best early in the day, before the wind picks up.

Great For...

☑ **Don't Miss**

Riding one of the most celebrated (and feared) waves in the country.

Surfboards, Playa Cocles

HEMIS/ALAMY STOCK PHOTO ©

❶ Need to Know

Waves peak from November to March, with a surfing miniseason in June and July.

✕ Take a Break

Sip a cold one and enjoy the view of the namesake break at Salsa Brava (p240).

★ Top Tip

The nearest medical facility is Hospital Tony Facio (☎ 2758-2222) in Puerto Limón.

Salsa Brava

One of the biggest breaks in Costa Rica, Salsa Brava is named for the heaping helping of 'spicy sauce' it serves up on the sharp, shallow reef, continually collecting its debt of fun in broken skin, boards and bones. The wave makes its regular, dramatic appearance when the swells pull in from the east, pushing a wall of water against the reef, in the process generating a thick and powerful curl.

There's no gradual build-up here: the water is transformed from swell to wave in a matter of seconds. Ride it out and you're golden. Wipe out and you'll rocket headfirst into the reef. In his memoir, *In Search of Captain Zero,* surfer and screenwriter

Allen Weisbecker describes it as 'vicious.' Some mordant locals have baptized it 'the cheese-grater.'

Surf Lessons

Several surf schools around town charge US$40 to US$50 for two hours of lessons. Stands around town rent boards from about US$20 per day.

Caribbean Surf School (☎8357-7703) Lessons by super-smiley surf instructor Hershel Lewis, widely considered the best teacher in the town. Recently he also started teaching paddle boarding.

One Love Surf School (☎8719-4654; jewell420@hotmail.com) Julie Hickey and her surfing sons Cedric and Solomon specialize in surf lessons, massage school and yoga classes for women and children.

Refugio Nacional de Vida Silvestre Gandoca-Manzanillo

This little-explored refuge – called Regama for short – protects nearly 70% of the southern Caribbean coast, extending from Manzanillo all the way to the Panama border.

Great For...

☑ Don't Miss

Swimming and snorkeling off the gorgeous beach in Manzanillo village.

Regama encompasses 50 sq km of land plus 44 sq km of marine environment. The peaceful, pristine stretch of sandy white beach stretches for miles in either direction – from Punta Uva in the west to Punta Mona in the east. Offshore, a 5-sq-km coral reef is a teeming habitat for lobsters, sea fans and long-spined urchins.

Hiking

A coastal trail heads 5.5km east out of Manzanillo to Punta Mona. The first part of this path, which leads from Manzanillo to Tom Bay (about a 40-minute walk), is well trammeled, clearly marked and doesn't require a guide. Once you pass Tom Bay, however, the path gets murky and it's easy to get lost. It's a rewarding walk with amaz-

Coral reef

CARIBBEAN SEA

Puerto Viejo de Talamanca

Bribri

Manzanillo

Refugio Nacional de Vida Silvestre Gandoca-Manzanillo

ⓘ Need to Know

☎2759-9100; ⏰8am-noon & 1-4pm

✕ Take a Break

Enjoy the hot food and cool vibe at Cool & Calm Cafe (p242).

★ Top Tip

Refugio Nacional de Vida Silvestre Gandoca-Manzanillo is an excellent photo book by Juan José Puccí.

ing scenery, as well as excellent (and safe) swimming and snorkeling at the end.

Recommended Guide

Local guide and former park ranger **Florentino Grenald** (Tino; ☎8841-2732, 2759-9043; 4hr tours per person from US$35) is one of the most knowledgeable naturalists on the Caribbean. Since 1992 he's been handing out rubber boots out and escorting guests through his yard, a veritable tropical Eden, before taking them into the Gandoca-Manzanillo reserve, where he quickly spots caimans, frogs, snakes and whatever else happens to be nearby.

Snorkeling & Diving

The undersea portion of the park cradles one of the two accessible living coral reefs in the country. Comprising five types of coral, the reefs begin in about 1m of water and extend 5km offshore to a barrier reef. Punta Mona is a popular destination for snorkeling, though it's a trek, so you may wish to hire a boat. Otherwise, you can snorkel offshore at Manzanillo at the eastern end of the beach (the riptide can be dangerous here; inquire about conditions before setting out). Also check out the Coral Reef Information Center at Bad Barts (p242) in Manzanillo.

Bad Barts also rents kayaks, in case you wish to kayak out to the reef.

Dolphin-Watching

In 1997 a group of local guides in Manzanillo identified tucuxi dolphins, a little-known species previously not found in Costa Rica, and began to observe their interactions with bottlenose dolphins. A third species – the Atlantic spotted dolphin – is also common in this area. For dolphin-watching trips in the reserve (from US$53), contact Bad Barts (p242), and keep in mind that it is illegal to swim with dolphins.

Puerto Viejo de Talamanca

SIGHTS

Jaguar Centro de Rescate
Wildlife Reserve

(☑2750-0710; www.jaguarrescue.com; Playa Chiquita; adult/child under 10yr US$20/free; ⊙tours 9:30am & 11:30am Mon-Sat; 🚼) ✐
Named in honor of its original resident, this well-run wildlife-rescue center in Playa Chiquita now focuses mostly on other animals, including raptors, sloths and monkeys. Founded by zoologist Encar and her partner, Sandro, a herpetologist, the center rehabilitates orphaned, injured and rescued animals for reintroduction into the wild whenever possible. Volunteer opportunities are available with a three-week minimum commitment.

The rescue center recently started additional tours at La Ceiba, 50 hectares of primary forest in the Gandoca-Manzanillo national wildlife refuge. Rehabilitated animals are released there, and tours are available in the morning and evening, with breakfast or dinner included. Prices range from US$55 to US$60.

Aiko-logi
Wildlife Reserve

(☑8997-6869, 2750-2084; www.aiko-logi-tours. com; day tours incl transport & lunch US$60, overnight stays per person incl meals US$99; P)
✐ Nestled into the Cordillera de Talamanca, 15km outside Puerto Viejo, this private 135-hectare reserve is centered on a former *finca* (farm), on land fringed with dense primary rainforest. It's ideal for birdwatching, hiking and splashing around in swimming holes. Day tours from Puerto Viejo (or Cahuita) can be arranged, as can overnight tent platform stays and yoga classes. Reserve ahead.

Finca La Isla
Gardens

(☑2750-0046, 8886-8530; self-guided/guided tours US$6/12; ⊙10am-4pm Fri-Mon; P)
✐ West of town, this farm and botanical garden has long produced organic pepper and cacao, along with more than 150 tropical fruits and ornamental plants.

Birds and wildlife abound, including sloths, poison-dart frogs and toucans. Informative guided tours (minimum three people) include admission, fruit tasting and a glass of fresh juice; alternatively, buy a booklet (US$1) and take a self-guided tour. Recently, the farm began making its own chocolate.

🎯 TOURS

Chocolate Forest Experience
Tour

(☑8836-8930, 8341-2034; www.caribeanscr. com/chocolate-tour; Playa Cocles; guided tours US$26; ⊙tours 10am Mon, 10am & 2pm Tue & Thu, 2pm Fri & Sat) ✐ Playa Cocles–based chocolate producer Caribeans leads tours of its sustainably managed cacao forest and chocolate-creation lab, accompanied by gourmet chocolate tastings.

Terraventuras
Tour

(☑2750-0750; www.terraventuras.com; ⊙7am-7pm) Offers overnights in Tortuguero, a shaman tour, and a Caribbean cooking class, along with the usual local tours. Also has its very own 23-platform, 2.1km-long canopy tour (US$58), complete with Tarzan swing.

Gecko Trail Costa Rica
Tour

(☑2756-8159, in USA & Canada 415-230-0298; www.geckotrail.com) This full-service agency arranges local tours as well as transportation, accommodations and tours throughout Costa Rica.

Reef Runner Divers
Diving

(☑2750-0480; www.reefrunnerdivers.net; 1-/2-tank dives US$65/100; ⊙8am-6pm) If you are not certified, you can do a discover dive course for US$155 (includes two tanks) or spring for the full PADI certification for US$375.

> *Chill a little. Party a little. Surf a little.*

Puerto Viejo de Talamanca

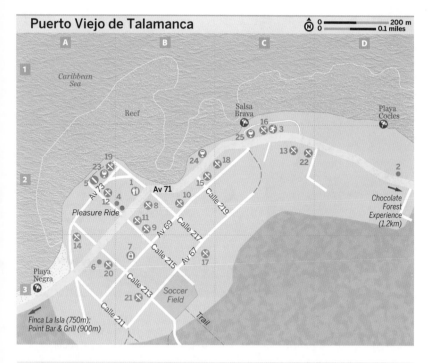

Puerto Viejo de Talamanca

🛍 SHOPPING

Lulu Berlu Gallery　　　　Crafts

(📞2750-0394; ⊙9am-9pm) On a backstreet parallel to the main road, this gallery carries folk art, clothing, jewelry, ceramics, embroidered purses and mosaic mirrors, among many other one-of-a-kind, locally made items. Out back, the popular restaurant Congo Reeff opened recently.

CARVERMOSTARD/ALAMY STOCK PHOTO ©

Fair-trade chocolate for sale

> *area vendors and growers sell snacks typical of the region*

Organic Market
Market

(🕐6:30-11am Sat) Don't miss the weekly organic market, when area vendors and growers sell snacks typical of the region, particularly tropical produce and chocolate. Arrive before 9am or the best stuff will be long gone.

🍴 EATING

With the most diverse restaurant scene on the Caribbean coast, Puerto Viejo has the cure for *casado* (set menu) overkill.

Don't miss the Saturday organic market, when area vendors and growers sell snacks typical of the region.

Como en mi
Casa Art Café
Cafe $

(📱6069-6337, 6069-6319; www.comoenmicasa-costarica.wordpress.com; cakes US$4, mains US$5-10; 🕐7am-4pm Thu-Tue; 🍴) Owned by a friendly bohemian expat couple, this charming vegetarian cafe makes everything from scratch, from the jams to the hot sauces to the gluten-free pancakes. The walls are covered in local art and 10% of the coffee profit helps buy supplies for local schools. Oddly enough, you'll find this place above the butcher shop in the center of town.

Popular items include raw cakes, homemade lentil-bean burgers and gluten-free avocado wraps.

Bread & Chocolate
Breakfast $

(📱2750-0723; cakes US$4, meals US$6-9; 🕐6:30am-6:30pm Wed-Sat, to 2:30pm Sun; 🍴) Ever had a completely homemade PB&J (bread, peanut butter and jelly, all made from scratch)? That and more can be yours at this dream of a gluten-lover's cafe.

Coffees are served in individual French presses; mochas come unconstructed so you have the pleasure of mixing your own homemade chocolate, steamed milk and coffee; and everything else – from the gazpacho to the granola to the biscuits – is lovingly and skillfully made in-house.

Café Rico
Cafe $

(☑2750-0510; caferico.puertoviejo@yahoo.com; breakfast US$3-8; ☺5:30am-1pm; 🛜) Home to some of Puerto Viejo's best home-roasted coffee, this cozy garden cafe serves breakfast accompanied by a plethora of other services: free wi-fi, a book exchange, a laundry, and rentals of bikes and snorkeling gear.

De Gustibus
Bakery $

(☑2756-8397; www.facebook.com/degustibus-bakery; baked goods from US$1; ☺6:45am-6pm) This bakery on Puerto Viejo's main drag draws a devoted following with its fabulous focaccia (US$1 a slice), along with slices of pizza, apple strudels, profiteroles and all sorts of other sweet and savory goodies. Eat in, or grab a snack for the beach.

Soda Shekiná
Caribbean $

(☑2750-0549; mains US$7-12; ☺11:30am-9pm Wed-Mon) Delicious traditional Caribbean home cooking can be found at this backstreet eatery with wooden slab tables on an open-air terrace, just northwest of the soccer field. Everything is served with coconut rice and beans, salad and caramelized fried bananas.

Sel & Sucre
French $

(☑2750-0636; meals US$4-10; ☺noon-9:30pm; 🍴) Dark coffee and fresh-fruit smoothies offer a nice complement to the menu of crepes, both savory and sweet. These delights are all prepared by the one and only chef Sebastien Flageul, meaning service can be slow. But it's worth the wait.

Pan Pay
Bakery $

(☑2750-0081; dishes US$3-6; ☺7am-5pm) This popular corner spot on the beachside road in town is excellent for strong coffee, fresh baked goods and hearty wedges of fluffy Spanish omelet served with crisp tomato bread. There are sandwiches and other

Out of Town Eating

Pita Bonita (☑2756-8173; Punta Uva; US$7-15; ☺1-9pm Mon-Sat) For Turkish coffee, hummus and the best pita bread in the Caribbean, this is the place. The open-air eatery is ensconced in a tropical garden across from the Tree House Lodge in Punta Uva, making it a great stop before or after the beach. For adventurous eaters there's also *shakshuka*, an African dish with poached eggs and spicy tomato sauce.

Selvin's Restaurant (☑2750-0664; Punta Uva; mains US$10-18; ☺noon-8pm Thu-Sun) Selvin is a member of the extensive Brown family, noted for their charm, and his place is considered one of the region's best, specializing in shrimp, lobster, a terrific *rondón* and a succulent chicken *caribeño* (chicken stewed in a spicy Caribbean sauce).

La Pecora Nera (☑2750-0490; Playa Cocles; mains US$10-30; ☺5:30-10pm Tue-Sun; 🍴) If you splurge for a single fancy meal during your trip, do it at this romantic eatery run by Ilario Giannoni. On a lovely, candlelit patio, deftly prepared Italian seafood and pasta dishes are served alongside unusual offerings such as the delicate *carpaccio di carambola*: transparent slices of starfruit topped with shrimp, tomatoes and balsamic vinaigrette.

El Refugio (☑2759-9007; Punta Uva; mains US$15-25; ☺5-9pm Thu-Tue) This tony Argentine-owned restaurant with only five tables is renowned for its rotating menu of three appetizers, five main dishes and three desserts. New offerings get chalked up on the board daily, anchored by perennial favorites such as red tuna in garlic, *bife de entraña* with chimichurri (beef in a marinade of parsley, garlic and spices) and *dulce de leche* crepes. Reserve ahead.

light meals, but it's the flaky chocolate croissants that make us want to jump out of bed in the morning.

Dee-Lite
Ice Cream $

(☎8935-6547; gelati US$3-5; ☉noon-8pm) Directly across from the bus stop, this authentic *gelateria* is the perfect place to cool off after a long, hot bus ride.

Laszlo's
Seafood $$

(mains US$16; ☉6-9:30pm) Whaddya get when you take a champion sport fisherman, born and raised in Transylvania, and transplant him in Puerto Viejo by way of New Jersey? Answer: an amazing, eclectic eatery with no sign and no menu that only opens when owner Laszlo catches enough fish. The day's catch comes with garlic and parsley, homemade French fries and grilled veggies. Yum.

Stashu's con Fusion
Fusion $$

(☎2750-0530; mains US$10-18; ☉5-10pm Thu-Tue; 🖐) Stroll 250m out of town toward Playa Cocles to this romantic low-lit patio cafe serving up creative fusion cuisine that combines elements of Caribbean, Indian, Mexican and Thai cooking. Steamed spicy mussels in red-curry sauce and tandoori chicken in coconut are just a couple of standouts. Excellent vegetarian and vegan items round out the menu. Owner and chef Stash Golas is an artist inside the kitchen and out.

Mopri
Seafood $$

(☎2756-8411; www.pescaderiaymariqueriamopri. com; mains US$6-14; ☉10am-10pm; 🖐) You'd never know it from Mopri's dingy facade or cheap plastic tables, but this place serves the best seafood in Puerto Viejo and possibly all of Costa Rica. The whole snapper and sizable lobster, which are also sold fresh at the adjacent fish market, are served up with a lip-smacking salsa *caribeño*.

Miss Lidia's Place
Caribbean $$

(☎2750-0598; dishes US$7-20; ☉11am-9:30pm Tue-Sun) A long-standing favorite for classic Caribbean flavors, Miss Lidia's has been around for years, pleasing the palates and satisfying the stomachs of locals and

tourists alike. Fruit-and-veggie lovers will appreciate the ice-cold *batidos* (fresh fruit drinks) and the delicious assortment of broccoli, green beans, cauliflower, corn-on-the-cob, carrots and mushrooms accompanying most dishes.

Bikini Restaurant
& Bar
Fusion $$

(☑2750-3061; mojitos US$3, mains US$5-15; ☺noon-10:30pm) If frozen mojitos are your thing, get thee to Bikini. This hip new restaurant and bar opened in 2015, quickly attracting a crowd of revelers with its affordable cocktails and varied menu. Caribbean dishes, pasta, salads and sushi all pair well with strong drinks and a convivial atmosphere.

Koki Beach
Latin American $$$

(☑2750-0902; www.kokibeach.com; mains US$11-24; ☺5-11pm Tue-Sun; 🛜) A high-end favorite for drinks and dinner, this sleek eatery cranks lounge music and sports colorful Adirondack chairs that face the ocean from an elevated wooden platform on the east end of town. Koki Beach has

a decent selection of Peruvian-inflected *ceviches* (marinated seafood), plus meat and other seafood dishes, but there are slim pickings for vegetarians.

Café Viejo
Italian $$$

(☑2750-0817; www.cafeviejo.com; mains US$10-28; ☺6-11:30pm Wed-Mon) This pricey, sceney Mediterranean lounge and restaurant stands out for its fresh pastas, tasty pizzas, fancy cocktails and upscale, romantic ambiance. Its main-street location makes for excellent people-watching.

🍷 DRINKING & NIGHTLIFE

Lazy Mon
Club

(☺12:30pm-2:30am) Puerto Viejo's most dependable spot for live music, Lazy Mon draws big crowds with reggae at happy hour (4pm to 7pm), then keeps things hopping with more of the same throughout the evening. The ping-pong and pool tables are popular gathering spots, and fire shows take place every Thursday night.

GREG RODEN/GETTY IMAGES ©

★ Top Caribbean Cooking

Selvin's Restaurant (p237), Punta Uva

Miss Lidia's Place (p238), Puerto Viejo de Talamanca

Stashu's con Fusion (p238), Puerto Viejo de Talamanca

Mopri (p238), Puerto Viejo

From left: Caribbean eatery, Puerto Viejo; Milkshake with starfruit garnish; Lulu Berlu Gallery (p235)

CHRISTER FREDRIKSSON/GETTY IMAGES ©

Safety First

Be aware that though the use of marijuana (and harder stuff) is common in Puerto Viejo, it is nonetheless illegal.

As in other popular tourist centers, theft can be an issue. Stay aware, use your hotel safe, and if staying outside of town avoid walking alone late at night.

Salsa Brava   Bar
(☎2750-0241; ⊙11am-3am) Specializing in fresh seafood and open-grill cooking, this popular spot is the perfect end-of-day cocktail stop – hit happy hour from 4pm to 6pm and you'll also catch two-for-one mojitos for sunset overlooking the Salsa Brava surf break. On Friday and Sunday they bring in DJs for the popular reggae nights.

Point Bar & Grill   Sports Bar
(☎2756-8491; Playa Negra; ⊙11am-11pm; 🛜) If you happen to be traveling during football season (or any other sport season, for that matter), you don't have to miss the big game. Just head to this convivial spot located on the beach northwest of town. Decent food, big screens and craft beer. Nuff said.

Johnny's Place   Club
(⊙11am-8pm, to 2am Wed, Fri & Sat) Once a beachside clubbing institution, Johnny's Place slowed after the party started getting out of control in 2015. The place shut down briefly and reopened under new ownership as a classy restaurant and bar with fancy cocktails. There are still DJs, dancing and occasional revelry on weekends, though.

ENTERTAINMENT

Live music or fire dancing happen almost nightly at Lazy Mon (p239). You can pop in during the day to find out who's performing.

🛈 GETTING THERE & AWAY

If you're driving your own vehicle, Puerto Viejo de Talamanca is a straight shot down the paved coastal highway from Puerto Limón.

An ever-growing number of companies offer convenient van shuttles from Puerto Viejo to other tourist hotspots around Costa Rica and down the coast to Bocas del Toro, Panama. For an exhaustive list, see Gecko Trail's very helpful website.

The following companies operate out of Puerto Viejo.

Caribe Shuttle (☎2750-0626; caribeshuttle. com/puerto-viejo-tours) Serves Bocas del Toro (Panama), San José and Tortuguero.

Gecko Trail Costa Rica (p234) Standard shuttle service to San José and Tortuguero; also offers good-value Adventure Connection packages that provide transport to San José or Arenal, with a half-day, 30km Río Pacuare rafting trip included in the price.

Interbus (☎4100-0888; www.interbusonline. com) Serves Arenal-La Fortuna, San José, Siquirres and Puerto Viejo de Sarapiquí.

Pleasure Ride (2750-2113) Operates tours and transportation in the Caribbean, and well as reliable private vans to the rest of the country. They also run an Airport Express to and from San José.

🛈 GETTING AROUND

A bicycle is a fine way to get around town, and pedaling out to beaches east of Puerto Viejo is one of the highlights of this corner of Costa Rica. You'll find rentals all over town for about US$5 per day.

Clockwise from top: The road to Puerto Viejo; A banana plantation; Biking to the beach

Selling fresh coconuts

Manzanillo

The chill village of Manzanillo has long been off the beaten track, even since the paved road arrived in 2003. This little town remains a vibrant outpost of Afro-Caribbean culture and has also remained pristine, thanks to the 1985 establishment of the Refugio Nacional de Vida Silvestre Gandoca-Manzanillo, which includes the village and imposes strict regulations on regional development.

Activities are of a simple nature, *in* nature: hiking, snorkeling and kayaking are king. (As elsewhere, ask about riptides before heading out.)

☺ ACTIVITIES

Bad Barts   Snorkeling
(☑2750-3091; www.badbartsmanzanillo.com) Near the bus stop in Manzanillo, this outfit rents snorkel gear and kayaks, boogie board, bicycles and scuba gear. Hours vary. Call ahead to confirm.

✖ EATING

There are few options but they are all fantastic in this small beach town; the best is Cool & Calm Cafe. The owner catches and prepares his outrageous lobster *caribeño* daily.

Cool & Calm Cafe   Caribbean $$
(☑8843-7460; mains US$10-24; ☺4-9pm Mon, 11am-9pm Wed-Sun) Directly across from Manzanillo's western beachfront, this front-porch eatery regales visitors with fine Caribbean cooking, from snapper to shrimp, and chicken to lobster, with a few extras like guacamole, tacos and veggie curry thrown in for good measure. Owner Andy offers Caribbean cooking classes and a 'reef-to-plate' tour where you dive for your own lobster or fish.

Maxi's Restaurant   Caribbean $$
(mains US$9-23, lobster US$24-80; ☺noon-10pm; ☑) Manzanillo's most famous restaurant draws a tourist crowd with large platters of grilled seafood, whole red snappers

(*pargo rojo*), steaks and Caribbean-style lobsters (expensive and not necessarily worth it). Despite the somewhat lackadaisical service, the open-air upstairs dining area is a wonderful seaside setting for a meal and a beer with views of the beach and the street below.

 DRINKING & NIGHTLIFE

You may find the occasional party at Maxi's Restaurant at the end of the road (where buses arrive).

 GETTING THERE & AWAY

A 13km road winds east from Puerto Viejo, through rows of coconut palms, alongside coastal lodges and through lush lowland rainforest before coming to a dead end at the sleepy town of Manzanillo. The road was paved for the

---

 Crazy Monkey Canopy Tour

Crazy Monkey Canopy Tour (www. almondsandcorals.com/activities/crazy-mon key-canopy-ride; per person US$45; ☺10am-2pm) is the region's only canopy tour, operated by **Almonds & Corals Lodge** (☎2271-3000, in USA 1-888-373-9042; www.almondsandcorals.com; r/master ste US$195/295, additional person from US$20, all incl breakfast; P@⊠) ✒ between Punta Uva and Manzanillo.

---

first time in 2003, dramatically shortening the amount of time it takes to travel this route. The roadway is narrow, however, so if you're driving, take your time and be alert for cyclists and one-lane bridges.

Traditional painted ox-cart wheel

In Focus

Costa Rica Today

Elation over Costa Rica reaching the 2014 World Cup quarterfinal having worn off, discontent over the presidency of Luis Guillermo Solís has grown due to growing unemployment and continuing economic woes. And while Costa Rica has emerged the victor in the long-standing border dispute with Nicaragua, relations between the two countries have worsened due to the Cuban immigrant crisis.

Changing of the Guard

Costa Rica acquired a new president after a runoff election (the second in history) in April 2014. Luis Guillermo Solís, affiliated with the center-left Citizens' Action Party (PAC), ran on promises to fight corruption and to address the country's social and economic inequality. As a scholar of Latin American studies, Solís was formerly a professor at the University of Costa Rica and a published writer specializing in Latin American politics and social issues. As such, he is still considered something of a political outsider, despite serving as an advisor to Óscar Arias as a foreign-ministry official.

Many Costa Ricans viewed Solís as an agent of much-needed yet not-too-radical change, but his government continues to face substantial problems such as the growing rate of inflation, growing unemployment and severe income inequality.

belief systems
(% of population)

76	14			3
		1	6	
Roman Catholic	Evangelical	Jehovah's Witnesses	None	Other

if Costa Rica were 100 people

94 would be white & mestizo
3 would be black
1 would be Chinese
1 would be Amerindian
1 would be other

population per sq km

≈ 2 people

COSTA RICA   UNITED STATES   CANADA

Carbon Neutrality

Back in 2009, then-president Óscar Arias set an ambitious goal – that Costa Rica achieve carbon neutrality by 2021. Meeting this goal would have made Costa Rica the first carbon-neutral country in the world.

Some measures have not yet been implemented as scheduled, and the numbers suggest that the 2021 target may have been overly ambitious. The first phase – as yet incomplete – addresses energy and agriculture, both major contributors to carbon-dioxide emissions. Proposed changes for the energy sector, for example, include transitioning buses and taxis to natural-gas, electric and hybrid vehicles, and imposing stricter emissions regulations on these companies. Agricultural changes include government-sponsored training programs for smaller farms, teaching them to implement organic methods.

One of the proposals announced by president Luis Guillermo Solís during his electoral campaign was an extension of the carbon-neutrality goal to 2025, yet when Costa Rica submitted its INDC (Intended Nationally Determined Contribution) with regards to the UN Framework Convention on Climate Change, it announced its long-term goal of becoming carbon-neutral by 2085. This was unexpected, given the Costa Rican government's recent announcement that it had already reached 81% of its carbon neutral target.

Río San Juan Saga

Forming the eastern stretch of the border between Nicaragua and Costa Rica is the Río San Juan, a silty river studded with small marshy islands. This quiet waterway has been the source of much discord between the two countries, to the extent that the International Court of Justice has had to preside over legal disputes and territory claims in the last 20 years.

The border area is complicated. The 1858 Cañas-Jerez Treaty asserts that Nicaragua owns the Río San Juan, but that Costa Rica retains navigation rights on its side of the river. Though spats have arisen over the years, and both countries have kept these tensions in relative check, they've been bubbling over recently. In December 2015 the International Court of Justice ruled that Costa Rica has sovereignty over the 3km patch of wetlands in Río San Juan, and Nicaragua promised to abide by the ruling.

There has also been an escalation of tensions between the two countries over Cuban immigrants, hundreds of whom have been trying to cross Central America in a bid to reach the US. Costa Rica has been granting Cubans short-term visas, only for them to be turned back at the Nicaraguan border. Costa Rica has requested that the Cubans be granted a 'humanitarian corridor' through the region. As of early 2016, talks with Nicaragua had broken down and Cuban immigrants were being flown from Costa Rica into Mexico.

Beach in Manzanillo (p242)

History

As in other Central American countries, European 'discovery' of the New World was followed by the subjugation and evangelization of Costa Rica's indigenous peoples. But in the mid-20th century this country departed from the standard Central American playbook by abolishing its army, diversifying its economy and brokering peace in the region.

11,000 BC
The first humans occupy Costa Rica and populations quickly flourish due to the rich land and marine resources.

1000 BC
The Huetar power base in the Central Valley is solidified following the construction and habitation of the ancient city of Guayabo.

100 BC
Costa Rica becomes part of an extensive trade network that extends from present-day Mexico down though to the Andean empires.

Lost Worlds of Ancient Rica

The coastlines and rainforests of Central America have been inhabited by humans for at least 10,000 years, but ancient civilizations in Costa Rica are largely the subject of speculation. It is thought that the area was something of a backwater straddling the two great ancient civilizations of the Andes and Mesoamerica, with the exception of the Diquís Valley along the Pacific coast, where archaeological finds suggest that a great deal of trading took place with their more powerful neighbors. On the eve of European discovery some 500 years ago, an estimated 400,000 people were living in today's Costa Rica, though sadly our knowledge about these pre-Columbian cultures is scant.

Unlike the massive pyramid complexes found throughout other parts of Latin America, the ancient towns and cities of Costa Rica (with the exception of Guayabo) were loosely organized and had no centralized government or ceremonial centers. The settlements fought among each other, but for the purpose of getting slaves rather than to extend their

1522
Spanish settlement develops in Costa Rica, though it will be several decades before the colonists can get a sturdy foothold on the land.

1540
The Spanish establish the Kingdom of Guatemala, which includes Costa Rica, Nicaragua, Honduras, El Salvador and Guatemala.

1562
Spanish conquistador Juan Vásquez de Coronado arrives in Costa Rica with the title of governor.

Ancient stones, Monumento Nacional Arqueológico Guayabo

★ **Pre-Columbian Sites**

Monumento Nacional Arqueológico Guayabo (Turrialba)

Hacienda Barú (Dominical)

Sitio Arqueológico Finca 6 (Sierpe)

Finca Cántaros (San Vito)

land territory. Not known for building edifices that would stand the test of time, Costa Rica's early inhabitants did, however, leave behind mysterious relics: enormous stone spheres, liberally scattered around the Diquís Valley.

Heirs of Columbus

On his fourth and final voyage to the New World in 1502, Christopher Columbus was forced to drop anchor near present-day Puerto Limón after a hurricane damaged his ship. While waiting for repairs, Columbus ventured into the verdant terrain and exchanged gifts with hospitable and welcoming chieftains. He returned from this encounter claiming to have seen 'more gold in two days than in four years in Española'. Columbus dubbed the stretch of shoreline from Honduras to Panama 'Veraguas,' but it was his excited descriptions of *costa rica* (the 'rich coast') that gave the region its lasting name. At least that's how the popular story goes.

Anxious to claim its bounty, Columbus petitioned the Spanish Crown to have himself appointed governor. But by the time he returned to Seville, his royal patron Queen Isabella was on her deathbed, which prompted King Ferdinand to award the prize to Columbus' rival, Diego de Nicuesa. Although Columbus became a very wealthy man, he never returned to the New World. He died in 1506 after being worn down by ill health and court politics.

To the disappointment of his conquistador heirs, Columbus' tales of gold were mostly lies and the locals were considerably less than affable. Nicuesa's first colony in present-day Panama was abruptly abandoned when tropical disease and warring tribes decimated its ranks. Successive expeditions launched from the Caribbean coast also failed as pestilent swamps, oppressive jungles and volcanoes made Columbus' paradise seem more like a tropical hell.

A bright moment in Spanish exploration came in 1513 when Vasco Núñez de Balboa heard rumors about a large sea and a wealthy, gold-producing civilization across the mountains of the isthmus – these almost certainly referred to the Inca empire of

1563	1737	1821
The first permanent Spanish colonial settlement in Costa Rica is established in Cartago by Juan Vásquez de Coronado.	The future capital of San José is established, sparking a rivalry with neighboring Cartago that will culminate in a civil war.	Following a unanimous declaration by Mexico on behalf of all of Central America, Costa Rica gains its independence from Spain.

present-day Peru. Driven by equal parts ambition and greed, Balboa scaled the continental divide, and on September 26, 1513, he became the first European to set eyes upon the Pacific Ocean. Keeping up with the European fashion of the day, Balboa immediately proceeded to claim the ocean and all the lands it touched for the king of Spain.

The thrill of discovery aside, the conquistadors now controlled a strategic western beachhead from which to launch their conquest of Costa Rica. In the name of God and king, aristocratic adventurers plundered indigenous villages, executed resisters and enslaved survivors throughout the Península de Nicoya. However, none of these bloodstained campaigns led to a permanent presence as intercontinental germ warfare caused outbreaks of feverish death on both sides. The indigenous people mounted a fierce resistance to the invaders, which included guerrilla warfare, destroying their own villages and killing their own children rather than letting them fall into Spanish hands.

New World Order

It was not until the 1560s that a Spanish colony was firmly established in Costa Rica. Hoping to cultivate the rich volcanic soil of the Central Valley, the Spanish founded the village of Cartago on the banks of the Río Reventazón. Although the fledgling colony was extremely isolated, it miraculously survived under the leadership of its first governor, Juan Vásquez de Coronado. Some of Costa Rica's demilitarized present was presaged in its early colonial government: preferring diplomacy over firearms to counter the indigenous threat, Coronado used Cartago as a base to survey the lands south to Panama and west to the Pacific, and secured deed and title over the colony.

Though Coronado was later lost in a shipwreck, his legacy endured. Costa Rica was an officially recognized province of the Viceroyalty of New Spain (Virreinato de Nueva España), which was the name given to the viceroy-ruled territories of the Spanish empire in North America, Central America, the Caribbean and Asia.

For roughly three centuries, the Captaincy General of Guatemala (also known as the Kingdom of Guatemala), which included Costa Rica, Nicaragua, Honduras, El Salvador, Guatemala and the Mexican state of Chiapas, was a loosely administered colony in the vast Spanish empire. Since the political and military headquarters of the kingdom were in Guatemala, Costa Rica became a minor provincial outpost that had little if any strategic significance or exploitable riches.

As a result of its status as a swampy, largely useless backwater, Costa Rica's colonial path diverged from the typical pattern in that a powerful landholding elite and slave-based economy never gained prominence. Instead of large estates, mining operations and coastal cities, modest-sized villages of smallholders developed in the interior Central Valley. According to national lore, the stoic, self-sufficient farmer provided the backbone for 'rural democracy' as Costa Rica emerged as one of the only egalitarian corners of the Spanish empire.

April 1823	December 1823	1824
The Costa Rican capital officially moves to San José after intense skirmishes with the conservative residents of Cartago.	The Monroe Doctrine formally declares the USA's intention to be the dominant imperial power in the Western Hemisphere.	The Nicoya-Guanacaste region votes to secede from Nicaragua and become a part of Costa Rica.

Bahía Drake's Plundered Treasure

British explorer, government-sponsored pirate and slaver Sir Francis Drake is believed to have anchored in Bahía Drake in 1579. Rumor has it that he buried some of his plundered treasure here, but the only solid memorial to the man is a monument that looks out to his namesake bay.

Equal rights and opportunities were not extended to the indigenous groups, and as Spanish settlement expanded, the local population decreased dramatically. From 400,000 at the time Columbus first sailed, the population was reduced to 20,000 a century later, and to 8000 a century after that. While disease was the main cause of death, the Spanish were relentless in their effort to exploit the natives as an economic resource by establishing the *encomienda* system that applied to indigenous males and gave the Spaniards the right to demand free labour, with many worked to death. Central Valley groups were the first to fall, though outside the valley several tribes managed to survive a bit longer under forest cover, staging occasional raids. However, as in the rest of Latin America, repeated military campaigns eventually forced them into submission and slavery, though throughout that period, many clergymen protested the brutal treatment of indigenous subjects and implored the Spanish Crown to protect them.

Fall of an Empire

Spain's costly Peninsular War with France from 1808 to 1814 – and the political turmoil, unrest and power vacuums that it caused – led Spain to lose all its colonial possessions in the first third of the 19th century.

In 1821 the Americas wriggled free of Spain's imperial grip following Mexico's declaration of independence for itself as well as the whole of Central America. Of course, the Central American provinces weren't too keen on having another foreign power reign over them and subsequently declared independence from Mexico. However, all of these events hardly disturbed Costa Rica, which learned of its liberation a month after the fact.

The newly liberated colonies pondered their fate: stay together in a United States of Central America or go their separate national ways. At first they came up with something in between, namely the Central American Federation (CAF), though it could neither field an army nor collect taxes. Accustomed to being at the center of things, Guatemala also attempted to dominate the CAF, alienating smaller colonies and hastening its demise. Future attempts to unite the region would likewise fail.

Meanwhile, an independent Costa Rica was taking shape under Juan Mora Fernández, the first head of state (1824–33). He tended toward nation building, and organized new towns, built roads, published a newspaper and coined a currency. His wife even partook in the effort by designing the country's flag.

1856	1889	1890
Costa Rica quashes the expansionist aims of the USA by defeating William Walker and his invading army at the epic Battle of Santa Rosa.	Costa Rica's first democratic elections are held, a monumental event given the long history of colonial occupation.	The construction of the railroad between San José and Puerto Limón is finally completed despite years of hardships and deaths.

Life returned to normal, unlike in the rest of the region, where post-independence civil wars raged on. In 1824 the Nicoya-Guanacaste region seceded from Nicaragua and joined its more easygoing southern neighbor, defining the territorial borders. In 1852 Costa Rica received its first diplomatic emissaries from the USA and Great Britain.

Coffee Rica

In the 19th century the riches that Costa Rica had long promised were uncovered when it was realized that the soil and climate of the Central Valley highlands were ideal for coffee cultivation. Costa Rica led Central America in introducing the caffeinated bean, which transformed the impoverished country into the wealthiest in the region.

When an export market was discovered, the government actively promoted coffee to farmers by providing free saplings. At first Costa Rican producers exported their crop to nearby South Americans, who processed the beans and re-exported the product to Europe. By the 1840s, however, local merchants had already built up domestic capacity and learned to scope out their own overseas markets. Their big break came when they persuaded the captain of HMS *Monarch* to transport several hundred sacks of Costa Rican coffee to London, percolating the beginning of a beautiful friendship.

The Costa Rican coffee boom was on. The drink's quick fix made it popular among working-class consumers in the industrializing north. The aroma of riches lured a wave of enterprising German immigrants, enhancing technical and financial skills in the business sector. By century's end, more than one-third of the Central Valley was dedicated to coffee cultivation, and coffee accounted for more than 90% of all exports and 80% of foreign-currency earnings.

The coffee industry in Costa Rica developed differently from those in the rest of Central America. As elsewhere, there arose a group of coffee barons, elites that reaped the rewards for the export bonanza. But Costa Rican coffee barons lacked the land and labor to cultivate the crop. Coffee production is labor intensive, with a long and painstaking harvest season. The small farmers became the principal planters. The coffee barons, instead, monopolized processing, marketing and financing. The coffee economy in Costa Rica created a wide network of high-end traders and small-scale growers, whereas in the rest of Central America a narrow elite controlled large estates worked by tenant laborers.

Coffee wealth became a power resource in politics. Costa Rica's traditional aristocratic families were at the forefront of the enterprise. At mid-century, three-quarters of the coffee barons were descended from just two colonial families. The country's leading coffee exporter at this time was President Juan Rafael Mora Porras (1849–59), whose lineage went back to the colony's founder, Juan Vásquez de Coronado. Mora was overthrown by his brother-in-law after the president proposed to form a national bank independent of the coffee barons. The economic interests of the coffee elite would thereafter become a priority in Costa Rican politics.

1900	**1914**	**1919**
Costa Rica begins to develop and prosper due to lucrative international coffee and banana trades.	Costa Rica is given an economic boost following the opening of the Panama Canal.	Federico Tinoco Granados is ousted as the dictator of Costa Rica.

Banana plantation, Puerto Viejo de Talamanca (p234)

Banana Empire

The coffee trade unintentionally gave rise to Costa Rica's next export boom – bananas. Getting coffee out to world markets necessitated a rail link from the central highlands to the coast, and Limón's deep harbor made an ideal port. Inland was dense jungle and insect-infested swamps, which prompted the government to contract the task to Minor Keith, nephew of an American railroad tycoon.

The project was a disaster. Malaria and accidents churned through workers as Tico recruits gave way to US convicts and Chinese indentured servants, who were in turn replaced by freed Jamaican slaves. To entice Keith to continue, the government turned over 3200 sq km of land along the route and provided a 99-year lease to run the railroad. In 1890 the line was finally completed and running at a loss.

Keith had begun to grow banana plants along the tracks as a cheap food source for the workers. Desperate to recoup his investment, he shipped some bananas to New Orleans in the hope of starting a side venture. He struck gold, or rather yellow. Consumers went crazy for the elongated finger fruit. By the early 20th century, bananas surpassed coffee as Costa Rica's most lucrative export and the country became the world's

1940	1940s	1948
Rafael Ángel Calderón Guardia is elected president and proceeds to improve working conditions in Costa Rica.	José Figueres Ferrer becomes involved in national politics and opposes the ruling conservatives.	Conservative and liberal forces clash, resulting in a six-week civil war that leaves 2000 Costa Ricans dead and many more wounded.

leading banana exporter. Unlike in the coffee industry, the profits were exported along with the bananas.

Costa Rica was transformed by the rise of Keith's banana empire. He joined another American importer to found the infamous United Fruit Company, known locally as Yunai, and soon the largest employer in Central America. To the locals, it was known as *el pulpo* (the octopus) – its tentacles stretched across the region, becoming entangled with the local economy and politics. United Fruit owned huge swaths of lush lowlands, much of the transportation and communication infrastructure and bunches of bureaucrats. The company drew a wave of migrant laborers from Jamaica, changing the country's ethnic complexion and provoking racial tensions. In its various incarnations as the United Brands Company and, later, Chiquita, Yunai was virulently anti-union and maintained control over its workforces by paying workers in redeemable scrips rather than cash for many years. Amazingly, the marks that *el pulpo* left on Costa Rica are still present, including the rusting train tracks and a locomotive engine in Palmares.

Bitter Fruit

For details on the role of Minor Keith and the United Fruit Company in lobbying for a CIA-led coup in Guatemala, pick up a copy of the highly readable *Bitter Fruit* by Stephen Schlesinger and Stephen Kinzer.

Birth of a Nation

The inequality of the early 20th century led to the rise of José Figueres Ferrer, a self-described farmer-philosopher and the father of Costa Rica's unarmed democracy. The son of Catalan immigrant coffee planters, Figueres excelled in school and went to Boston's MIT to study engineering. Upon returning to Costa Rica to set up his own coffee plantation, he organized the hundreds of laborers on his farm into a utopian socialist community and appropriately named the property La Luz Sin Fin (The Struggle Without End).

In the 1940s Figueres became involved in national politics as an outspoken critic of President Calderón. In the midst of a radio interview in which he badmouthed the president, police broke into the studio and arrested Figueres. He was accused of having fascist sympathies and was banished to Mexico. While in exile he formed the Caribbean League, a collection of students and democratic agitators from all over Central America who pledged to bring down the region's military dictators. When he returned to Costa Rica, the Caribbean League, now 700-men strong, went with him and helped protest against the powers that be.

When government troops descended on the farm with the intention of arresting Figueres and disarming the Caribbean League, it touched off a civil war. The moment had arrived: the diminutive farmer-philosopher now played the man on horseback. Figueres emerged victorious from the brief conflict and seized the opportunity to put into place his

1949

The temporary government abolishes the army, desegregates the country, and grants women and blacks the right to vote.

1963

Reserva Natura Absoluta Cabo Blanco becomes Costa Rica's first federally protected conservation area.

1977

The Indigenous Law of 1977 is passed, protecting the rights of indigenous communities to ownership of their territories.

The Little Drummer Boy

During your travels through the countryside, you may notice statues of a drummer boy from Alajuela named Juan Santamaría. He is one of Costa Rica's most beloved national heroes.

In April 1856 the North American mercenary William Walker and his ragtag army attempted to invade Costa Rica during an ultimately unsuccessful campaign to conquer all of Central America. Walker had already managed to seize control of Nicaragua, taking advantage of the civil war that was raging there. It didn't take him long after that to decide to march on Costa Rica, though Costa Rican president Juan Rafael Mora Porras guessed Walker's intentions and managed to recruit a volunteer army of 9000 civilians. They surrounded Walker's army as they lay waiting in an old *hacienda* (estate) in present-day Parque Nacional Santa Rosa. The Costa Ricans won the battle and Walker was forever expelled from Costa Rican soil. During the fighting, Santamaría was killed while daringly setting fire to Walker's defenses – and a national legend was born.

vision of Costa Rican social democracy. After dissolving the country's military, Figueres quoted HG Wells: 'The future of mankind cannot include the armed forces.'

As head of a temporary junta government, Figueres enacted nearly a thousand decrees. He taxed the wealthy, nationalized the banks and built a modern welfare state. His 1949 constitution granted full citizenship and voting rights to women, African-Americans, indigenous groups and Chinese minorities. Today Figueres' revolutionary regime is regarded as the foundation of Costa Rica's unarmed democracy.

The American Empire

Throughout the 1970s and '80s, the sovereignty of the small nations of Central America was limited by their northern neighbor, the USA. Big sticks, gunboats and dollar diplomacy were instruments of a Yankee policy to curtail socialist politics, especially the military oligarchies of Guatemala, El Salvador and Nicaragua.

In 1979 the rebellious Sandinistas toppled the American-backed Somoza dictatorship in Nicaragua. Alarmed by the Sandinistas' Soviet and Cuban ties, fervently anticommunist president Ronald Reagan decided it was time to intervene. Just like that, the Cold War arrived in the hot tropics.

The organizational details of the counterrevolution were delegated to Oliver North, an eager-to-please junior officer working out of the White House basement. North's can-do creativity helped to prop up the famed Contra rebels to incite civil war in Nicaragua. While both sides invoked the rhetoric of freedom and democracy, the war was really a turf battle between left-wing and right-wing forces.

1987
President Óscar Arias Sánchez wins the Nobel Peace Prize for his work on the Central American peace accords.

1994
The indigenous people of Costa Rica are finally granted the right to vote.

2006
Óscar Arias Sánchez is elected president for the second time on a pro-Cafta (Central American Free Trade Agreement) platform.

Under intense US pressure, Costa Rica was reluctantly dragged in. The Contras set up camp in northern Costa Rica, from where they staged guerrilla raids. Not-so-clandestine CIA operatives and US military advisers were dispatched to assist the effort. A secret jungle airstrip was built near the border to fly in weapons and supplies. To raise cash for the rebels, North allegedly used his covert supply network to traffic illegal narcotics through the region.

The war polarized Costa Rica. From conservative quarters came a loud call to re-establish the military and join the anticommunist crusade, which was largely under-written by the US Pentagon. In May 1984 more than 20,000 demonstrators marched through San José to give peace a chance, though the debate didn't climax until the 1986 presidential election. The victor was 44-year-old Óscar Arias Sánchez, who, despite being born into coffee wealth, was an intellectual reformer in the mold of Figueres, his political patron.

Once in office, Arias affirmed his commitment to a negotiated resolution and reasserted Costa Rican national independence. He vowed to uphold his country's pledge of neutrality and to vanquish the Contras from the territory. The sudden resignation of the US ambassador around this time was suspected to be a result of Arias' strong stance. In a public ceremony, Costa Rican schoolchildren planted trees on top of the CIA's secret airfield. Most notably, Arias became the driving force in uniting Central America around a peace plan, which ended the Nicaraguan war and earned him the Nobel Peace Prize in 1987.

In 2006 Arias once again returned to the presidential office, winning the popular election by a 1.2% margin and subsequently ratifying the controversial Central American Free Trade Agreement (Cafta), which Costa Rica entered into in 2009.

When Laura Chinchilla became the first female president of Costa Rica in 2010, she promised to continue with Arias' free-market policies, in spite of the divisive Cafta agreement (the referendum in 2007 barely resulted in a 'yes' vote at 51%). She also pledged to tackle the rise of violent crime and drug trafficking, on the rise due to Costa Rica being used as a halfway house by Colombian and Mexican cartels. Ironically, a month after discussing the drug cartel problem with US President Barack Obama during his visit to Costa Rica, Chinchilla became embroiled in a drug-related scandal over the use of a private jet belonging to a man under investigation by Costa Rican intelligence for possible links to international drug cartels.

2010
Costa Rica elects its first female president, National Liberation Party candidate Laura Chinchilla.

2013
The murder of 26-year-old environmentalist Jairo Mora Sandoval in Limón Province attracts international attention.

2015
The International Criminal Court in the Hague settles the land dispute between Costa Rica and Nicaragua in Costa Rica's favor.

Hanging bridge, Parque Nacional Volcán Arenal (p128)

JEFF DIENER/GETTY IMAGES ©

Costa Rica Outdoors

Miles of shoreline, endless warm water and a diverse array of national parks and reserves provide an inviting playground for active travelers. Whether it's the solitude of absolute wilderness, hiking and rafting adventures kids can enjoy, or surfing and jungle trekking you seek, Costa Rica offers fun to suit everyone.

Hiking & Trekking

Hiking opportunities around Costa Rica are seemingly endless. With extensive mountains, canyons, dense jungles, cloud forests and two coastlines, this is one of Central America's best and most varied hiking destinations.

Hikes come in an enormous spectrum of difficulty. At tourist-packed destinations such as Monteverde, trails are clearly marked and sometimes paved. This is fantastic if you're traveling with kids or aren't confident about route-finding. For long-distance trekking, there are many more options in the remote corners of the country.

Opportunities for moderate hiking are typically plentiful in most parks and reserves. For the most part, you can rely on signs and maps for orientation, though it helps to have some navigational experience. Good hiking shoes, plenty of water and confidence in your

Surfing in Costa Rica

abilities will enable you to combine several shorter day hikes into a lengthier expedition. Tourist-information centers at park entrances are great resources for planning your intended route.

If you're properly equipped with camping essentials, the country's longer and more arduous multiday treks are at your disposal. Costa Rica's top challenges are scaling Cerro Chirripó, traversing Corcovado and penetrating deep into the heart of La Amistad. While Chirripó can be undertaken independently, local guides are required for much of La Amistad and for all of Corcovado.

Make It Happen

If you're planning your trip around long-distance trekking, it's best to visit during the dry season (December to April). Outside this time frame, rivers become impassable and trails are prone to flooding. In the highlands, journeys become more taxing in the rain, and the bare landscape offers little protection.

Costa Rica is hot and humid: hiking in these tropical conditions, harassed by mosquitoes, can really take it out of you. Remember to wear light clothing that will dry quickly. Overheating and dehydration are the main sources of misery on the trails, so be sure to bring plenty of water and take rest stops. Make sure you have sturdy, comfortable footwear and a lightweight rain jacket.

Unfortunately there are occasional stories of people getting robbed while on some of the more remote hiking trails. Although this rarely happens, it is always advisable to hike in a group for added safety. Hiring a local guide is another excellent way to enhance your

Howler monkey (p277)

KRYSIA CAWPOS/GETTY IMAGES ©

experience, avoid getting lost and learn an enormous amount about the flora and fauna around you.

Some of the local park offices have maps, but this is the exception rather than the rule. If you are planning to do independent hiking on long-distance trails, be sure to purchase your maps in San José in advance.

A number of companies offer trekking tours in Costa Rica:

Osa Wild (p199) Offers a huge variety of hikes in the Osa, in partnership with a sustainability organization.

Costa Rica Trekking Adventures (p222) Offers multiday treks in Chirripó, Corcovado and Tapanti.

Osa Aventura (p199) Specializes in treks through Corcovado.

Surfing

Point and beach breaks, lefts and rights, reefs and river mouths, warm water and year-round waves make Costa Rica a favorite surfing destination. For the most part, the Pacific coast has bigger swells and better waves during the latter part of the rainy season, but the Caribbean cooks from November to May. Basically, there is a wave waiting to be surfed at any time of year.

For the uninitiated, lessons are available at almost all of the major surfing destinations – especially popular towns include Jacó, Dominical and Tamarindo on the Pacific coast. Surfing definitely has a steep learning curve, and can be potentially dangerous if the currents are strong. With that said, the sport is accessible to children and novices, though it's advisable to start with a lesson and always inquire locally about conditions before you paddle out.

Throughout Costa Rica, waves are big (though not massive), and many offer hollow and fast rides that are perfect for intermediates. As a bonus, Costa Rica is one of the few places on the planet where you can surf two different oceans in the same day. Advanced surfers with plenty of experience can contend with some of the world's most famous waves. The top ones include Ollie's Point and Witch's Rock, off the coast of the Santa Rosa sector of the Área de Conservación Guanacaste; Mal País and Santa Teresa, with a groovy scene to match the powerful waves; Playa Hermosa, whose bigger, faster curls attract a more determined (and experienced) crew of wave-chasers; Pavones, a legendary long left across the sweet waters of the Golfo Dulce; and the infamous Salsa Brava in Puerto Viejo de Talamanca, for experts only.

Make It Happen

Most international airlines accept surfboards (they must be properly packed in a padded board bag) as one of the two pieces of checked luggage, though this is getting more difficult and pricier in the age of higher fuel tariffs. Domestic airlines offer more of a challenge; they will accept surfboards for an extra charge, but the board must be under 2.1m in length. On full flights, there's a chance your board won't make it on because of weight restrictions.

An alternative is to buy a new or used board in Costa Rica and then sell it before you leave. Great places to start your search include Jacó, Mal País and Santa Teresa, and Tamarindo. It's usually possible to buy a cheap longboard for about US$250 to US$300, and a cheap shortboard for about US$150 to US$200. Many surf shops will buy back your board for about 50% of the price you paid.

Outfitters in many of the popular surf towns rent all kinds of boards, fix dings, give classes and organize excursions. Jacó, Tamarindo, Pavones and Puerto Viejo de Talamanca are good for these types of activities.

Costa Rica Surf Camp (☑8812-3625, 2787-0393; www.crsurfschool.com; Hotel DiuWak; all-inclusive packages per week from US$1190) Excellent teachers with safety certification and low teacher-student ratios.

Dominical Surf Adventures (☑2787-0431; www.dominicalsurfadventures.com; ☺8am-5pm Mon-Sat, 9am-3pm Sun) An excellent source of surf lessons in Dominical.

Iguana Surf (☑2653-0091; www.iguanasurf.net; board rental US$20, group/semiprivate/private lessons US$45/65/80; ☺8am-6pm) Playa Tamarindo's stalwart surf shop has lessons, rentals and good tips.

Caribbean Surf School (p231) Based in Puerto Viejo de Talamanca, Hershel is widely considered to be one of the best teachers on the Caribbean.

Pura Vida Adventures (☑in USA 415-465-2162; www.puravidaadventures.com; Playa del Carmen) An excellent women-only surf-and-yoga camp at Playa El Carmen.

Wildlife-Watching & Birding

Costa Rica's biodiversity is legendary, and the country delivers unparalleled opportunities for wildlife- and birdwatching. Most people are already familiar with the most famous, yet commonly spotted, animals. You'll instantly recognize monkeys bounding through the treetops, sloths clinging to branches and toucans gliding beneath the canopy. Young children, even if they have been to the zoo dozens of times, typically love the thrill of spotting creatures in the wild.

For the slightly older, keeping checklists is a fun way to add an educational element to your travels. If you really want to know what you're looking at, pick up wildlife and bird guides before your trip – look for ones with color plates for easy positive IDs.

A quality pair of binoculars is highly recommended and can really make the difference between far-off movement and a veritable face-to-face encounter. For expert birders, a spotting scope is essential, and multipark itineraries will allow you to quickly add dozens of new species to your all-time list.

White-water rafting, Río Pacuare

★ **Top 5 for Rafting & Kayaking**

Río Sarapiquí (p78)

La Virgen (p80)

Parque Nacional Manuel Antonio
(p182)

Parque Nacional Tortuguero (p92)

Bahía Drake (p208)

Make It Happen

It's worth pointing out that Costa Rica is brimming with avian life at every turn, but sometimes it takes an experienced guide to help you notice it.

Aratinga Tours (p222) Some of the best bird tours in the country are led by Belgian ornithologist Pieter Westra.

Tropical Feathers (www.costaricabirdingtours.com; cnr Barrio Laboratorio & Calle Mariposa) Local owner and guide Noel Ureña has over 16 years' experience leading birding tours.

Bird Treks (📞in USA 717-548-3303; www.birdtreks.com) An international bird-tour company with highly entertaining and qualified guides in Costa Rica.

White-Water Rafting & Kayaking

White-water rafting has remained one of Costa Rica's top outdoor pursuits since the '80s. Ranging from family-friendly Class I riffles to nearly unnavigable Class V rapids, the country's rivers offer highly varied white-water experiences.

First-time runners are catered for year-round, while seasoned enthusiasts arrive en masse during the wildest months from June to October. There is also much regional variation, with gentler rivers located near Manuel Antonio along the central Pacific coast, and world-class runs along the Río Pacuare in the Central Valley. Since all white-water rafting in Costa Rica requires the presence of a certified guide, you will need to book trips through a reputable tour agency.

River kayaking has its fair share of loyal fans. The tiny village of La Virgen in the northern lowlands is the unofficial kayaking capital of Costa Rica and the best spot to hook up with other paddlers. The Río Sarapiquí has an impressive variety of runs that cater to all ages and skill levels.

With 1228km of coastline, two gulfs and plentiful mangrove estuaries, Costa Rica is also an ideal destination for sea kayaking. This is a great way for paddlers to access remote areas and catch glimpses of rare birds and wildlife. Difficulty of access varies considerably, and is largely dependent on tides and currents.

Make It Happen

June to October are considered peak season for river rafting and kayaking, though some rivers offer good runs all year. Government regulation of outfitters is shoddy, so ask lots of questions about your guide's water-safety, emergency and medical training. If you suspect they're bluffing, move along – there are plenty of legit outfits.

River kayaking can be organized in conjunction with white-water rafting trips if you are experienced; sea kayaking is popular year-round.

Aguas Bravas (☏2479-7645; www.costaricaraftingvacation.com; rafting US$80-100, kayaking US$60; ☺7am-7pm) In La Virgen, this is the best outfitter on Costa Rica's best white water.

Exploradores Outdoors (p96) This outfit offers one- and two-day trips on the Ríos Pacuare, Reventazón and Sarapiquí.

Pineapple Kayak Tours (☏8362-7655, 8873-3283; www.pineapplekayaktours.com; tours US$20-75) Exciting half-day kayak trips go through caves and mangrove channels.

H2O Adventures (p182) Arranges two- and five-day adventures on the Río Savegre.

Ríos Tropicales (☏2233-6455, in USA 866-722-8273; www.riostropicales.com) Multiday adventures on the Río Pacuare and two days of kayaking in Tortuguero.

Costa Rica Expeditions (☏2521-6099; www.costaricaexpeditions.com) This outfitter handles small groups and offers rafting trips that cater to foodies.

Gulf Islands Kayaking (☏in Canada 250-539-2442; www.seakayak.ca) Tours on offer include five days of sea kayaking in Corcovado.

Diving & Snorkeling

The good news is that Costa Rica offers body-temperature water with few humans and abundant marine life. The bad news is that visibility is low because of silt and plankton, and soft corals and sponges are dominant.

However, if you're looking for fine opportunities to see massive schools of fish, as well as larger marine animals such as turtles, sharks, dolphins and whales, then jump right in. It's also worth pointing out that there are few places in the world where you could feasibly dive in the Caribbean and the Pacific on the same day, though why not take your time?

The Caribbean Sea is better for novice divers and snorkelers, with the beach towns of Manzanillo and Cahuita particularly well suited to youngsters. Puerto Viejo lays claim to a few decent sites that can be explored on a discovery dive. Along the Pacific, Isla del Caño ups the ante for those with solid diving experience.

Isla del Coco is the exception to the rule – this remote island floating in the deep Pacific is regarded by veteran divers as one of the best spots on the planet. To dive the wonderland of Coco, you'll need to visit on a liveaboard and have logged some serious time underwater.

Make It Happen

Generally, visibility isn't great during the rainy months, when rivers swell and their outflow clouds the ocean. At this time, boats to offshore locations offer better viewing opportunities.

The water is warm – around 24°C (75°F) to 29°C (84°F) at the surface, with a thermocline at around 20m below the surface, where it drops to 23°C (73°F). If you're keeping it shallow, you can skin-dive.

If you're interested in diving but aren't certified, you can usually do a one-day introductory course that will allow you to do one or two accompanied dives. If you love it, which most people do, certification courses take three to four days and cost from around US$350 to US$500.

To plan a trip to Isla del Coco, get in touch with the liveaboard operation **Undersea Hunter** (☏2228-6613, in USA 800-203-2120; www.underseahunter.com).

Mountain Biking & Cycling

Although the winding, pot-holed roads and aggressive drivers can be a challenge, cycling is on the rise in Costa Rica. Numerous less-trafficked roads offer plenty of adventure – from scenic mountain paths with sweeping views to rugged trails that take riders through streams and past volcanoes.

The best long-distance rides are along the Pacific coast's Interamericana, which has a decent shoulder and is relatively flat, and on the road from Montezuma to the Reserva Natural Absoluta Cabo Blanco, on the southern Península de Nicoya.

Mountain biking has taken off in recent years and there are good networks of trails around Corcovado and Arenal, as well as more rides in the central mountains.

Make It Happen

Most international airlines will fly your bike as a piece of checked baggage for an extra fee. Pad it well, because the box is liable to be roughly handled.

Alternatively, you can rent mountain bikes in almost any tourist town, but the condition of the equipment varies greatly. For a monthly fee, **Trail Source** (www.trailsource.com) can provide you with information on trails all over Costa Rica and the world.

Outfitters in Costa Rica and the US can organize multiday mountain-biking trips. If you want to tour Costa Rica by bicycle, be forewarned that the country's cycling shops are decidedly more geared toward utilitarian concerns. Bring any specialized equipment (including a serious lock) from home.

Companies organizing bike tours in Costa Rica include the following:

Backroads (☑in USA 800-462-2848, in USA 510-527-1555; www.backroads.com)

Coast to Coast Adventures (☑2280-8054; www.ctocadventures.com)

Costa Rica Expeditions (p263)

Lava Tours (☑2281-2458; www.lava-tours.com)

Serendipity Adventures (☑2556-2222, in USA & Canada 877-507-1358; www.serendipity adventures.com).

Picnic at Playa Dominical

The Tico Way of Life

Blessed with natural beauty and a peaceful, military-free society, it's no wonder that Costa Rica has long been known as the Switzerland of Central America. While the country is certainly challenged by its lofty eco-conscious goals, and modern intercontinental maladies such as drug trafficking and a disparity in wealth, the Tico attitude remains sunny and family-centered.

Pura Vida

Pura vida (pure life) is more than just a slogan that rolls off the tongues of Ticos (Costa Ricans) and emblazons souvenirs; in the laid-back tone in which it is constantly uttered, the phrase is a bona fide mantra for the Costa Rican way of life. Perhaps the essence of the pure life is something better lived than explained, but hearing *pura vida* again and again while traveling across this beautiful country – as a greeting, a stand-in for goodbye, 'cool,' and an acknowledgement of thanks – makes it evident that the concept lives deep within the DNA of this country.

The living seems particularly pure when Costa Rica is compared with its Central American neighbors such as Nicaragua and Honduras; there's little poverty, illiteracy or political tumult, the country is crowded with ecological jewels, and the standard of living is high. What's more, Costa Rica has flourished without an army for the past 60 years. The sum of the parts is a country that's an oasis of calm in a corner of the world that has been continuously degraded by warfare. And though the Costa Rican people are justifiably proud hosts, a compliment to the country is likely to be met simply with a warm smile and an enigmatic two-word reply: *pura vida*.

Daily Life

With its lack of war, long life expectancy and relatively sturdy economy, Costa Rica enjoys the highest standard of living in Central America. For the most part, Costa Ricans live fairly affluent and comfortable lives, even by North American standards.

As in many places in Latin America, the family unit in Costa Rica remains the nucleus of life. Families socialize together and extended families often live near each other. When it's time to party it's also largely a family affair; celebrations, vacations and weddings are a social outlet for rich and poor alike, and those with relatives in positions of power – nominal or otherwise – don't hesitate to turn to them for support.

Given this mutually cooperative environment, it's no surprise that life expectancy in Costa Rica is slightly higher than in the US. In fact, most Costa Ricans are more likely to die of heart disease or cancer than the childhood diseases that plague many developing nations. A comprehensive socialized health-care system and excellent sanitation systems account for these positive statistics, as do a generally stress-free lifestyle, tropical weather and a healthy and varied diet – the *pura vida*.

Still, the divide between rich and poor is broad. The middle and upper classes largely reside in San José, as well as in the major cities of the Central Valley highlands (Heredia, Alajuela and Cartago), and enjoy a level of comfort similar to their economic brethren in Europe and the US. City dwellers are likely to have a maid and a car or two, and the lucky few have a second home on the beach or in the mountains.

The home of an average Tico is a one-story construction built from concrete blocks, wood or a combination of both. In the poorer lowland areas, people often live in windowless houses made of *caña brava* (a local cane). For the vast majority of *campesinos* (farmers) and *indígenas* (people of indigenous origin), poverty levels are higher and standards of living are lower than in the rest of the country. This is especially true along the Caribbean coast, where the descendants of Jamaican immigrants have long suffered from lack of attention by the federal government, and in indigenous reservations. However, although poor families have few possessions and little financial security, every member assists with working the land or contributing to the household, which creates a strong safety net.

As in the rest of the world, globalization is having a dramatic effect on Costa Ricans, who are increasingly mobile, international and intertwined in the global economy – for better or for worse. These days, society is increasingly geographically mobile – the Tico who was born in Puntarenas might end up managing a lodge on the Península de Osa. And, with the advent of better-paved roads, cell-phone coverage, and the increasing presence of North American and European expats (and the accompanying malls and big box stores), the Tico family unit is subject to the changing tides of a global society.

Women in Costa Rica

By the letter of the law, Costa Rica's progressive stance on women's issues makes the country stand out among its Central American neighbors. A 1974 family code stipulated equal duties and rights for men and women. Additionally, women can draw up contracts, assume loans and inherit property. Sexual harassment and sex discrimination are also against the law, and in 1996 Costa Rica passed a landmark law against domestic violence that was one of the most progressive in Latin America. With women holding more and more roles in political, legal, scientific and medical fields, Costa Rica has been home to some historic firsts: in 1998 both vice presidents (Costa Rica has two) were women, and in February 2010 Arias Sánchez's former vice president, Laura Chinchilla, became the first female president.

Still, the picture of sexual equality is much more complicated than the country's bragging rights might suggest. A thriving legal prostitution trade has fueled illicit underground activities such as child prostitution and the trafficking of women. Despite cultural reverence for the matriarch (Mother's Day is a national holiday), traditional Latin American machismo is hardly a thing of the past; anti-discrimination laws are rarely enforced. Particularly in the countryside, many women maintain traditional roles: raising children, cooking, and running the home.

Sport

From the scrappy little matches that take over the village pitch to the breathless exclamations of 'Goal!' that erupt from San José bars on the day of a big game, no Costa Rican sporting venture can compare with *fútbol* (soccer). Every town has a soccer field (which usually serves as the most conspicuous landmark) where neighborhood aficionados play in heated matches.

The *selección nacional* (national selection) team is known affectionately as La Sele. Legions of rabid Tico fans still recall La Sele's most memorable moments, including an unlikely showing in the quarterfinals at the 1990 World Cup in Italy and a solid (if not long-lasting) performance in the 2002 World Cup. More recently, La Sele's failure to qualify in 2010 led to a top-down change in leadership and the reinstatement of one-time coach Jorge Luis Pinto, a Colombian coach who has had mixed results on the international stage. In general, Pinto seems to be a good fit for the team's ferocious young leaders, such as record-setting scorer Álvaro Saborío, goalkeeper Keylor Navas and forward Bryan

 Tico versus Nica

Ticos have a well-deserved reputation for friendliness, and it's rare for travelers of any sex, race or creed to experience prejudice in Costa Rica. However, it's unfortunate and at times upsetting that the mere mention of anything related to Nicaragua is enough to turn an average Tico into a stereotype-spewing anti-Nicaraguan. Despite commonalities in language, culture, history and tradition, Nica-versus-Tico relations are at an all-time low, and rhetoric (on both sides) isn't likely to improve any time soon.

Why is there so much hostility between Nicaraguans and Ticos? The answer is as much a product of history as it is of misunderstanding, though economic disparities between the countries are largely to blame.

Though Nicaragua was wealthier than Costa Rica as recently as 25 years ago, decades of civil war and a US embargo quickly bankrupted it, and today Nicaragua is the second-poorest country in the Western Hemisphere (after Haiti).

Nicaraguans are crossing the border in record numbers, drawn to Costa Rica by its growing economy and impressive education and health systems. However, immigration laws in Costa Rica make it difficult for Nicaraguans to find work, and the majority end up living in shantytowns and doing poorly paid manual labor. Also, crime is on the rise throughout Costa Rica, and some Ticos are quick to point the finger at Nicaraguans.

Costa Rica is currently at loggerheads with Nicaragua over the Cuban immigrant crisis, since Nicaragua refuses to grant them passage to the US after they have been granted temporary Costa Rican visas. Nicaragua, on the other hand, has also passed a law requiring all visiting Ticos to be in possession of a valid visa. As with all instances of deep-rooted prejudice, the solution is anything but clear.

Ruiz. And in fact, Pinto led the team to qualify for the 2014 World Cup in Brazil, where the team reached the quarterfinals, making them national heroes.

With such perfect waves, surfing has steadily grown in popularity among Ticos, especially those who grow up shredding in surf towns. Costa Rica hosts numerous national and international competitions annually that are widely covered by local media, as well as holding regular local competitions such as the weekly contest at Playa Hermosa (south of Jacó).

Bullfighting is also popular, particularly in the Guanacaste region, though the bull isn't killed in the Costa Rican version.

Arts

Literature

Costa Rica has a relatively young literary history and few works of Costa Rican writers or novelists are available in translation. Carlos Luis Fallas (1909–66) is widely known for *Mamita Yunai* (1940), an influential 'proletarian' novel that took the banana companies to task for their labor practices, and he remains very popular among the Latin American left.

Carmen Naranjo (1928–2012) is one of the few contemporary Costa Rican writers who have risen to international acclaim. She is a novelist, poet and short-story writer who also served as ambassador to India in the 1970s, and a few years later as minister of culture. In 1996 she was awarded the prestigious Gabriela Mistral medal by the Chilean government. Her collection of short stories, *There Never Was a Once Upon a Time,* is widely available in English. Two of her stories can also be found in *Costa Rica: A Traveler's Literary Companion.*

José León Sánchez (1929–) is an internationally renowned memoirist of Huetar descent from the border of Costa Rica and Nicaragua. After being convicted for stealing from the famous Basílica de Nuestra Señora de los Angeles in Cartago, he was sentenced to serve his term at Isla San Lucas, one of Latin America's most notorious jails. Illiterate when he was incarcerated, Sánchez taught himself how to read and write, and clandestinely authored one of the continent's most poignant books: *La isla de los hombres solos* (the English translation is titled *God Was Looking the Other Way*).

Music & Dance

Although there are other Latin American musical hotbeds of more renown, Costa Rica's central geographical location and colonial history have resulted in a varied musical culture that incorporates elements from North and South America and the Caribbean islands.

San José features a regular lineup of domestic and international rock, folk and hip-hop artists, but you'll find that the regional sounds also survive, each with their own special rhythms, instruments and styles. For instance, the Península de Nicoya has a rich musical history, most of it made with guitars, maracas and marimbas. The traditional sound on the Caribbean coast is calypso, which has roots in Afro-Caribbean slave culture.

Popular dance music includes Latin dances, such as salsa, merengue, bolero and *cumbia*. Guanacaste is also the birthplace of many traditional dances, most of which depict courtship rituals between country folk. The most famous dance – sometimes considered the national dance – is the *punto guanacasteco*. What keeps it lively is the *bomba,* a funny (and usually racy) rhymed verse shouted by the male dancers during the musical interlude.

Visual Arts

The visual arts in Costa Rica first took on a national character in the 1920s, when Teodórico Quirós, Fausto Pacheco and their contemporaries began painting landscapes that differed from traditional European styles, depicting the rolling hills and lush forest of the

Costa Rican countryside, often sprinkled with characteristic adobe houses.

The contemporary scene is more varied and it is difficult to define a unique Tico style. Several individual artists have garnered acclaim for their work, including the magical realism of Isidro Con Wong, the surreal paintings and primitive engravings of Francisco Amighetti and the mystical female figures painted by Rafa Fernández. The Museo de Arte y Diseño Contemporáneo in San José is the top place to see this type of work, and its permanent collection is a great primer.

Many art galleries are geared toward tourists and specialize in brightly colored, whimsical folk paintings depicting flora and fauna that evoke the work of French artist Henri Rousseau.

Folk art and handicrafts are not as widely produced or readily available here as in other Central American countries. However, the dedicated souvenir hunter will have no problem finding the colorful Sarchí oxcarts that have become a symbol of Costa Rica. Indigenous crafts, which include intricately carved and painted masks made by the Boruca, as well as handwoven bags and linens and colorful Chorotega pottery, can also be found in San José and more readily along Costa Rica's Pacific coast.

Film

Artistically, while film is not a new medium in Costa Rica, young filmmakers have been upping the ante in this arena. Over the last decade or so, a handful of Costa Rican filmmakers have submitted their work for Oscar consideration, and many others have received critical acclaim for their pictures nationally and internationally. These films range from adaptations of Gabriel García Márquez's magical-realism novel *Del amor y otro demonios* (Of Love and Other Demons, 2009), directed by Hilda Hidalgo, and a comedic coming-of-age story of contemporary young Ticos on the cusp of adulthood in *El cielo rojo* (The Red Sky, 2008), written and directed by Miguel Alejandro Gomez, to a light-hearted story of a Costa Rican farmer who embarks on the journey to Europe to raise money to avoid losing his farm in *Maikol Yordan de Viaje Perdido* (Maikol Yordan Traveling Lost, 2014), directed by Miguel Alejandro Gomez.

A film-festival calendar has also been blossoming in Costa Rica, though dates vary from year to year. Sponsored by the Ministerio de Cultura y Juventud, the Costa Rica Festival Internacional de Cine (www.costaricacinefest.go.cr) takes place in San José (check the website for current dates) and features international films fitting the year's theme. The longer-running Costa Rica International Film Festival (CRIFF; www.filmfestivallife.com) hits Montezuma in early June, with an associated documentary film festival the week following.

Hot off the Press: Marriage Equality

Since 1998 there have been laws on the books to protect 'sexual option,' and discrimination is generally prohibited in most facets of society, including employment. And though the country is becoming increasingly more gay friendly, this traditional culture has not always been quick to adopt equal protection.

Legal recognition of same-sex partnerships has been a hot topic since 2006 and was a major point of contention in the 2010 presidential race. In January 2012 Costa Rica's primary newspaper *La Nación* conducted a poll in which 55% of the respondents believed that same-sex couples should have the same rights as heterosexual couples. Then in July 2013 the Costa Rican legislature 'accidentally' passed a law legalizing gay marriage, due to a small change in the bill's wording. In 2015 a Costa Rican judge granted a same-sex common-law marriage, making it the first country in Central America to recognise gay relationships. The current president, Luis Guillermo Solís, has expressed support for gay rights, and even flew the rainbow flag at the presidential house.

Manzanillo (p242)

MATTHEW MICAH WRIGHT/GETTY IMAGES ©

Costa Rican Landscapes

Despite its diminutive size Costa Rica's land is an astounding collection of different habitats. On one coast are the breezy skies and big waves of the Pacific, while only 119km away lie the shores of the Caribbean. In between are active volcanoes, alpine peaks and crisp high-elevation forest. Few places on earth can compare with Costa Rica's spectacular natural, geological and climactic forces.

The Land

Pacific Coast

Two major peninsulas hook out into the ocean along the 1016km-long Pacific coast: Nicoya in the north and Osa in the south. Although they look relatively similar from space, on the ground they could hardly be more different. Nicoya is one of the driest places in the country and holds some of Costa Rica's most developed tourist infrastructure; Osa is wet and rugged, run through by wild, seasonal rivers and rough dirt roads that are always under threat from the creeping jungle.

Crater of Volcán Poás (p66)

Just inland from the coast, the landscapes of the Pacific lowlands are a narrow strip of land backed by mountains. This area is equally dynamic, ranging from dry deciduous forests and open cattle country in the north to misty, mysterious tropical rainforests in the south.

Central Costa Rica

Move a bit inland from the Pacific coast and you immediately ascend the jagged spine of the country: the majestic Cordillera Central in the north and the rugged, largely unexplored Cordillera de Talamanca in the south. Continually being revised by tectonic activity, these mountains are part of the majestic Sierra Madre chain that runs north through Mexico.

A land of active volcanoes, clear trout-filled streams and ethereal cloud forest, these mountain ranges generally follow a northwest-to-southeast line, with the highest and most dramatic peaks in the south near the Panamanian border. The highest in the country is the windswept 3820m peak of Cerro Chirripó.

In the midst of this powerful landscape, surrounded on all sides by mountains, are the highlands of the Meseta Central – the Central Valley. This fertile central plain, some 1000m above sea level, is the agricultural heart of the nation and enjoys abundant rainfall and mild temperatures. It includes San José and cradles three more of Costa Rica's five largest cities, accounting for more than half of the country's population.

Caribbean Coast

Cross the mountains and drop down the eastern slope and you'll reach the elegant line of the Caribbean coastline – a long, straight 212km along low plains, brackish lagoons and

Diving with an eagle ray

WILDEST ANIMAL/GETTY IMAGES ©

★ **Top Sites for Diving & Snorkeling**

Parque Nacional Cahuita, Cahuita

Refugio Nacional de Vida Silvestre Gandoca-Manzanillo

Reserva Biológica Isla del Caño, Bahía Drake

Islas Murciélago, Península de Nicoya

waterlogged forests. A lack of strong tides allows plants to grow right over the water's edge along coastal sloughs. Eventually, these create the walls of vegetation along the narrow, murky waters that characterize much of the region. As if taking cues from the slow-paced, Caribbean-influenced culture, the rivers that rush out of the central mountains take on a languid pace here, curving through broad plains toward the sea.

Compared with the smoothly paved roads and popular beaches of the Pacific coast, much of the land here is still largely inaccessible, except by boat or plane.

Out on the Reef

Compared with the rest of the Caribbean, the coral reefs of Costa Rica are not a banner attraction. Heavy surf and shifting sands along most of the Caribbean coast produce conditions that are unbearable to corals. The exceptions are two beautiful patches of reef in the south that are protected on the rocky headlands of Parque Nacional Cahuita and Refugio Nacional de Vida Silvestre Gandoca-Manzanillo. These diminutive but vibrant reefs are home to more than 100 species of fish and many types of coral and make for decent snorkeling and diving.

Unfortunately, the reefs themselves are in danger due to sediment washing downriver from logging operations and toxic chemicals that wash out of nearby agricultural fields. Although curbed by the government, these factors persist. Also, a major earthquake in 1991 lifted the reefs as much as 1.5m, stranding and killing large portions of this fragile ecosystem. More recently, climate change has led to warmer water in the Caribbean, which puts the reefs at the greatest peril – scientists released a report in 2008 that found that over half of Caribbean reefs were dead due to increased temperatures.

National Parks & Protected Areas

The national-park system began in the 1960s, and has since been expanded into a National Conservation Areas System with an astounding 186 protected areas, including 27 national parks, eight biological reserves, 32 protected zones, 13 forest reserves and 58 wildlife refuges. At least 10% of the land is strictly protected and another 17% is included in various multiple-use preserves. Costa Rican authorities enjoy their claim that more than 27% of the country has been set aside for conservation, but multiple-use zones still allow farming, logging and other exploitation, so the environment within them is not totally protected. The smallest number might be the most amazing of all: Costa Rica's parks are safe haven to approximately 5% of the world's wildlife species.

In addition to the system of national preserves, there are hundreds of small, privately owned lodges, reserves and haciendas (estates) that have been set up to protect the land. Many belong to longtime Costa Rican expats who decided that this country was the last stop in their journey along the 'gringo trail' in the 1970s and '80s. The abundance of foreign-owned protected areas is a bit of a contentious issue with Ticos. Although these are largely nonprofit organizations with keen interests in conservation, they are private and often cost money to enter. There's also a number of animal rescue and rehabilitation centers (also largely set up by expats), where injured and orphaned animals and illegal pets are rehabilitated and released into the wild, or looked after for life if they cannot be released.

Although the national-park system appears glamorous on paper, national conservation body the Sistema Nacional de Areas de Conservación (Sinac) still sees much work to be done. A report from several years ago amplified the fact that much of the protected area is, in fact, at risk. The government doesn't own all of this land – almost half of the areas are in private hands – and there isn't the budget to buy it. Technically, the private lands are protected from development, but there have been reports that many landowners are finding loopholes in the restrictions and selling or developing their properties, or taking bribes from poachers and illegal loggers in exchange for access.

On the plus side there is a project by Sinac that links national parks and reserves, private reserves and national forests into 13 conservation areas. This strategy has two major effects. First, these 'megaparks' allow greater numbers of individual plants and animals to exist.

When Worlds Collide

If all this wildly diverse beauty makes Costa Rica feel like the crossroads between vastly different worlds, that's because it is. Part of the thin strip of land that separates two continents with hugely divergent wildlife and topographical character and right in the middle of the world's two largest oceans, it's little wonder that Costa Rica boasts such a colorful collision of climates, landscapes and wildlife.

The country's geological history began when the Cocos Plate, a tectonic plate that lies below the Pacific, crashed headlong into the Caribbean Plate, which is off the isthmus' east coast. Since the plates travel about 10cm every year, the collision might seem slow by human measure, but it was a violent wreck by geological standards, creating the area's subduction zone. The plates continue to collide, with the Cocos Plate pushing the Caribbean Plate toward the heavens and making the area prone to earthquakes and ongoing volcanic activity.

Despite all the violence underfoot, these forces have blessed the country with some of the world's most beautiful and varied tropical landscapes.

Second, the administration of the national parks is delegated to regional offices, allowing a more individualized management approach. Each conservation area has regional and subregional offices charged with providing effective education, enforcement, research and management, although some regional offices play what appear to be only obscure bureaucratic roles.

In general, support for land preservation remains high in Costa Rica because it provides income and jobs to so many people, plus important opportunities for scientific investigation.

Sloth (p277)

Wildlife Guide

Costa Rica's reputation as a veritable Eden precedes it – with its iconic blue morpho butterflies, four species each of monkey and sea turtle, scarlet and great green macaws, two- and three-toed sloths, a rainbow of poison-dart frogs, mysterious tapirs and cute coatis.

Birds

Toucan Six species of this classic rainforest bird are found in Costa Rica. Huge bills and vibrant plumage make the commonly sighted chestnut-mandibled toucan and keel-billed toucan hard to miss. Listen for the keel-billed's song: a repetitious 'carrrick!'

Scarlet Macaw Of the 16 parrot species in Costa Rica, none is as spectacular as the scarlet macaw. Unmistakable for its large size, bright-red body and ear-splitting squawk, it's common in Parque Nacional Carara and the Península de Osa. Macaws have long, monogamous relationships and can live 50 years.

Keel-billed toucan

DANIEL PARENT/500PX ©

Resplendent Quetzal The most dazzling bird in Central America, the quetzal once held great ceremonial significance for the Aztecs and the Maya. Look for its iridescent-green body, red breast and long green tail at high elevations and near Parque Nacional Los Quetzales.

Roseate Spoonbill This wading bird has a white head and a distinctive spoon-shaped bill, and feeds by touch. Common around the Península de Nicoya, Pacific lowlands and on the Caribbean side at the Refugio Nacional de Vida Silvestre Caño Negro.

Tanager There are 42 species of tanager in the country – many are brightly colored and all have bodies about the size of an adult fist. Look for them everywhere except at high elevation. Their common name in Costa Rica is *viuda* (meaning widow).

Hummingbird More than 50 species of hummingbird have been recorded – and most live at high elevations. The largest is the violet sabrewing, with a striking violet head and body and dark-green wings.

Reptiles & Amphibians

Green iguana The stocky green iguana is regularly seen draping its 2m-long body along a branch. Despite their enormous bulk, iguanas are incessant vegetarians, and prefer to eat young shoots and leaves. You'll see them just about everywhere in Costa Rica – in fact, if you're driving, beware of iguanas sunning on or skittering across the roads.

Red-eyed tree frog The unofficial symbol of Costa Rica, the red-eyed tree frog has red eyes, a green body, yellow and blue side stripes, and orange feet. Despite this vibrant coloration, they're well camouflaged in the rainforest and rather difficult to spot. They are widespread except for the Península de Nicoya, which is too dry for them. You'll have a particularly good chance of seeing them at Estación Biológica La Selva.

Poison-dart frog Among the several species found in Costa Rica, the blue-jeans or strawberry poison-dart frog is the most commonly spotted, from Arenal to the Caribbean coast. These colorful, wildly patterned frogs' toxic excretions were once used to poison indigenous arrowheads. The Golfo Dulce poison-dart frog is endemic to Costa Rica.

Crocodile Impressive specimens can be seen from Crocodile Bridge on the central Pacific coast or in a more natural setting on boat trips along the Tortuguero canals.

Viper Three serpents you'll want to avoid are the fer-de-lance pit viper, which lives in agricultural areas of the Pacific and Caribbean slopes, the black-headed bushmaster (endemic to Costa Rica) and the beautiful eyelash pit viper, which lives in low-elevation rainforest. To avoid serious or fatal bites, watch your step and look before you grab onto any vines when hiking.

Marine Animals

Olive ridley turtle The smallest of Costa Rica's sea turtles, the olive ridley is easy to love – it has a heart-shaped shell. Between September and October they arrive to nest at Ostional beach in Guanacaste Province and near Ojochal on the Pacific coast.

Leatherback turtle The gigantic 360kg leatherback sea turtle is much, much bigger than the olive ridley, and is distinguished by its soft, leathery carapace, which has seven ridges. It nests on the Pacific beaches of the Osa and Nicoya peninsulas.

Whale Migrating whales, which arrive from both the Northern and Southern Hemispheres, include orca, blue and sperm whales and several species of relatively unknown beaked whale. Humpback whales are commonly spotted along the Pacific coast and off the Península de Osa.

Bottle-nose dolphin These charismatic, intelligent cetaceans are commonly sighted, year-round residents of Costa Rica. Keep a lookout for them on the boat ride to Bahía Drake.

Whale shark Divers may encounter this gentle giant in the waters off Reserva Biológica Isla del Caño, the Golfo Dulce or Isla del Coco. The world's biggest fish, whale sharks can reach 6m long and over 2000kg.

Manta ray With a wingspan that can reach 7m, the elegant manta ray is common in warm Pacific waters, especially off the coast of Guanacaste and around the Bat and Catalina islands.

Hammerhead shark The intimidating hammerhead has a unique cephalofoil that enables it to maneuver with incredible speed and precision. Divers can see enormous schools of hammerheads around the remote Isla del Coco.

Land Mammals

Sloth Costa Rica is home to the brown-throated, three-toed sloth and Hoffman's two-toed sloth. Both species tend to hang seemingly motionless from branches, their coats growing moss. Look for them in Parque Nacional Manuel Antonio.

Howler monkey The loud vocalizations of a male mantled howler monkey can carry for more than 1km even in dense rainforest, and echoes through many of the nation's national parks.

White-faced capuchin The small and inquisitive white-faced capuchin has a prehensile tail that is typically carried with the tip coiled – one is likely to steal your lunch near Volcán Arenal or Parque Nacional Manuel Antonio.

Squirrel monkey The adorable, diminutive squirrel monkey travels in small- to medium-sized groups during the day, in search of insects and fruit. They live only along the Pacific coast and are common in Parque Nacional Manuel Antonio and on the Península de Nicoya.

Jaguar The king of Costa Rica's big cats, the jaguar is extremely rare, shy and well camouflaged, so the chance of seeing one is virtually nonexistent (but the best chance is in Parque Nacional Corcovado).

White-nosed coati A frequently seen member of the raccoon family, with a longer, slimmer and lighter body than your average raccoon. It has a distinctive pointy, whitish snout and a perky, striped tail.

Baird's tapir A large browsing mammal related to the rhinoceros, the tapir has a characteristic prehensile snout and lives deep in forests ranging from the Península de Osa to Parque Nacional Santa Rosa.

Insects & Arachnids

Blue morpho butterfly The blue morpho butterfly flutters along tropical rivers and through openings in the forests. When it lands, the electric-blue upper wings close, and only the mottled brown underwings become visible, an instantaneous change from outrageous display to modest camouflage.

Tarantula Easily identified by its enormous size and hairy appendages, the Costa Rican red tarantula is an intimidating arachnid that can take down a mouse, but it is completely harmless to humans. They are most active at night while foraging and seeking mates.

Hercules beetle Turn on your flashlight while visiting one of Costa Rica's old-growth forests and you might draw out the Hercules beetle, one of the largest bugs in the world, a terrifying-looking but utterly harmless scarab beetle that can be as big as a cake plate. Fun fact: it can carry over 100 times its own body weight.

Leaf-cutter ant Long processions of busy leaf-cutter ants traverse the forest floors and trails of Costa Rica, appearing like slow-moving rivulets of green leaf fragments. Leaf-cutter ants are actually fungus farmers – in their underground colonies, the ants chew the harvested leaves into a pulp to precipitate the growth of fungus, which feeds the colonies. Don't confuse them with the predatory army ants!

Gallo pinto (rice and beans)

Food & Drink

Traditional Costa Rican fare, for the most part, is comfort food. The diet consists largely of beans and rice, fried plantains and the occasional slab of chicken, fish or beef. But in the last few years, locals have started to experiment more with the country's fresh, exotic and plentiful produce. The results have been inspiring and delicious.

What to Eat

Meals

Breakfast for Ticos is usually *gallo pinto* (literally 'spotted rooster'), a stir-fry of last night's rice and beans. When combined, the rice gets colored by the beans, and the mix obtains a speckled appearance. Served with eggs, cheese or *natilla* (sour cream), *gallo pinto* is generally cheap, filling and sometimes downright tasty. If you plan to spend the whole day surfing or hiking, you'll find that *gallo pinto* is great energy food. If you aren't keen on rice and beans, many hotels offer a tropical-style continental breakfast, usually consisting of toast with butter and jam, accompanied by fresh fruit. American-style

Traditional pork *casado* (set meal)

CHRIS FERTNIG/GETTY IMAGES ©

breakfasts are also available in many eateries and are, needless to say, heavy on the fried foods and fatty meats.

Most restaurants offer a set meal at lunch and dinner called a *casado* (literally 'married'), a cheap, well-balanced plate of rice, beans, meat, salad and sometimes *plátanos maduros* (fried sweet plantains) or *patacones* (twice-fried plantains), which taste something like french fries.

Specialties

Considering the extent of the coastline, it is no surprise that seafood is plentiful, and fish dishes are usually fresh and delicious. While not traditional Tico fare, *ceviche* (seafood marinated in lemon or lime juice, garlic and seasonings) is on most menus, usually made from *pargo* (red snapper), *dorado* (mahi-mahi), octopus or tilapia. Raw fish is marinated in lime juice with some combination of chilis, onions, tomatoes and herbs. Served chilled, it is a delectable way to enjoy fresh seafood. Emphasis is on 'fresh' here – it's raw fish, so if you have reason to believe it is not fresh, don't risk eating it.

Most bars also offer the country's most popular *boca* (snack), *chifrijo*, which derives its name from two main ingredients: *chicharrón* (fried pork) and frijoles (beans). Diced tomatoes, spices, rice, tortilla chips and avocado are also thrown in for good measure. Fun fact about *chifrijo:* in 2014 a restaurant owner named Miguel Cordero claimed he officially invented it. He brought lawsuits against 49 businesses and demanded a cool US$15 million in damages. So far he has not been able to collect.

Caribbean cuisine is the most distinctive in Costa Rica, having been steeped in indigenous, *criollo* (Creole) and Afro-Caribbean flavors. It's a welcome cultural change of pace

🍴 Gallo Pinto

No other dish in Costa Rica inspires Ticos quite like their national dish of *gallo pinto,* that ubiquitous medley of rice, beans and spices. You might even hear Costa Ricans refer to themselves as '*más Tico que gallo pinto*' (literally, 'more Costa Rican than *gallo pinto*'). Exactly what type and amount of this holy trinity makes up authentic *gallo pinto* is the subject of intense debate, especially since it is also the national dish of neighboring Nicaragua.

Both countries claim that *gallo pinto* originated on their soil. Costa Rican lore holds that the dish and its iconic name were coined in 1930 in the neighborhood of San Sebastián, on the southern outskirts of San José. Nicaraguans claim that it was brought to the Caribbean coast of their country by Afro-Latinos long before it graced the palate of any Costa Rican.

The battle for the rights to this humble dish doesn't stop here, especially since the two countries can't even agree on the standard recipe. Nicaraguans traditionally prepare it with small red beans, whereas Costa Ricans swear by black beans. And let's not even get into the subtle complexities of balancing cilantro, salt and pepper.

Nicaragua officially holds the world record for making the biggest-ever pot of *gallo pinto*. On September 15, 2007, a seething vat of it fed 22,000 people, which firmly entrenched Nicaragua's name next to *gallo pinto* in the *Guinness Book of World Records.* Costa Rica responded in 2009 by cooking an even more massive avalanche of the stuff, feeding a small crowd of 50,000. Though the event was not officially recognized as setting any records, that day's vat of *gallo pinto* warmed the hearts and bellies of many a proud Tico.

after seemingly endless *casados* (set meals). Regional specialties include *rondón* (whose moniker comes from 'rundown,' meaning whatever the chef can run down), a spicy seafood gumbo; Caribbean-style rice and beans, made with red beans, coconut milk and curry spices; and *patí,* the Caribbean version of an *empanada* (savory turnover), the best street food, bus-ride snack and picnic treat.

Vegetarians

If you don't mind rice and beans, Costa Rica is a relatively comfortable place for vegetarians to travel.

Most restaurants will make veggie *casados* (a cheap set meal) on request and many are now including them on the menu. They usually include rice and beans, cabbage salad and one or two selections of variously prepared vegetables or legumes.

With the high influx of tourism, there are also many specialty vegetarian restaurants or restaurants with a veggie menu in San José and tourist towns. In remote areas lodges that offer all-inclusive meal plans can accommodate vegetarians with advance notice.

Vegans, macrobiotic and raw-food-only travelers will have a tougher time, as there are fewer outlets accommodating those diets, although this is slowly changing. If you intend to keep to your diet, it's best to choose a lodging where you can prepare food yourself. Many towns have *macrobióti-cas* (health-food stores), but the selection varies. Fresh vegetables can be hard to come by in isolated areas and will often be quite expensive, although farmers markets are cropping up throughout the country.

What to Drink

Coffee

Coffee is probably the most popular beverage in the country, and wherever you go, someone is likely to offer you a *cafecito*. Traditionally, it is served strong and mixed with hot milk to taste, also known as *café con leche*. Purists can get *café negro* (black coffee); if you want a little milk, ask for *leche al lado* (milk on the side). Many trendier places serve espresso drinks.

Nonalcoholic Drinks

For a refresher, nothing beats *batidos* – fresh fruit shakes made either *al agua* (with water) or *con leche* (with milk). The array of available tropical fruit can be intoxicating and includes mango, papaya, *piña* (pineapple), *sandía* (watermelon), *melón* (cantaloupe), *mora* (blackberry), *carambola* (starfruit), *cas* (a type of tart guava), *guanabana* (soursop or cherimoya) or *tamarindo* (fruit of the tamarind tree). If you are wary about the condition of the drinking water, ask that your *batido* be made with *agua enbotellada* (bottled water) and *sin hielo* (without ice), though water is generally safe to drink throughout the country.

Pipas are green coconuts that have had their tops hacked off with a machete and been spiked with a straw for drinking the coconut water inside – super refreshing when you're wilting in the tropical heat. If you're lucky enough to find it, *agua dulce* is sugarcane water, a slightly grassy, sweet juice that's been pressed through a heavy-duty, hand-cranked mill. On the Caribbean coast, look for *agua de sapo* (literally 'toad water'), a beautiful lemonade laced with fresh ginger juice and *tapa de dulce* (brown sugar; also known as *tapa dulce*). *Resbaladera,* found mostly in the Guanacaste countryside, is a sweet milk – much like *horchata* (Mexican rice drink) – made from rice, barley, milk and cinnamon. Other local drinks you may encounter include *linaza* (a flaxseed drink said to aid digestion) and *chan* (a drink made from chia seed and lemon), which can be an acquired taste due to its slimy (yum!) texture.

Beer

The most popular alcoholic drink is *cerveza* (beer; aka *birra* locally), and there are several national brands. Imperial is the most popular – either for its smooth flavor or for the ubiquitous merchandise emblazoned with the eagle-crest logo. Pilsen, which has a higher alcohol content, is known for its saucy calendars featuring *las chicas Pilsen* (the Pilsen girls). Both are tasty pilsners. Bavaria produces a lager and Bavaria Negro, a delicious, full-bodied dark beer; this brand is harder to find. A most welcome burgeoning craft-beer scene is broadening the variety of Costa Rican beers and deepening the tastes of local palates.

Guaro

After beer, the poison of choice is *guaro*, which is a colorless alcohol distilled from sugarcane and usually consumed as a sour or by the shot, oftentimes with hot sauce and lime juice. This spicy concoction is called a *chili guaro,* and in the last few years it has become a staple in San José and certain beach towns. *Guaro* goes down mighty easily but leaves one hell of a hangover.

Rum

As in most of Central America, the local rums are inexpensive and worthwhile, especially the Ron Centenario, which recently shot to international fame. And at the risk of alienating the most patriotic of Ticos, we would be remiss not to mention the arguably tastier Flor de Caña from Nicaragua (pause for rotten tomatoes). The most popular rum-based tipple is a *cuba libre* (rum and cola), which hits the spot on a hot, sticky day, especially when served with a fresh splash of lime. Premixed cans of *cuba libre* are also available in stores, but it'd be a lie to say the contents don't taste weirdly like aluminum.

Baby three-toed sloth (p277)

MARK KOSTICH/GETTY IMAGES ©

Survival Guide

Directory A–Z

Accommodations

Accommodations come at every price and comfort level: from luxurious ecolodges and sparkling all-inclusive resorts and backpacker palaces to spartan rooms with little more than a bed and four cinderblock walls. The variety and number of rooms on offer means that booking is not usually mandatory.

The term *cabina* (cabin) is a catch-all that can define a wide range of prices and amenities – from very rustic to very expensive.

Pricing

Rates provided in this guide are for the high (dry) season, generally from December to April. Many lodgings lower their prices during the low (rainy) season, from May to November. Prices change quickly and many hotels charge per person rather than per room – read rates carefully and always check ahead. Expect to pay a premium during Christmas, New Year and Easter week (Semana Santa).

US dollars is the preferred currency for listing rates in Costa Rica. However, colones are accepted everywhere and are usually exchanged at current rates without an additional fee. Paying with a credit card will sometimes incur a surcharge.

Booking Services

Costa Rica Innkeepers Association (www.costaricainnkeepers.com) A nonprofit association of B&Bs, small hotels, lodges and inns.

Escape Villas (www.villascostarica.com) High-end accommodations across Costa Rica, most near Parque Nacional Manuel Antonio, which are suitable for

> ### Book Your Stay Online
>
> For more accommodation reviews by Lonely Planet authors, check out http://hotels.lonelyplanet.com/costarica. You'll find independent reviews, as well as recommendations on the best places to stay. Best of all, you can book online.

Climate

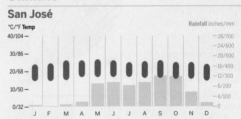

San José

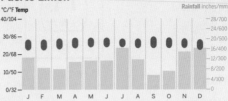

Puerto Limón

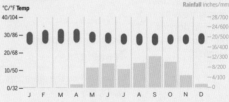

Puntarenas

families and honeymooners looking for luxury.

Lonely Planet (www.lonely planet.com/costa-rica/hotels) Recommendations and bookings.

Customs Regulations

○ All travelers over the age of 18 are allowed to enter the country with 5L of wine or spirits and 500g of processed tobacco (400 cigarettes or 50 cigars).

○ Camera gear, binoculars, and camping, snorkeling and other sporting equipment are readily allowed into the country.

○ Dogs and cats are permitted entry providing they have obtained both general health and rabies vaccination certificates.

○ Pornography and illicit drugs are prohibited.

Electricity

While Costa Rica uses a 110V/60Hz power system that is compatible with North American devices, power surges and fluctuation are frequent.

120V/60Hz

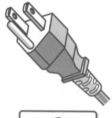

120V/60Hz

Gay & Lesbian Travelers

In Costa Rica the situation facing gay and lesbian travelers is better than in most Central American countries and some areas of the country – particularly Quepos and Parque Nacional Manuel Antonio – have been gay vacation destinations for two decades. Homosexual acts are legal, and in 2015 Costa Rica became the first country in Central America to recognise gay relationships. Still, most Costa Ricans are tolerant of homosexuality only at a 'don't ask, don't tell' level. Same-sex couples are unlikely to be the subject of harassment, though public displays of affection might attract unwanted attention.

The undisputed gay and lesbian capital of Costa Rica is Manuel Antonio; while there, look for the gay magazine *Playita*. The monthly newspaper *Gayness* and the magazine *Gente 10* (in Spanish) are both available at gay bars in San José.

Agua Buena Human Rights Association (☎2280-3548; www.aguabuena.org) This noteworthy nonprofit organization has campaigned steadily for fairness in medical treatment for people living with HIV/AIDS in Costa Rica.

Center of Investigation & Promotion of Human Rights in Central America (CIPAC; ☎2280-7821; www.cipacdh. org) The leading gay activist organization in Costa Rica.

Toto Tours (☎800-565-1241, in USA 773-274-8686; www. tototours.com) Gay-travel specialists who organize regular trips to Costa Rica, among other destinations.

Health

Travelers to Central America need to be vigilant about food- and mosquito-borne infections. Most of these illnesses are not life-threatening, but they can certainly ruin your trip. Besides getting the proper vaccinations, it's important to use a good insect repellent and exercise care in what you eat and drink.

Before You Go

Health Insurance

Should you wish to take part in high-risk adventure activities or water sports such as diving, make sure you pay for the appropriate level of insurance coverage. Some insurance companies may cover basic activities, such as hiking, but not zip-lining or surfing; if diving, you may only be able to get cover you up to a certain depth. If in doubt, check with your insurance company before setting off on your trip.

A list of medical evacuation and travel insurance companies can be found on the website of the **US State Department** (www.travel.state.gov) under the 'Before You Go' tab.

Recommended Vaccinations

○ Get necessary vaccinations four to eight weeks before departure.

○ Ask your doctor for an International Certificate of Vaccination (otherwise known as the 'yellow booklet'), which will list all the vaccinations you've received. This is mandatory for countries that require proof of yellow-fever vaccination upon entry. (Costa Rica only requires such proof if you are entering from a country that carries a risk of yellow fever.)

In Costa Rica

Health Care

○ Good medical care is available in most major cities but may be limited in rural areas.

○ For an extensive list of physicians, dentists and hospitals visit http://costarica.usembassy.gov and search for 'medical practitioners'.

○ Most pharmacies are well supplied and a handful are open 24 hours. Pharmacists are licensed to prescribe medication. If you're taking any medication on a regular basis, make sure you know its generic (scientific) name, since many pharmaceuticals go under different names in Costa Rica.

Infectious Diseases

Dengue fever (breakbone fever) Dengue is transmitted by *Aedes aegypti* mosquitoes, which often bite during the daytime and are usually found close to human habitations, often indoors. Dengue is especially common in densely populated urban environments. It usually causes flulike symptoms including fever, muscle aches, joint pains, headaches, nausea and vomiting, often followed by a rash. Most cases resolve uneventfully in a few days. There is no treatment for dengue fever except taking analgesics such as acetaminophen/paracetamol (Tylenol) and drinking plenty of fluids. Severe cases may require hospitalization for intravenous fluids and supportive care. There is no vaccine. The key to prevention is taking insect-protection measures.

Hepatitis A The second most common travel-related infection (after traveler's diarrhea). It's a viral infection of the liver that is usually acquired by ingestion of contaminated water, food or ice, though it may also be acquired by direct contact with infected persons. Symptoms may include fever, malaise, jaundice, nausea, vomiting and abdominal pain. Most cases resolve without complications, though hepatitis A occasionally causes severe liver damage. There is no treatment. The vaccine for hepatitis A is extremely safe and highly effective.

Leishmaniasis This is transmitted by sand flies. Most cases occur in newly cleared forest or areas of secondary growth; the highest incidence is in Talamanca. It causes slow-growing ulcers over exposed parts of the body. There is no vaccine. To protect yourself from sand flies, follow the same precautions as for mosquitoes.

Malaria Malaria is very rare in Costa Rica, occurring only occasionally in rural parts of the Limón Province. It's transmitted by mosquito bites, usually between dusk and dawn. Taking malaria pills is not necessary unless you are making a long stay in the province of Limón (not Puerto Limón). Protection against mosquito bites is most effective.

Traveler's diarrhea Tap water is safe and of high quality in Costa Rica, but when you're far off the beaten path it's best to avoid tap water unless it has been boiled, filtered or chemically disinfected (with iodine tablets). To prevent diarrhea, be wary of dairy products that might contain unpasteurized milk and be highly selective when eating food from street vendors. If you develop diarrhea, be sure to drink plenty of fluids, preferably with an oral rehydration solution containing lots of salt and sugar. If diarrhea is bloody or persists for more than 72 hours, or is accompanied by fever, shaking chills or severe abdominal pain, seek medical attention.

Typhoid Caused by ingestion of food or water contaminated by a species of salmonella known as *Salmonella typhi*. Fever occurs in virtually all cases. Other symptoms may include headache, malaise, muscle aches, dizziness, loss of appetite, nausea and abdominal pain. Possible complications include intestinal perforation, intestinal bleeding, confusion, delirium or (rarely) coma. A pretrip vaccination is recommended.

Zika virus At the time of research, pregnant women are advised against traveling to Costa Rica, as the virus may be linked to microcephaly, a birth defect that affects a baby's brain development. Zika is primarily transmitted by mosquitoes, but it can also be transmitted by a man to his sex partner or by a woman to her fetus. Be aware that symptoms are usually mild in adults, and many people may not realize that they are infected.

Environmental Hazards

Animal bites Do not attempt to pet, handle or feed any animal. Any bite or scratch by a mammal, including bats, should be promptly and thoroughly cleansed with large amounts of soap and water, and an antiseptic such as iodine or alcohol should be applied. Contact a local health authority in the event of such an injury.

Insect bites No matter how much you safeguard yourself, getting bitten by mosquitoes is part of every traveler's experience here. The best prevention is to stay covered up – wear long pants, long sleeves, a hat, and shoes, not sandals. Invest in a good insect repellent, preferably one containing DEET. Apply to exposed skin and clothing (but not to eyes, mouth, cuts, wounds or irritated skin). Compounds containing DEET should not be used on children under the age of two and should be used sparingly on children under 12. Invest in a bug net to hang over beds (along with a few thumbtacks

or nails with which to hang it). Many hotels in Costa Rica don't have windows (or screens), and a cheap little net will save you plenty of nighttime aggravation. The mesh size should be less than 1.5mm. Dusk is the worst time for mosquitoes, so take extra precautions.

Sun Stay out of the midday sun, wear sunglasses and a wide-brimmed hat, and apply sunblock with SPF 15 or higher, with both UVA and UVB protection. Drink plenty of fluids and avoid strenuous exercise when the temperature is high.

Tap Water

❍ It's generally safe to drink tap water in Costa Rica, except in the most rural and undeveloped parts of the country. However, if you prefer to be cautious, buying bottled water is your best bet.

❍ If you have the means, vigorous boiling for one minute is the most effective means of water purification. At altitudes greater than 2000m, boil for three minutes.

❍ Another option is to disinfect water with iodine pills: add 2% tincture of iodine to 1L of water (five drops to clear water, 10 drops to cloudy water) and let stand for 30 minutes. If the water is cold, longer times may be required.

❍ Alternatively, carry a SteriPen that destroys most bacteria, viruses and protozoa with UV light.

Insurance

It is vital that travelers purchase the right type of travel insurance before coming to Costa Rica. Basic insurance tends to cover medical expenses, baggage loss, trip cancelation, accidents and personal liability, but it's worth spending extra to make sure you're covered in the event of natural disasters. If you intend to take part in adventure sports, make sure that those particular sports are covered by your policy; some policies only cover divers up to a certain depth.

Worldwide travel insurance is available at www.lonelyplanet.com/travel-insurance. You can buy, extend and claim online anytime – even if you're already on the road.

Internet Access

○ The number of internet cafes in Costa Rica has greatly decreased with the advent of smartphones and wi-fi in restaurants and cafes.

○ Expect to pay US$1 to US$2 per hour in San José and tourist towns.

○ Wi-fi is common in all midrange and top-end hotels, and in the vast majority of budget hotels and hostels. Some hostels still have computers for guest use and/or wi-fi.

Legal Matters

○ If you are arrested, your embassy can offer limited assistance. Embassy officials will not bail you out and you are subject to Costa Rican laws, not the laws of your own country.

○ The use of recreational substances, other than tobacco and alcohol, is illegal in Costa Rica and punishable by imprisonment.

○ In Costa Rica the legal age for driving and voting is 18 years.

○ Keep in mind that travelers may be subject to the laws of their own country in regard to sexual relations.

Maps

Unfortunately detailed maps are hard to come by in Costa Rica, so it's best to purchase one online before your trip.

○ The excellent water-resistant 1:350,000 *Costa Rica Adventure Map* published by National Geographic also has an inset map of San José. Available online or in various book and gift shops in San José.

○ Another quality option is the 1:330,000 Costa Rica sheet produced by International Travel Map, which is waterproof and includes a San José inset.

○ The **Fundación Neotrópica** (☏2253-2130; www.neotropica.org) publishes a 1:500,000 map showing national parks and other protected areas; available online and in San José bookstores.

○ The ICT (Instituto Costarricense de Turismo) publishes a 1:700,000 Costa Rica map with a 1:12,500 Central San José map on the reverse; it's free at the ICT office in San José.

○ **Maptak** (www.maptak.com) has maps of Costa Rica's seven provinces and their capitals.

○ Few national-park offices or ranger stations have maps for hikers. Topographical maps are available for purchase from **Instituto Geográfico Nacional** (IGN; ☏2257-7798; Calle 9 btwn Avs 20 & 22, San José; ⊙7:30am-noon & 1-3pm Mon-Fri).

○ The *Mapa-Guía de la Naturaleza Costa Rica* is an atlas no longer published by Incafo, and included 1:200,000 topographical sheets, as well as English and Spanish descriptions of Costa Rica's natural areas. Out-of-print used copies can be purchased online.

Money

Both US dollars and Costa Rican colones are accepted everywhere and dispensed from ATMs across the country. With the exception of the smallest towns and shops in rural areas, credit cards are accepted.

ATMs

ATMs are ubiquitous, typically dispensing colones or US dollars. They are not easily found in rural and remote areas.

Cash & Currency

o The Costa Rican currency is the colón (plural colones), named after Cristóbal Colón (Christopher Columbus).

o Bills come in 1000, 2000, 5000, 10,000, 20,000 and 50,000 notes, while coins come in denominations of five, 10, 20, 25, 50, 100 and 500.

o Paying for things in US dollars is common, and at times is encouraged, since the currency is viewed as being more stable than colones.

o In US-dollar transactions the change will usually be given in colones.

o Newer US dollars (ie big heads) are preferred throughout Costa Rica.

o When paying in US dollars at a local restaurant, bar or shop the exchange rate can be unfavorable.

Changing Money

All banks will exchange US dollars, and some will exchange euros and British pounds; other currencies are more difficult. Most banks have excruciatingly long lines, especially at the state-run institutions (Banco Nacional, Banco de Costa Rica, Banco Popular), though they don't charge commission on cash exchanges. Private banks (Banex, Banco Interfin, Scotiabank) tend to be faster. Make sure the bills you want to exchange are in good condition or they may be refused.

Credit Cards

o Cards are widely accepted at midrange and top-end hotels, as well as at top-end restaurants and some travel agencies; they are less likely to be accepted in small towns and remote areas.

o A transaction fee (around 3% to 5%) on all international credit-card purchases is often added.

o Holders of credit and debit cards can buy colones in some banks, though expect to pay a high transaction fee.

o All car-rental agencies require drivers to have a credit card. It's possible to hire a car with just a debit card, but only on the condition that you pay for full insurance.

Exchange Rates

Australia	A$1	₡374
Canada	C$1	₡375
Euro zone	€1	₡581
Japan	¥100	₡453
New Zealand	NZ$1	₡372
UK	£1	₡761
USA	US$1	₡534

For current exchange rates, see www.xe.com.

Dollars versus Colones

While colones are the official currency of Costa Rica, US dollars are virtually legal tender. Case in point: most ATMs in large towns and cities will dispense both currencies. However, it pays to know where and when you should be paying with each currency.

In Costa Rica you can use US dollars to pay for hotel rooms, midrange to top-end meals, admission fees for sights, tours, domestic flights, international buses, car hire, private shuttle buses and large-ticket purchase items. Local meals and drinks, domestic bus fares, taxis and small-ticket purchase items should be paid for in colones.

Tipping

Restaurants Your bill at many restaurants will usually include a 10% service charge. If not, you might leave a small tip to show your appreciation, but it is not required.

Hotels It is customary to tip the bellhop/porter (US$1 to US$5 per service) and the housekeeper (US$1 to US$2 per day) in top-end hotels, less in budget places.

Taxis Taxi drivers are not usually tipped unless some special service is provided.

Guides On guided tours, tip the guide US$5 to US$15 per person per day. Tip the tour driver about half of what you tip the guide. Naturally, tips depend upon quality of service.

Opening Hours

Opening hours vary throughout the year. The following are high-season opening hours; hours will generally decrease in the shoulder and low seasons. Unless otherwise stated, count on sights, activities and restaurants to be open daily.

Banks 9am to 4pm Monday to Friday, sometimes 9am to noon Saturday.

Bars & clubs 8pm to 2am

Government offices 8am to 5pm Monday to Friday. Often closed between 11.30am and 1.30pm.

Restaurants 7am to 9pm. Upscale places may open only for dinner. In remote areas, even the small *sodas* (inexpensive eateries) might open only at specific meal times.

Shops 8am to 6pm Monday to Saturday.

Public Holidays

Días feriados (national holidays) are taken seriously in Costa Rica. Banks, public offices and many stores close. During these times, public transport is tight and hotels are heavily booked. Many festivals coincide with public holidays.

New Year's Day January 1

Semana Santa (Holy Week; March or April) The Thursday and Friday before Easter Sunday is the official holiday, though most businesses shut down for the whole week. From Thursday to Sunday bars are closed and alcohol sales are prohibited; on Thursday and Friday buses stop running.

Día de Juan Santamaría (April 11) Honors the national hero who died fighting William Walker in 1856; major events are held in Alajuela, his hometown.

Labor Day May 1

Día de la Madre (Mother's Day; August 15) Coincides with the annual Catholic Feast of the Assumption.

Independence Day September 15

Día de la Raza (Columbus Day, October 12)

Christmas Day (December 25) Christmas Eve is also an unofficial holiday.

Last week in December The week between Christmas and New Year is an unofficial holiday; businesses close and beach hotels are crowded.

Safe Travel

Costa Rica is largely a safe country, but petty crime (bag snatchings, car break-ins etc) is common and muggings do occur, so it's important to be vigilant. Many of Costa Rica's dangers are nature-related: rip tides, earthquakes and volcanic eruptions are among them. Predatory and venomous wildlife can also pose a threat, so a wildlife guide is essential if trekking in the jungle.

Smoking

Smoking is banned in all public places, restaurants, bars and casinos and on public transport. There are no separate 'smoking areas.' Some hotels in Costa Rica are non-smoking only.

Telephone

○ Mobile service now covers most of the country and nearly all of the country that is accessible to tourists.

○ Public phones are found all over Costa Rica, and chip or Colibrí phonecards are available in 1000-, 2000- and 3000-colón denominations.

○ Chip cards are inserted into the phone and scanned. Colibrí cards (more common) require you to dial a toll-free number (☏199) and enter an access code. Instructions are provided in English or Spanish.

○ The cheapest international calls from Costa Rica are direct-dialed using a phonecard. To make international calls, dial '00' followed by the country code and number.

○ Pay phones cannot receive international calls.

○ To call Costa Rica from abroad, use the country code (☏506) before the eight-digit number.

○ Due to the widespread popularity of voice-over IP services such as Skype, and more reliable ethernet connections, traveling with a smartphone or tablet can be the cheapest and easiest way to call internationally.

Time

Costa Rica is six hours behind GMT, so Costa Rican time is equivalent to Central Time in North America. There is no daylight-saving time.

Toilets

○ Public restrooms are rare, but most restaurants and cafes will let you use their facilities, sometimes for a small charge – never more than 500 colones.

○ Bus terminals and other major public buildings usually have toilets, also for a charge.

○ Don't flush your toilet paper. Costa Rican plumbing is often poor and has very low pressure.

○ Dispose of toilet paper in the rubbish bin inside the bathroom.

Tourist Information

○ The government-run tourism board, the **Instituto Costarricense de Turismo** (ICT; Map p48; ☏2222-1090, in USA & Canada 866-267-8274; www.visitcostarica.com; Edificio de las Academias, Av Central btwn Calles 1 & 3; ☺8am-5pm Mon-Fri), has an office in the capital; English is spoken.

○ The ICT can provide you with free maps, a master bus schedule, information on road conditions in the hinterlands, and a helpful brochure with up-to-date emergency numbers for every region.

○ Consult its English-language website for information.

○ From the USA call the ICT's toll-free number for brochures and information.

Travelers with Disabilities

Independent travel in Costa Rica is difficult for anyone with mobility constraints. Although Costa Rica has an equal-opportunity law, the law applies only to new or newly remodeled businesses and is loosely enforced. Therefore, very few hotels and restaurants have features specifically suited to wheelchair use. Many don't have ramps, and room or bathroom doors are rarely wide enough to accommodate a wheelchair.

Streets and sidewalks are potholed and poorly paved, making wheelchair use frustrating at best. Public buses don't have provisions to carry wheelchairs, and most national parks and outdoor tourist attractions don't have trails suited to wheelchair use. Notable exceptions include **Parque Nacional Volcán Poás** (☎2482-1226; admission US$15; ◷8am-3:30pm), **INBioparque** (☎2507-8107; www.inbioparque.com/en; Santo Domingo; adult/student/child US$25/19/15, serpentarium admission adult/child US$3/2; ◷9am-3pm Fri, 9am-4pm Sat & Sun) ✎ and the **Rainforest Aerial Tram** (☎2257-5961, in USA 1-866-759-8726; www.rainforestadventure.com; adult/student & child tram US$60/30, zip line US$50/35).

Download Lonely Planet's free Accessible Travel guide from http://lptravel.to/AccessibleTravel.

Visas

Passport-carrying nationals of the following countries are allowed 90 days' stay with no visa: Argentina, Australia, Canada, Chile, Iceland, Ireland, Israel, Japan, Mexico, New Zealand, Panama, South Africa, the US and most Western European countries.

Most other visitors require a visa from a Costa Rican embassy or consulate.

For the latest info on visas, check the websites of the ICT or the **Costa Rican Embassy** (www.costarica-embassy.org).

Women Travelers

Most female travelers experience little more than a *'mi amor'* ('my love') or an appreciative hiss from the local men. But, in general, Costa Rican men consider foreign women to have looser morals and to be easier conquests than Ticas (female Costa Ricans). Men will often make flirtatious comments to single women, particularly blondes, and women traveling together are not exempt. The best response is to do what Ticas do: ignore it completely. Women who firmly resist unwanted verbal advances from men are normally treated with respect.

○ In small highland towns, dress is usually conservative. Women rarely wear shorts, but belly-baring tops are all the rage. On the beach, skimpy bathing suits are OK, but topless and nude bathing are not.

○ Solo women travelers should avoid hitchhiking.

○ Do not take unlicensed 'pirate' taxis (licensed taxis are red and have medallions) as there have been reports of assaults on women by unlicensed drivers.

○ Birth-control pills are available at most pharmacies without a prescription.

○ Sanitary products can be found at any pharmacy.

Transport

Getting There & Away

Costa Rica can be reached via freqent, direct international flights from the US, Canada and other Central American countries. You can also cross a land border into Costa Rica from Panama or Nicaragua. Flights, cars and tours can be booked online at lonelyplanet.com/bookings.

Air

Costa Rica is well connected by air to other Central and South American countries, as well as the USA.

Arriving in Costa Rica

Aeropuerto Internacional Juan Santamaria (San José)
Alajuela–San José buses (US$1.10) from the airport to central San José run between 5am and 10pm. Taxis charge from US$25 to US$30 (depending on your destination in San José) and depart from the official stand; the trip takes 20 minutes to an hour. **Interbus** (☎4100-0888; www.interbusonline.com) runs between the airport and San José accommodations (US$15 per adult, US$7 per child under 12). Many rental-car agencies have desks at the airport.

Aeropuerto Internacional Daniel Oduber Quirós (Liberia)
Buses run to the Mercado Municipal (30 minutes, hourly) between 6am and 7pm, Monday through Friday only. Taxis from Liberia to the airport are about US$20. There are no car-rental desks at the airport; make reservations in advance and your company will meet you at the airport with a car.

Airports & Airlines

Aeropuerto Internacional Juan Santamaría (☑2437-2400; fly2sanjose.com) International flights arrive here, 17km northwest of San José, in the town of Alajuela.

Aeropuerto Internacional Daniel Oduber Quirós (LIR; www.liberiacostaricaairport.net) This airport in Liberia also receives international flights from the USA, the Americas and Canada. It serves a number of American and Canadian airlines and some charters from London, as well as regional flights from Panama and Nicaragua.

Avianca (part of the Central American airline consortium Grupo TACA; www.avianca.com) The national airline, flies to the USA and Latin America, including Cuba.

The US Federal Aviation Administration has assessed Costa Rica's aviation authorities to be in compliance with international safety standards.

Departure Tax

○ There is a US$29 departure tax on all international outbound flights, payable in dollars or colones, though most carriers now include it in the ticket price.

○ At the Juan Santamaría and Liberia airports this tax can be paid in cash or by credit card; Banco de Costa Rica has an ATM by the departure-tax station. Note that credit-card payments are processed as cash advances, which often carry hefty fees.

○ Travelers will not be allowed through airport security without paying.

Sea

Cruise ships stop in Costa Rican ports and enable passengers to make a quick foray into the country. Typically, ships dock at either the Pacific ports of Caldera, Puntarenas, Quepos and Bahía Drake, or the Caribbean port of Puerto Limón.

It is also possible to arrive in Costa Rica by private yacht.

Getting Around

Air Inexpensive domestic flights between San José and popular destinations such as Puerto Jiménez, Quepos and Tortuguero will save you the driving time.

Bus Very reasonably priced, with extensive coverage of the country, though travel can be slow and some destinations have infrequent service.

Private shuttle For door-to-door service between popular destinations, private and shared shuttles like Interbus or Gray Line can save time by allowing you to schedule to your needs

Car Renting a car allows you to access more remote destinations that are not served by buses, and frees you to cover as much ground as you like, within a limited time frame. Cars can be rented in most towns. Renting a 4WD vehicle is advantageous (and essential in some parts of the country); avoid driving at night.

Air

○ Costa Rica's domestic airlines are **Nature Air** (☑2220-3054; www.natureair.com) and **Sansa** (☑2290-4100; www.flysansa.com). Sansa is linked with Grupo TACA.

○ Both airlines fly small passenger planes, and you're allocated a baggage allowance of no more than 12kg.

○ Space is limited and demand is high in the dry season, so reserve and pay for tickets in advance.

○ In Costa Rica schedules change constantly and delays are frequent because of inclement weather. You should not arrange a domestic flight that makes a tight connection with an international flight.

○ Domestic flights (excepting charter flights) originate and terminate at San José.

Charter Flights

o Travelers on a larger budget or in a larger party should consider chartering a private plane, which is by far the quickest way to travel around the country.

o It takes under 90 minutes to fly to most destinations, though weather conditions can significantly speed up or delay travel time.

o The two most reputable charters in the country are **Nature Air** (☑2220-3054; www.natureair.com) and **Alfa Romeo Aero Taxi** (☑2735-5353; www.alfaromeoair.com). Both can be booked directly through the company, a tour agency or some high-end accommodations.

o Luggage space on charters is extremely limited.

Bicycle

With an increasingly large network of paved secondary roads and heightened awareness of cyclists, Costa Rica is emerging as one of Central America's most comfortable cycle-touring destinations. That said, many roads are narrow and winding and there are no designated cycle lanes, so there's an element of risk involved.

Mountain bikes and beach cruisers can be rented in towns with a significant tourist presence, for US$10 to US$20 per day. A few companies organize bike tours around Costa Rica.

Boat

o In Costa Rica there are some regular coastal services and safety standards are generally good.

o Ferries cross the Golfo de Nicoya, connecting the central Pacific coast with the southern tip of Península de Nicoya.

o The **Coonatramar Ferry** (☑2661-1069; www.coonatramar.com; adult/child/bicycle/motorcycle/car US$2/1/4/6/18) links the port of Puntarenas with Playa Naranjo four times daily. The **Ferry Naviera Tambor** (☑2661-2084; www.navieratambor.com; adult/child/bicycle/motorcycle/car US$1.65/1/4.50/7/23) travels between Puntarenas and Paquera every two hours, for a bus connection to Montezuma.

o On the Golfo Dulce a daily passenger ferry links Golfito with Puerto Jiménez on the Península de Osa. On the other side of the Península de Osa, water taxis connect Bahía Drake with Sierpe.

o On the Caribbean coast there is a bus and boat service that runs several times a day, linking Cariari and Tortuguero via La Pavona, while another links Parismina and Siquirres (transfer in Caño Blanco).

o Boats ply the canals that run along the coast from Moín to Tortuguero, although no regular service exists. A weekly water taxi connects Puerto Viejo de Sarapiquí with Trinidad on the Río San Juan on Tuesday afternoons. The San Juan is Nicaraguan territory, so take your passport. You can try to arrange boat transportation for Barra del Colorado in any of these towns.

Bus (Shuttle)

The tourist-van shuttle services (aka gringo buses) are a pricier alternative to the standard intercity buses. Shuttles are provided by **Gray Line** (www.graylinecostarica.com), **Easy Ride** (www.easyridecr.com), **Monkey Ride** (www.monkeyridecr.com) and **Interbus** (www.interbusonline.com).

o All four companies run overland transportation from San José to the most popular destinations, as well as directly between other destinations (see the

Driving in Costa Rica

o Drivers should carry their passport and driver's license at all times.

o If you have an accident, call the police immediately to make a report (required for insurance purposes).

o Leave the vehicles in place until the report has been made and do not make any statements except to members of law-enforcement agencies.

websites for the comprehensive list).

• These services will pick you up at your hotel, and reservations can be made online, or through local travel agencies and hotel owners.

• Popular destinations they serve include Quepos, Monteverde/Santa Elena, Manuel Antonio, Jacó, Dominical, Uvita, Puerto Jiménez, Arenal, Montezuma, and Mal País.

• Easy Ride offers international services directly from Jacó, Tamarindo and Liberia to Granada and Managua in Nicaragua and from Monteverde to Managua.

Car & Motorcycle

• Drivers in Costa Rica are required to have a valid driver's license from their home country. Many places will also accept an International Driving Permit (IDP), issued by the automobile association in your country of origin. After 90 days, however, you will need to get a Costa Rican driver's license.

• Gasoline (petrol) and diesel are widely available, and 24-hour service stations are along the Interamericana. At the time of research, fuel prices averaged US$1.01 per liter.

• In more remote areas, fuel will be more expensive and might be sold at the neighborhood *pulpería* (corner store).

• Spare parts may be hard to find, especially for vehicles with sophisticated electronics and emissions-control systems.

Hire & Insurance

• There are car-rental agencies in San José and in popular tourist destinations on the Pacific coast.

• All of the major international car-rental agencies have outlets in Costa Rica, though you can sometimes get better deals from local companies.

• Due to road conditions, it is necessary to invest in a 4WD unless travel is limited only to the Interamericana.

• Many agencies will insist on 4WD in the rainy season, when driving through rivers is a matter of course.

• To rent a car you need a valid driver's license, a major credit card and a passport. The minimum age for car rental is 21 years. It's possible to rent with a debit card, but only if you agree to pay full insurance.

• Carefully inspect rented cars for minor damage and make sure that any damage is noted on the rental agreement. If your car breaks down, call the rental company. Don't attempt to get the car fixed yourself – most companies won't reimburse expenses without prior authorization.

• Prices vary considerably; on average you can expect to pay over US$200 per week for a standard SUV, including *kilometraje libre* (unlimited mileage). Economy cars are much cheaper, as little as US$80 a week. The price of mandatory insurance makes this more expensive, often doubling the rate.

• Costa Rican insurance is mandatory, even if you have insurance at home. Expect to pay about US$12 to US$25 per day. Many rental companies won't rent you a car without it. The basic insurance that all drivers must buy is from a government monopoly, the Instituto Nacional de Seguros. This insurance does not cover your rental car at all, only damages to other people, their cars, or property. It is legal to drive only with this insurance, but it can be difficult to negotiate with a rental agency to allow you to drive away with only this minimum standard. Full insurance through the rental agency can be up to US$50 a day.

• Some roads in Costa Rica are rough and rugged, meaning that minor accidents or car damage are common.

• Note that if you pay basic insurance with a gold or platinum credit card, the card company will usually take responsibility for damages to the car, in which case you can forgo the cost of the full insurance. Make sure you verify this with your credit-card company ahead of time.

• Most insurance policies do not cover damage caused by flooding or driving through a river, so be aware of the extent of your policy.

○ Rental rates fluctuate wildly, so shop around. Some agencies offer discounts for extended rentals. Note that rental offices at the airport charge a 12% fee in addition to regular rates.

○ Thieves can easily recognize rental cars. Never leave anything in sight in a parked car – nothing! – and remove all luggage from the trunk overnight. If possible, park the car in a guarded parking lot rather than on the street.

○ Motorcycles (including Harleys) can be rented in San José and Escazú.

Road Conditions & Hazards

○ The quality of roads varies, from the quite smoothly paved Interamericana to the barely passable, bumpy, potholed, rural back roads. Any can suffer from landslides, sudden flooding and fog.

○ Most roads are single-lane and winding, lacking hard shoulders; others are dirt-and-mud affairs that climb mountains and traverse rivers.

○ Drive defensively and expect a variety of obstructions in the roadway, from cyclists and pedestrians to broken-down cars and cattle. Unsigned speed bumps are placed on some stretches of road without warning.

○ Roads around major tourist areas are adequately marked; all others are not.

○ Always ask about road conditions before setting out, especially in the rainy season when a number of roads become impassable.

Road Rules

○ There are speed limits of 100km/h or less on all primary roads and 60km/h or less on secondary roads.

○ Traffic police use radar, and speed limits are sometimes enforced with speeding tickets.

○ Tickets are issued to drivers operating vehicles without a seat belt.

○ It's illegal to stop in an intersection or make a right turn on a red.

○ At unmarked intersections, yield to the car on your right.

○ Drive on the right. Passing is allowed only on the left.

○ If you are issued with a ticket, you have to pay the fine at a bank; instructions are given on the ticket. If you are driving a rental car, the rental company may be able to arrange your payment for you – the amount of the fine should be on the ticket. A portion of the money from these fines goes to a children's charity.

○ Police have no right to ask for money, and they shouldn't confiscate a car, unless the driver cannot produce a license and ownership papers, the car lacks license plates, the driver is drunk, or the driver has been involved in an accident causing serious injury.

○ If you are driving and see oncoming cars with headlights flashing, it often means that there is a road problem or a radar speed trap ahead. Slow down immediately.

Taxis

In San José taxis have *marías* (meters) and it is illegal for a driver not to use it. Outside San José, however, most taxis don't have meters and fares tend to be agreed upon in advance. Bargaining is quite acceptable.

In some towns there are *colectivos* (taxis that several passengers are able to share). Although *colectivos* are becoming increasingly difficult to find, the basic principle is that the driver charges a flat fee (usually about US$0.50) to take passengers from one end of town to the other.

In rural areas, 4WDs are often used as taxis and are a popular means for surfers (and their boards) to travel from their accommodations to the break. Prices vary wildly depending on how touristy the area is, though generally speaking a 10-minute ride costs between US$5 and US$15.

Taxi drivers are not normally tipped unless they assist with your luggage or have provided an above-average service.

Language

Spanish pronunciation is not difficult as most of the sounds are also found in English. You can read our pronunciation guides below as if they were English and you'll be understood just fine. And if you pronounce 'kh' in our guides as a throaty sound and remember to roll the 'r,' you'll even sound like a real Costa Rican.

To enhance your trip with a phrasebook, visit **lonelyplanet.com**. Lonely Planet iPhone phrasebooks are available through the Apple App store.

Basics

Hello.
Hola.   *o·*la

How are you?
¿Cómo está? (pol)   *ko·*mo es·*ta
¿Cómo estás? (inf)   *ko·*mo es·*tas

I'm fine, thanks.
Bien, gracias.   byen *gra·*syas

Excuse me. (to get attention)
Con permiso.   kon per·*mee·*so

Yes./No.
Sí./No.   see/no

Thank you.
Gracias.   *gra·*syas

You're welcome./That's fine.
Con mucho gusto.   kon *moo·*cho *goo·*sto

Goodbye./See you later.
Adiós./Nos vemos.   a·*dyos/nos ve·*mos

Do you speak English?
¿Habla inglés? (pol)   *a·*bla een·*gles
¿Hablas inglés? (inf)   *a·*blas een·*gles

I don't understand.
No entiendo.   no en·*tyen·*do

How much is this?
¿Cuánto cuesta?   *kwan·*to *kwes·*ta

Can you reduce the price a little?
¿Podría bajarle el   po·*dree·*a ba·*khar·*le
el precio?   el *pre·*syo

Accommodations

I'd like to make a booking.
Quisiera reservar   kee·*sye·*ra re·ser·*var
una habitación.   *oo·*na a·bee·ta·*syon

Do you have a room available?
¿Tiene una habitación?   *tye·*ne *oo·*na a·bee·ta·*syon

How much is it per night?
¿Cuánto es por noche?   *kwan·*to es por *no·*che

Eating & Drinking

I'd like ..., please.
Quisiera ..., por favor.   kee·*sye·*ra ... por fa·*vor

That was delicious!
¡Estuvo delicioso!   es·*too·*vo de·lee·*syo·*so

Bring the bill/check, please.
La cuenta, por favor.   la *kwen·*ta por fa·*vor

I'm allergic to ...
Soy alérgico/a al ... (m/f)   soy a·*ler·*khee·ko/a al ...

I don't eat ...
No como ...   no *ko·*mo ...

   chicken   *pollo*   *po·*yo
   fish   *pescado*   pes·*ka·*do
   (red) meat *carne (roja)* *kar·*ne (*ro·*kha)

Emergencies

I'm ill.
Estoy enfermo/a. (m/f)   es·*toy en·*fer·*mo/a

Help!
¡Socorro!   so·*ko·*ro

Call a doctor!
¡Llame a un doctor!   *ya·*me a oon dok·*tor

Call the police!
¡Llame a la policía!   *ya·*me a la po·lee·*see·*a

Directions

Where's a/the ...?
¿Dónde está ...?   *don·*de es·*ta ...

   bank
   el banco   el *ban·*ko
   ... embassy
   la embajada de ...   la em·ba·*kha·*da de ...
   market
   el mercado   el mer·*ka·*do
   museum
   el museo   el moo·*se·*o
   restaurant
   un restaurante   oon res·tow·*ran·*te
   toilet
   el baño   el *ba·*nyo

Behind the Scenes

Acknowledgements

Climate map data adapted from Peel MC, Finlayson BL & McMahon TA (2007) 'Updated World Map of the Koppen-Geiger Climate Classification', *Hydrology and Earth System Sciences*, 11, pp1633–44.

This Book

This book was curated by Mara Vorhees and researched and written by Ashley Harrell, Anna Kaminski and Mara Vorhees. This guidebook was produced by the following:
Destination Editor Bailey Johnson
Product Editor Kate Mathews
Cartographers Julie Dodkins, Wayne Murphy
Book Designer Virginia Moreno
Assisting Editors Victoria Harrison, Kate James
Cover Researcher Naomi Parker
Thanks to Liz Heynes, Indra Kilfoyle, Campell McKenzie, Jenna Myers, Katie O'Connell, Dianne Schallmeiner, John Taufa, Juan Winata

Send Us Your Feedback

We love to hear from travelers – your comments keep us on our toes and help make our books better. Our well-traveled team reads every word on what you loved or loathed about this book. Although we cannot reply individually to postal submissions, we always guarantee that your feedback goes straight to the appropriate authors, in time for the next edition. Each person who sends us information is thanked in the next edition, the most useful submissions are rewarded with a selection of digital PDF chapters.

Visit lonelyplanet.com/contact to submit your updates and suggestions or to ask for help. Our award-winning website also features inspirational travel stories, news and discussions.

Index

Symbols & Map Key

Look for these symbols to quickly identify listings:

- ◎ Sights
- ✪ Activities
- ❺ Courses
- ◉ Tours
- ✪ Festivals & Events
- ✪ Eating
- ◑ Drinking
- ✪ Entertainment
- ⊙ Shopping
- ⓘ Information & Transport

These symbols and abbreviations give vital information for each listing:

- ✔ Sustainable or green recommendation
- **FREE** No payment required

☏ Telephone number	☒ Bus
☺ Opening hours	☒ Ferry
Ⓟ Parking	☒ Tram
☺ Nonsmoking	☒ Train
❄ Air-conditioning	🄸 English-language menu
@ Internet access	🄵 Vegetarian selection
☏ Wi-fi access	
☰ Swimming pool	🄵 Family-friendly

Find your best experiences with these Great For... icons.

- 💳 Budget
- 🍽 Food & Drink
- 🍸 Drinking
- 🚲 Cycling
- 🛍 Shopping
- 🏀 Sport
- 🖼 Art & Culture
- ✨ Events
- 📷 Photo Op
- 🔭 Scenery
- 👪 Family Travel

- 🎟 Short Trip
- 🗺 Detour
- 🚶 Walking
- 💬 Local Life
- 📖 History
- 🎫 Entertainment
- 🏖 Beaches
- ❄ Winter Travel
- ☕ Cafe/Coffee
- 🐦 Nature & Wildlife

Sights

- 🅑 Beach
- 🅑 Bird Sanctuary
- 🅑 Buddhist
- 🅑 Castle/Palace
- 🅑 Christian
- 🅑 Confucian
- 🅑 Hindu
- 🅒 Islamic
- 🅙 Jain
- 🅙 Jewish
- 🅞 Monument
- 🏛 Museum/Gallery/ Historic Building
- 🅡 Ruin
- 🅢 Shinto
- 🅢 Sikh
- 🅣 Taoist
- 🅦 Winery/Vineyard
- 🅩 Zoo/Wildlife Sanctuary
- ◎ Other Sight

Points of Interest

- 🄑 Bodysurfing
- 🄒 Camping
- 🄒 Cafe
- 🄒 Canoeing/Kayaking
- ● Course/Tour
- 🄓 Diving
- 🄓 Drinking & Nightlife
- ✪ Eating
- 🄔 Entertainment
- 🄢 Sento Hot Baths/ Onsen
- 🄢 Shopping
- 🄢 Skiing
- 🄢 Sleeping
- 🄢 Snorkelling
- 🄢 Surfing
- 🄢 Swimming/Pool
- 🄦 Walking
- 🄦 Windsurfing
- ✪ Other Activity

Information

- 🅢 Bank
- 🅔 Embassy/Consulate
- ➕ Hospital/Medical
- @ Internet
- 🅟 Police
- 🅟 Post Office
- 🅣 Telephone
- 🅣 Toilet
- ⓘ Tourist Information
- ● Other Information

Geographic

- 🅑 Beach
- ⤜ Gate
- 🅗 Hut/Shelter
- 🅛 Lighthouse
- 🅛 Lookout
- ▲ Mountain/Volcano
- 🅞 Oasis
- 🅟 Park
-)(Pass
- 🅟 Picnic Area
- 🅦 Waterfall

Transport

- 🅐 Airport
- 🅑 BART station
- ⊗ Border crossing
- 🅣 Boston T station
- 🅑 Bus
- ⊕ Cable car/Funicular
- ⊚ Cycling
- 🅕 Ferry
- 🅜 Metro/MRT station
- 🅜 Monorail
- 🅟 Parking
- 🅟 Petrol station
- 🅢 Subway/S-Bahn/ Skytrain station
- 🅣 Taxi
- 🅣 Train station/Railway
- 🅣 Tram
- 🅔 Tube Station
- 🅤 Underground/ U-Bahn station
- ● Other Transport

Our Story

A beat-up old car, a few dollars in the pocket and a sense of adventure. In 1972 that's all Tony and Maureen Wheeler needed for the trip of a lifetime – across Europe and Asia overland to Australia. It took several months, and at the end – broke but inspired – they sat at their kitchen table writing and stapling together their first travel guide, *Across Asia on the Cheap*. Within a week they'd sold 1500 copies. Lonely Planet was born.

Today, Lonely Planet has offices in Franklin, London, Melbourne, Oakland, Dublin, Beijing and Delhi, with more than 600 staff and writers. We share Tony's belief that 'a great guidebook should do three things: inform, educate and amuse'.

Our Writers

Mara Vorhees

In 20 years of travel to Costa Rica, Mara has spotted 162 species of birds, all four New-World monkeys, anteaters, sloths, tapirs, peccaries, coatis, agoutis, a kinkajou and a jaguarundi. None of it, she attests, is quite as wild as her five-year-old twins, who accompanied her while hiking, snorkeling, surfing, zipping, rafting, birding and horseback riding around Costa Rica. Mara has written many guidebooks for Lonely Planet, including *Central America on a Shoestring* and *Belize*. When not spying on sloths, she lives in Somerville, Massachusetts, with her husband, two kiddies and two kitties. Follow her adventures at www.havetwinswilltravel.com.

Ashley Harrell

When Ashley was 12, her dad took her on a medical mission to León, Nicaragua, where she remembers diving into a muddy swimming hole, devouring whole fried fish (eyeballs included) and downing her first beer. Twenty years later, Central America enticed her again, and she moved to Costa Rica to be closer to sloths and to work as a journalist, eventually enlisting with Lonely Planet. Research for this guidebook involved sampling the capital's new farm-to-table restaurants, befriending a crocodile whisperer and exploring far-flung corners of the Caribbean.

Anna Kaminski

This was Anna's second research trip to Costa Rica and on this occasion she was lucky enough to tackle the southern part of the country – with the best dining scene, most rugged mountain and jungle trekking and the best opportunities to delve into indigenous culture. With a university background in the history and culture of Latin America, Anna has been traveling all over this part of the world for nearly 15 years. She tweets at @ACKaminski.

STAY IN TOUCH
lonelyplanet.com/contact

AUSTRALIA Levels 2 & 3, 551 Swanston St, Carlton, Victoria 3053
☏ 03 8379 8000,
fax 03 8379 8111

USA 150 Linden Street, Oakland, CA 94607
☏ 510 250 6400,
toll free 800 275 8555,
fax 510 893 8572

UK 240 Blackfriars Road, London SE1 8NW
☏ 020 3771 5100,
fax 020 3771 5101

twitter.com/
lonelyplanet

facebook.com/
lonelyplanet

instagram.com/
lonelyplanet

youtube.com/
lonelyplanet

lonelyplanet.com/
newsletter